LYBEAUS DESCONUS

MIDDLE ENGLISH TEXTS SERIES

The Middle English Texts Series is designed for classroom use. Its goal is to make available to teachers, scholars, and students texts that occupy an important place in the literary and cultural canon but have not been readily available in student editions. The series does not include those authors, such as Chaucer, Langland, or Malory, whose English works are normally in print in good student editions. The focus is, instead, upon Middle English literature adjacent to those authors that teachers need in compiling the syllabuses they wish to teach. The editions maintain the linguistic integrity of the original work but within the parameters of modern reading conventions. The texts are printed in the modern alphabet and follow the practices of modern capitalization, word formation, and punctuation. Manuscript abbreviations are silently expanded, and *u/v* and *j/i* spellings are regularized according to modern orthography. Yogh (ȝ) is transcribed as *g, gh, y,* or *s,* according to the sound in Modern English spelling to which it corresponds; thorn (þ) and eth (ð) are transcribed as *th.* Distinction between the second person pronoun and the definite article is made by spelling the one *thee* and the other *the,* and final *-e* that receives full syllabic value is accented (e.g., *charité*). Hard words, difficult phrases, and unusual idioms are glossed either in the right margin or at the foot of the page. Explanatory and textual notes appear at the end of the text, often along with a glossary. The editions include short introductions on the history of the work, its merits and points of topical interest, and brief working bibliographies.

This series is published in association with the University of Rochester.

Medieval Institute Publications is a program of
The Medieval Institute, College of Arts and Sciences

WESTERN MICHIGAN UNIVERSITY

Lybeaus Desconus

Edited by
Eve Salisbury and James Weldon

TEAMS • Middle English Texts Series

MEDIEVAL INSTITUTE PUBLICATIONS
Western Michigan University
Kalamazoo

Library of Congress Cataloging-in-Publication Data are available from the Library of Congress.

P 5 4 3 2 1

Contents

ACKNOWLEDGMENTS   vii

INTRODUCTION   1

LYBEAUS DESCONUS (LAMBETH PALACE, MS 306)   31

LIBIOUS DISCONIOUS (BIBLIOTECA NAZIONALE, MS XIII.B.29)   85

EXPLANATORY NOTES   139

TEXTUAL NOTES (LAMBETH)   185

TEXTUAL NOTES (NAPLES)   191

LIST OF NAMES, PLACE-NAMES, AND VARIANT SPELLINGS   197

BIBLIOGRAPHY   199

GLOSSARY   209

LIST OF ILLUSTRATIONS

FIGURE 1. LAMBETH PALACE, MS 306   30

FIGURE 2. EVE AND DRAGON-SERPENT IN EDEN   83

FIGURE 3. NAPLES, BIBLIOTECA NAZIONALE, MS XIII.B.29   84

ACKNOWLEDGMENTS

As so often happens in the world of medieval studies, the idea for putting together a volume on *Lybeaus Desconus* featuring two manuscript versions of the same poem began to take shape at a session at the International Congress on Medieval Studies at Kalamazoo. During the course of a wide-ranging Q & A in a session dedicated to critical readings of the Middle English *Bevis of Hampton*, the name of the Fair Unknown came up in a comment by James Weldon. After the session had ended he introduced himself and described his work on an underappreciated recension of the poem located in the Biblioteca Nazionale in Naples. Since Eve Salisbury had been working on a volume based exclusively on a single manuscript, Lambeth MS 306, the conversation proved to be of great interest and grew ever more so when Weldon outlined the value of a manuscript that would fill in scenes omitted from Lambeth and the other versions. That conversation marked the beginning of a collaboration designed to bring this little-known English narrative to the attention of the academic community. Soon afterward, a revised proposal was drafted, presented, and ultimately accepted by METS/TEAMS. What had erupted so spontaneously in a brief encounter in Kalamazoo was ultimately set in motion; the result is a dual edition that we hope will provoke additional commentary and scholarly work in a field and genre in need of attention.

Since putting together one of these compendious volumes involves a number of knowledgeable and dedicated people, the collaboration that began at that session continued as the volume developed. First and foremost we would like to thank the general editor of the series, Russell A. Peck, who recognized the potential contribution a dual edition would make to the nearly negligible discourse on the Fair Unknown, and his willingness to take a chance on something METS had never done before, to generate interest among our target audiences — "eager beginners, information-hungry graduate students, and scholars." There was firm guidance right from the beginning and enthusiastic support all during the process, with a blend of the occasional pat on the back in appreciation of our labors and critical commentary where and when needed. Editorial assistants John Chandler and Martha M. Johnson-Olin enhanced the quality of the project from its inception by reading with fresh eyes, asking the right sorts of questions at the right times, and adding our copious changes accurately and without complaint. In addition, we would like to thank Sharon E. Rhodes, Kara L. McShane, and Pamela M. Yee for noting nuances that two sets of tired eyes had not seen, Alan Lupack, curator of the Robbins Library, who served as final reader to the completed volume, for his scholarly insight and guidance, and Patricia Hollahan, the managing editor of Medieval Institute Publications, and her staff. Thanks also go to the libraries holding the original manuscripts — Lambeth Palace in London and the Biblioteca Nazionale in Naples — as well as the National Endowment for the Humanities grant that supports the entire METS/TEAMS project. On a personal note: Eve would like to thank David Bleich and daughter Meghan for their encouragement and support of her diverse academic (ad)ventures and students who have made the making and teaching of METS/TEAMS volumes a pleasure. Jim would like to thank Eve Salisbury, with whom it has been a pleasure to work, for her continual generosity, kindness, and guidance throughout our preparations. Jim's deepest appreciation goes to Emmy Misser for her unfailing support over the years, and thanks, too, go to Don Mahoney, whose passion for literature made his possible. Jim is also grateful to his students, whose enthusiasm and inquisitiveness encouraged and sustained him in many ways.

❧ INTRODUCTION

Lybeaus Desconus belongs to a widely disseminated intertextual network of narratives in which a handsome and mysterious young outsider comes to the Arthurian court to prove himself worthy of inclusion. Raised in the wilderness and given the nickname Bewfiz (Beautiful Son) by his mother in most versions of the tale, the young man lacks any "real" identity; when he appears before the king unable to articulate a name deemed appropriate for a reputable chevalier, he receives a temporary designation — Lybeaus Desconus, the Fair Unknown — along with an opportunity to demonstrate his physical prowess and intrinsic nobility. The young knight is then tested in the ways in which nearly all medieval romance heroes are tested, and in the course of his quest he learns about chivalric codes of behavior and the truth of his birthright as Guinglain, the illegitimate son of one of the most famous of Arthur's knights — Sir Gawain.

By whichever name this young man is known in the tale's many variants, individual, familial, and communal identities form a nexus of recurring medieval concerns. The mode of chivalry practiced by Arthurian knights and the potentiality for an illegitimate young man to discover who he is, who his parents are, where he belongs, and what he is destined to do, all make for compelling narration. That the aspiring youth achieves his reputation and social status not merely on his good looks but rather by earning recognition as one of Arthur's most notable retainers suggests an appreciation for the role that determination and courage play in the making of a respectable knight, especially one who has been excluded from the court by circumstances beyond his control. The story of the illegitimate but chivalric son not only imagines a place for any disenfranchised youth in courtly society but provides the means by which estranged parents may be reunited and kinship relations legitimated.

The closest analogue to the Middle English *Lybeaus Desconus* is Renaut de Bâgé's 6,266-line, late twelfth-century Old French poem, *Li Biaus Descouneüs* (*Le Bel Inconnu*), which perhaps explains why the story is repeatedly referred to as "the Frensshe tale."[1] Other analogues typically associated with the Fair Unknown tradition, which vary in length and emphasis as well as in language and culture, are the Middle High German *Wigalois* by Wirnt von Grafenberg; its own close analogue, the anonymous *Wigamur* (both exceeding 6,000 lines); and the Italian *Carduino*, which consists of two cantari in ottava rima of a mere thirty-five and seventy-two stanzas respectively.[2] While the German and Italian variants may be

---

[1] Renaut de Bâgé, *Le Bel Inconnu*. Renaut de Bâgé, formerly known as Renaut de Beujeu, is thought to have written his poem c. 1195.

[2] von Grafenberg, *Wigalois*; *Wigamur*, ed. Busch; *Cantari di Carduino*, ed. Branca; see also *I Cantari di Carduino*, ed. Rajna.

considered adaptations of Renaut's poem,[3] as to some extent is Malory's "Tale of Sir Gareth," many other retellings may be more aptly described as episodic parallels or the products of transformative motifs or "memes" with the capacity, as Helen Cooper suggests, "to adapt, mutate, and therefore survive in different forms and cultures."[4] Narratives as diverse as the Middle English *Sir Perceval of Galles*, the Irish/Scottish *Laoidh an Amadain Mhoir* (a goatskin-clad simpleton raised outside of civilization), and the Welsh *Peredur, Son of Evrawg*, whose mother whisks him away from court and raises him in the wilderness, reflect diverse recast-ings of this oft-told tale.[5] Accounts of the Fair Unknown prompt additional stories that move in different directions, in other words, whether by translation and adaptation or by more subtle shifts in emphasis, characterization, and narrative framing. Memes such as the illegit-imate/orphaned/abandoned child, the sovereign/loathly lady, or the supernatural/bestial/ human hybrid, to name a few, have the capacity to mutate and reemerge as autonomous narratives in different cultures at different times.

LI BIAUS DESCOUNEÜS AND *LYBEAUS DESCONUS*

While the Old French *Li Biaus Descouneüs* and the Middle English *Lybeaus Desconus* resemble one another in terms of basic narrative structure, there are a number of differ-ences that distinguish the later Middle English poem from its French predecessor.[6] The French poem is controlled by the voice of a courtly narrator who dedicates his creative work to his lady, indulges in frequent interjections, and revels in lengthy ethical asides on the ne-cessity for a knight's courtesy to the ladies and taking matters of the heart seriously. This apparatus is omitted in the English poem, whose poet establishes instead a distinctly omni-scient distance, adhering to the facts of the events with minimal interpretive and/or philo-sophical commentary, particularly in relation to love and the women so integral to its expression. Rather than beginning with an encomium to a lady and setting the stage for the courtliness of romance, the English *Lybeaus* begins in a way commensurate with many English and Scottish tail-rhyme romances, that is, with an explicit invocation to "Jhesus Criste oure Savyour / and His Moder, that swete floure" (Lambeth, lines 1–2).[7] Moreover, the

---

[3] Predelli, *Bel Gherardino*, argues that elements of the Fair Unknown story circulated in Europe earlier than Renaut's version. Renaut drew on these, of course, but so did the *Lybeaus* poet and the *Carduino* poet (p. 227).

[4] H. Cooper, *English Romance in Time*, p. 3.

[5] Still other analogues named as part of the Fair Unknown tradition with various degrees of resemblance include an Old Yiddish narrative called *Widwilt*, the Old French *Le Chevalier du Papegau*, Claude Platin's *L'hystoire de Giglan*, Robert de Blois's *Beaudos*, *Le Roman de Belris*, a 140-line fragment called "Gogulor," *Bel Gherardino*, *Ponzela Gaia*, the English *Ipomadon*, and Ulrich Von Zatzikhoven's *Lanzelet*.

[6] The two narratives resemble each other structurally in the first part only, as the Middle English romance omits the second part, which continues the story after the disenchantment of the Lady of Synadoun. Also, only major differences in plot and characterization are noted in this introduction; minor variations and other details appear in the Explanatory Notes.

[7] According to Carol Fewster, *Traditionality and Genre*, such invocations form part of the self-consciousness of English romances and constitute a deliberate realignment of the narrative away from the French tradition (p. 32).

English poem's brevity and focus upon the action-adventure components of the narrative underscore a modest narrative economy. The elaborate detail of the French poem — the list of knights at court and at tournament, lengthy descriptions of clothing, armor, décor, urban and natural landscapes, and material wealth — gives way to concision in an English work that intensifies the progressive complexities of the episodic plot. In a move toward a more prescriptive and streamlined retelling of the Fair Unknown story, in other words, the English *Lybeaus* poet concentrates on pivotal scenes among fewer characters refashioned in accordance with the poem's emphasis and concerns. These reconstructed figures appear in episodes that reveal the inexperienced nature of the novice chevalier often referred to as a "child" until he proves himself worthy of inclusion in Arthur's retinue. In its emphasis on the youthful knight's bumbling attempts at courtesy and his eventual acquisition of experience in love and chivalry, the narrative takes on characteristics of a medieval conduct book for a popular rather than an aristocratic audience.[8]

Another notable variation between the French and the English versions of the poem is in the account of the early childhood experience of the hero (his *enfances*) outside the Arthurian court. In the French version, his identity as the illegitimate son of Gawain is kept in abeyance until later in the poem, at the moment he is called upon to proffer the transformative kiss that only Gawain or a kinsman of Gawain can provide. In the English version, however, the revelation to the audience of the hero's "real" name and his relationship to Gawain occurs early, immediately foregrounding the matters of identity so central to Fair Unknown narratives.[9] The young man appears before the court not knowing his legitimate name, whereupon Arthur, apparently equating nobility, integrity, and success with the boy's good looks, dubs him the Fair Unknown and promises him the first boon to come along. When a maiden (Helie in the French, Elene in the English) comes to court to procure a champion who will liberate her lady (la Blonde Esmeree in the French, the Lady of Synadoun in the English), the inexperienced knight reminds Arthur of his earlier promise and receives the king's permission to participate in the quest, much to the maiden's dismay. Another important difference between the two poems is embedded in this scene — when the maiden asks for a knight in the French version she describes him as one who must not only be combat-ready but prepared to withstand the infamous *fier baiser* (fearsome kiss) in order to break the magic spell cast upon her lady. Judged by the maiden to be too young and inexperienced, the Fair Unknown appears unqualified to endure such dangerous intimacy. In the English version, the achievement of the fearsome kiss is not listed among the hero's expected qualifications at the poem's beginning; we must wait until Lybeaus is ready to stand up to the test before considering the maturity of his valor.

Nonetheless, the audacious young man accompanies the lady and her dwarf (a character given greater license to speak in the English version) and soon engages in combat with a series of formidable opponents. Beginning with the guard of the Perilous Ford, Blioblïeris and his cohort, followed in the next scene by two giants caught in the act of raping a young woman (Clarie in the French version, Violet in the English), Lybeaus's successes impress all

---

[8] *Lybeaus Desconus* and other verse romances are often categorized as popular romances, a frequently pejorative classification that colors both style and audience. For a recent discussion of the problems associated with the idea of popular romance audience, see Field, "Popular Romance," and Radulescu, "Genre and Classification."

[9] See M. Dickson, "Female Doubling and Male Identity in Medieval Romance."

who watch him vanquish his opponents with methodical aplomb. In the French version, the rescued maiden's presence carries over into the next episode in a dispute over a lost dog, which turns out to be a test of the knight's willingness to take up what amounts to a trivial challenge. Li Biaus's attempts to persuade Clarie to return the brachet to its rightful owner (l'Orguillous de la Lande) are met with adamant refusal, at which point its master prepares to retrieve his property by force. In the English version, the dog episode occurs later, where it is the messenger Elene, not Violet/Clarie, who claims the animal. When Lybeaus and Elene encounter the whelp (lost for eight years) Elene admires its beauty, and Lybeaus bestows the dog upon her. When they come upon the original owner, in a gesture of chivalric courtesy, Lybeaus defends the right of Elene to keep the wandering whelp and fights for the claim on her behalf. Whether this act constitutes an error in judgment is left to the audience to decide.

The episode of the sparrowhawk in the French poem is likewise markedly different from its English counterpart. The custom associated with the prized bird is as follows: "any maiden who gains possession of the hawk by taking it from its perch will be renowned as the most beautiful of women. But the maiden who wishes to have this hawk must bring with her a knight who will maintain that she is more beautiful than any other lady or maiden," and challenge by force of arms his claim against the reigning champion.[10] Seeing the hawk, desired by a lady named Margery whose own beloved knight has died in an effort to acquire the bird, persuades Li Biaus to take up her cause. In an astonishing twist in the French narrative, however, the presumably beautiful lady, who is defended by the Knight of the Falcon, is actually "quite ugly and wrinkled," a revelation that prompts the poet's rationalization: "Love makes the ugliest woman seem a beauty, so skilled are her ways of deceit and enchantment."[11] In the English version the scene has been cast into a beauty contest grounded in the mercantile realities of the marketplace, omitting reference to love's deceptive powers. Unfairly and unilaterally pitted against the lady of the Knight of the Falcon in order to provoke combat, Elene, while not unattractive, is nevertheless judged inferior in beauty by the townspeople. The English Lybeaus's lack of chivalric courtesy is notable in this episode. While the French poem exalts a knight's commitment to his lady and love's notorious blindness, the English poem exposes Lybeaus's lack of genuine feeling for Elene and insensitivity to chivalric protocols; his motive for combat derives from a beauty contest to which a mature knight would never have subjected his lady.

Points of departure in plot are significant to be sure, but there are also variations in the ways in which some characters are portrayed that underscore differing poetic agendas and emphases. The suitor of la Pucele as Blances Mains (the Maiden of the White Hands) — Malgiers li Gris, in Renaut's version — is transformed from a hostile knight into Maugis, a menacing giant. Malgiers's mission is to defend the causeway to the island for a period of seven years, as local custom requires, at which point he earns the right to marry la Pucele. In the English version, this character becomes a stereotypical Saracen giant whose defense of the lady of the Golden Isle (Dame Amoure) appears to be driven not by a desire to protect her interests but rather to inflict harm whenever another knight approaches. His function

---

[10] Renaut de Bâgé, *Le Bel Inconnu*, p. 95. The French reads: "Cele qui l'esprevier ara / et a le perce le prendra / si ara los de la plus biele" (lines 1589–91).

[11] Renaut de Bâgé, *Le Bel Inconnu*, p. 103. The French reads: "Molt estoit et laide et frencie!" (line 1727); "Amor ne l face bestorner; / la laide fait biele sanbler, / tant set de guile et d'encanter" (lines 1733–35).

in the English narrative, moreover, shifts from unwanted lover of the mistress of the Golden Isle to a serious impediment to Lybeaus's quest.

In a comparable transformation and variation between the French and English versions, a beneficent enchantress such as la Pucele becomes the malevolent sorceress Dame Amoure, who, like her guardian Maugis, threatens Lybeaus by means of her captivating spells, until Elene wakes him out of his stupor and he continues to Synadoun. Once there he encounters Lambard, the steward to the Lady of Synadoun in the English version, who, like Maugis, appears as a giant defender of her castle and therefore just another opponent who stands in Lybeaus's way.[12] While discernible shifts in characterization of these otherwise chivalric figures appear to be in keeping with changes in the portrayals of the enchantresses of the poem, so too is another dimensïon of meaning added to the English retelling. When the hero defeats the evil enchanters Mabon and Iran (Mabons and Evrain in the French), he enters the castle where the lady, transformed through sorcery into a dragon (a serpent in the French version), is imprisoned. In Renaut's telling, the disclosure of the young knight's identity comes from a disembodied voice (we learn later that it is la Pucele who speaks here) after the transformative kiss has taken place, and he is told that only the son of Gawain could accomplish such a deed.[13] This disclosure fulfills the requisites set out by Helie at the beginning—that the knight who rescues her lady must be able to endure the *fier baiser* to break the magic spell. At this point in the French narrative Li Biaus (a.k.a. Guinglain) learns who his parents are and that his mother, Blancemal la Fee, had armed and sent him to Arthur's court rather than choosing to resist his desire to become one of Arthur's knights as in the English version. The understandably grateful Blonde Esmeree (French version) offers Li Biaus her love, her kingdom, and a very political marriage, to which the astonished young knight agrees. But before the wedding takes place, Li Biaus returns to la Pucele where he learns, among other things, that she had known about him from the beginning and was, in fact, the disembodied voice that divulged his identity. The knight lingers with his "true love" in amorous bliss until a call to a tournament at the Castle of Maidens proves too much for him to ignore. Knowing that he will lose la Pucele forever if he leaves her to compete in

---

[12] There are two orders of giants in *Lybeaus Desconus*, the typical villainous giant who often opposes the knight with unchivalric weapons, such as a club or a grilling spit, and the giant as merely an extraordinarily large human being, who retains chivalric values for the most part, such as Sir Lambard. Although Lambard is called a "giant," he has neither the feral characteristics of the malevolent red and black giants who threaten Violet nor the animal features of Maugis; these are stereotypical giants of romance, and thus no match for Lybeaus. Lambard appears as a giant because of his size, and in this, he is more akin to Sir Valentine in *Sir Launfal* (lines 505–12). Lambard has no associations with violence against women, treacherous and unchivalric behavior, or unorthodox fighting as do the stereotypical giants: instead he tests knights for the task of rescuing the Lady of Synadoun, and once defeated in combat by Lybeaus, he identifies Lybeaus ("Thowe arte of Sir Gawynes kynne," Lambeth, line 1708) and with many expressions of courtesy welcomes him as the deliverer of his Lady. In Naples, Lybeaus's mother is said to be "a giantis lady" (line 2249). See also Explanatory Note to line 1708.

[13] At that moment, the Fair Unknown in Renaut de Bâgé's version discovers his real name, given to him at baptism: la Pucele tells him that, "King Arthur called you by the wrong name / he called you the Fair Unknown, / but Guinglain is the name you were given at baptism" – "Li rois Artus mal te nonma: / Bel Descouneü t'apiela, / Guinglains as non es batestire" (lines 3231–33). In the English version, Lybeaus discovers from Lambard and the Lady of Synadoun that he is related to Sir Gawain, but his mother reveals his full identity as Gawain's son only in the Naples and Ashmole manuscripts.

this prestigious event, he departs nonetheless and subsequently wins the praise of all who witness his prodigious expertise on the field. When the tournament is over, the king urges the now-proven Arthurian knight to agree to marry Blonde Esmeree, an arrangement that will make him the king of Wales. All the while, he longs to return to his true love — la Pucele.

The Middle English romance omits the second part of Renaut's story with the hero's conflict between two women, la Pucele and Blonde Esmeree (a conventional tension between passionate love and marriage), his return to la Pucele after his rescue of Blonde Esmeree, and the narrator's suggestion at the conclusion that Li Biaus's love for la Pucele might unfold as a narrative sequel. Instead, *Lybeaus Desconus* concludes with the eponymous hero's marriage to the Lady of Synadoun, though the marriage in the English tale is always the conclusion of the tale. Rather, a final reconciliation scene, present in only two of six redactions, brings Lybeaus's mother to Arthur's court where, in a dramatic face-to-face with Gawain, she announces that the newly validated knight is their son. Neither attempting denial nor rejecting accountability, Gawain responds affirmatively, and in a poignant narrative moment father and son reunite. Such an emotional scene is rare even in romances driven by familial reunion (*Sir Degaré*, *Southern* and *Northern Octavian*, *Emaré*, *Lai of Le Freine*, and *Sir Isumbras* come to mind here). The *Lybeaus* poet solves the problem of the hero's identity and place in the world through reconciliation with his separated and heretofore "lost" biological parents in a memorable way.

MANUSCRIPTS AND PROVENANCE

There are six manuscripts containing *Lybeaus Desconus*: London, British Library, MS Cotton Caligula A.ii (C, c. 1400); Naples, Biblioteca Nazionale, MS XIII.B.29 (N, 1457); London, Lambeth Palace, MS 306 (L, c. 1460); Oxford, Bodleian Library, MS 6922, also known as Ashmole 61 (A, c. 1490); London, Lincoln's Inn, MS 150 (LI, c.1400); and London, British Library, MS Additional 27879 (P, the Percy Folio, c. 1650). The poem is thought to have been written in the mid-fourteenth century (c. 1350), though the precise date is still a matter of speculation. Correspondences with a number of romances in the Auchinleck collection, "so exact as to rule out the possibility of mere coincidence," suggest that the work was influenced as much by the literary environment of the time as it was by its continental analogues.[14] That there is "evident borrowing from several earlier London romances," including *Guy of Warwick*, *Bevis of Hampton*, *Sir Degaré*, and *Otuel and Roland*, appears in the battles with giants, the descriptions of dwarves, some phrasing, and the atypical three-stress line that binds the poem together. All of these romances are contained

---

[14] Loomis, *Development of Arthurian Romance*, cites correspondences between *Lybeaus* and several popular romances: "In *Libeaus* we find correspondences to phrases and sequences of detail in *Sir Tristrem*, *Sir Launfal*, *Guy of Warwick*, *Bevis of Hampton*, *Sir Degaré*, and *Roland and Vernagu* — correspondences so exact as to rule out the possibility of mere coincidence." His exempla are from *Bevis of Hampton* and *Degaré*, but he goes on to say that "all six romances which show these correspondences with *Libeaus* are, or were, contained in the Auchinleck manuscript" (pp. 136–37). See also Purdie, *Anglicising Romance*, p. 212.

in the Auchinleck collection, although *Lybeaus Desconus*, once thought to have been included, now appears to be conspicuously absent.[15]

Among those to whom the story and its fair protagonist are known is Chaucer, who first mentions the narrative by including "sir Lybeux" (line 900) in a list of "romances of prys" (line 897) in The Tale of Sir Thopas. The Host's noteworthy interruption of the tale suggests to J. A. Burrow that Chaucer must have had the structure of the Canterbury journey in mind when *Sir Thopas* was written, which would make this first reference to *Lybeaus* after 1386.[16] Whether the English version of the Fair Unknown's story was originally included in the Auchinleck manuscript thought to have been in Chaucer's possession, or existed in a now-lost exemplar of the redaction included in the fifteenth-century Cotton Caligula A.ii manuscript, is a matter yet to be resolved.[17]

Evidence that an earlier, possibly Anglo-Norman version of the poem was in circulation in England is found in a list of romances that includes *Beu Desconu* in Shrewsbury School MS 7, a mid-thirteenth-century manuscript held in the library of the Benedictine Abbey of St. Werburg in Chester. And while it is important to note that the Shrewsbury list is *not* a modern-day table of contents literally noting items contained in the text but rather an individual folio added toward its end, probably sometime after 1270, it is also important to recognize that some version of the Fair Unknown was known in England earlier than originally thought.[18] Though the title is Anglo-Norman in spelling, the question of whether this *Beu Desconu* refers to a French or Anglo-Norman narrative cannot be answered definitively. As is the case with other such manuscript evidence, the narrative to which the citation appears to refer is non-extant, a status that places it in the company of other such documents, including the one referred to by Chaucer, a "lost antecedent" of the version attributed to Thomas Chestre circulating from about 1350 on, and an apparently lost printed version circulating from the

---

[15] Derek Pearsall and I. C. Cunningham suggest that *Lybeaus Desconus* was originally included in the Auchinleck manuscript but ultimately lost. See *Auchinleck Manuscript*, p. viii. The prevailing view now, however, is that *Lybeaus* was influenced by the Auchinleck manuscript but written afterward. Rhiannon Purdie comments: "this metropolitan literary circuit was clearly also drawn upon by *Lybeaus Desconus*, a later fourteenth-century London-area tail-rhyme romance which is almost certainly the referent of Chaucer's 'sir Lybeux' in his *Tale of Sir Thopas* (line 900). *Sir Degaré* has lent some battle scenes and a description of a dwarf; a version of *Guy* has lent details from Guy's battles with Amoraunt and Colbrond; *Bevis* appears to have contributed some phrasing. *Otuel and Roland* may have been the inspiration for *Lybeaus'* usual stanza of three-stress lines throughout since these (and *Roland and Vernagu* after line 425) are the only romances to use such a pattern, albeit partially masked by an inevitable scribal drift towards the more usual four stresses in the couplet lines" (*Anglicising Romance*, pp. 124–25).

[16] See Burrow, "Explanatory Notes: Sir Thopas," p. 918.

[17] Despite Pearsall's claim that the poem was originally in the Auchinleck manuscript only to be excised later (see note 14 above), Purdie thinks that Chaucer's knowledge of the work comes from another source entirely, a "later fourteenth-century London-area tail-rhyme romance" (*Anglicising Romance*, p. 124). Burrow, in the explanatory notes to Sir Thopas, says "Chaucer perhaps read these [*Sir Launfal* as well as *Lybeaus*] in a lost antecedent of the fifteenth-century MS B.L. Cotton Caligula A.ii, in which they both appear along with *Sir Eglamour* and *Ypotis*" ("Explanatory Notes: Sir Thopas," p. 917).

[18] Archibald, "Breton Lay in Middle English," p. 59. See also Brereton, "Thirteenth-Century List of French Lays"; Ker and Piper, *Medieval Manuscripts in British Libraries*, pp. 296–97.

late fifteenth century to the seventeenth century, the version from which the Percy Folio is thought to have been copied.[19]

In a different sort of evidence both extant and prominently displayed, the name "Lybyus Descony[us]" appears along with the names of twenty-four other knights inscribed on the Winchester Round Table sanctioned by Henry VIII in the sixteenth century.[20] Lybeaus's name is painted on the wood in the left hand margin of a table large enough to name twenty-three other knights. Literally written as "S[ir] lybyus dyscony[us]," the Fair Unknown's name is located in the twenty-second position in a sequence that includes Galahad, Lancelot, Gawain, and Perceval.[21] Although this artifact was repainted in 1749, the names of the knights are the same as on the original painting in 1516.[22] The style of the script, the *textura precissa* used for display in manuscripts and adopted for early printed texts, may or may not bear witness to another lost document, the early printed edition of *Lybeaus Desconus* thought to have served as the exemplar for the Percy Folio. Another possibility is that there is a connection to the Naples and Percy manuscripts to which the spelling of the hero's name corresponds.[23] Whether there is a tangible link between the Winchester inscription and these versions of the poem remains to be seen. What the inscription indicates without further verification, however, is public acknowledgment and familiarity with the story of the Fair Unknown.

GENRE, STYLE, AND FORM

Lybeaus Desconus belongs to a group of Middle English literary works identified as tail-rhyme romances not only because of their stanzaic form (typically twelve lines) and distinctive rhyme scheme — *aabccbddbeeb* or *aabaabccbddb* — but because of their association with French "romaunz," that is, poetry written in vernacular French. By the fourteenth century the meaning of romance had changed from a mere signification of the vernacular language in which a narrative was written into a literary genre with identifiable patterns of plot, structure,

---

[19] This is according to Max Kaluza, the earliest editor of the poem. See Kaluza, *Libeaus Desconus*, pp. x–xi. Helen Cooper, *English Romance in Time*, concludes that Kaluza's surmise has merit on two grounds — the accuracy of the Percy texts and Skelton's allusions: "Skelton lists [*Lybeaus Desconus*] among other romances known to have been printed in *Philip Sparrow*" (lines 649–50, in Skelton, *Complete English Poems*; see H. Cooper, *English Romance in Time*, p. 490n19). In other words, because all of Skelton's allusions are known to be printed versions, it stands to reason that his allusion to *Lybeaus* came from a printed version as well.

[20] Although controversy surrounds the date of its original construction, Henry's Round Table was painted in its current design with the names inscribed in 1516 or shortly thereafter. See Badham and Biddle, "Inscriptions in the Painting," p. 256. The spelling, Lybyus Dyscony[us] — a Latin abbreviation for "us" follows the "y" — corresponds to the spelling of the Naples and Percy manuscripts. The Winchester inscription, in other words, attests to the popularity of the literary text and provides further evidence of the continued and wide circulation of *Lybeaus Desconus* in the sixteenth century.

[21] See Badham and Biddle, "Inscriptions in the Painting," p. 255.

[22] Badham and Biddle, "Inscriptions in the Painting," pp. 256, 268.

[23] For the spelling on the Winchester Round Table, see Fleming, "Round Table in Literature and Legend," pp. 5–30.

and narrative style.[24] Despite their obvious associations with French antecedents, however, the English tail-rhyme romances distinguish themselves enough from prior influences to be considered a "unique" poetic corpus, although not a distinct "school of writing" as Trounce believed.[25] Certainly the rhyme scheme and stanzaic structure differentiate tail-rhyme poetics from early Anglo-Saxon alliteration and its subsequent revival in the alliterative long line of *Piers Plowman* or *Sir Gawain and the Green Knight* or the rime royal and early iambic pentameter of Chaucer.

Each rhyming unit of this unique form of Middle English poetry is comprised of a four-stress couplet, usually followed by a short, three-stress line, in a stanzaic pattern that calls attention to the short line as the primary element holding the structure together. Tail-rhyme romance may be rough around the edges, even amateurish or "hack" writing as so many critics have alleged, but it is a significant poetic form acknowledged for its ability to transform old stories into a distinctive literary corpus. That Chaucer parodied tail-rhyme romances in *Sir Thopas* in a negative way is generally accepted by Chaucerians, though perhaps too uncritically. When the tail-rhyme romances are accepted as a significant collective enterprise, however flawed in their execution and design, the mockery may be understood in a more positive sense, that is, as Chaucer's acknowledgment of the presence of a competing native poetic, fresh in its approaches to the retelling of tales in a style in accordance with popular interests and a newly recognized need for vernacular reading materials.

A feature of tail-rhyme poetry particularly relevant to a discussion of *Lybeaus Desconus* is its tendency toward piety. As the shifts in emphasis from the French to the Middle English *Lybeaus* suggest, the English poem demonstrates a more self-conscious recognition of a theo-centric environment than its courtly-oriented French antecedent. One of the first differences noted between the two is, in fact, in the framing of the narrative and *Lybeaus Desconus*'s prayerlike invocations at the poem's beginning as well as the "Amen" at its conclusion.[26] Such narrative framing, when considered in relation to the pious asides and enunciations to various saints throughout the poem, creates the impression of an underlying devotional consciousness that validates the poem's otherwise secular concerns.[27] Indeed, as Susan Crane suggests, "piety enriches and broadens the importance of heroic action, and in so doing it becomes in some ways merely an attribute of secular heroism."[28] That the pious framework of *Lybeaus* has the effect of catapulting secular heroism into the realm of the divine is sug-

---

[24] Furrow, *Expectations of Romance*, pp. 43–94.

[25] Trounce, "English Tail-Rhyme Romances," p. 88, and Purdie, *Anglicising Romance*, p. 1. See Calin, *French Tradition*, who observes: "Recent scholars, especially Dürmüller (1975) and Fewster (1987), have made the point that the composers of tail-rhyme consciously employ a conventional, indeed archetypal style and diction and thus constitute a school of writing. According to this thesis, conventional metre and diction ought not to be condemned; they are inherently no better and no worse than other sorts of metre and diction. This formulaic, stylized, distinctive style is formed by and appeals to pre-established audience expectations. It appeals to generic awareness and is, to some extent, self-referential as a code signaling archaic authenticity, narrative pleasure, and the actual presence of romance" (pp. 440–41).

[26] All versions of *Lybeaus* end with Amen but two, the Percy Folio (which ends with *ffine*) and MS Hale 150, which ends with *Explicit Libeaus Desconus*, followed by two lines in a later hand.

[27] See Dalrymple, *Language and Piety in Middle English Romance*, pp. 29–34.

[28] Crane, *Insular Romance*, p. 93.

gested by the implicit sanctification of a hero watched over by Christ and "heven's queene" and protected by a coterie of influential saints.

But there is something more specific to note about the piety found in tail-rhyme poetry, namely, the influence of Latin hymnody. As Rhiannon Purdie observes, "the primary associations accumulated by the tail-rhyme stanza from the twelfth to the early fourteenth centuries were, as one might expect with a verse form related to that of hymns, almost exclusively with didactic and religious material. The authors of the first Middle English tail-rhyme romances may therefore have been attracted to this stanza form precisely because its associations hitherto had been entirely *separate* from those of the romance genre, or indeed any other overtly secular form of literature."[29] While this theory is somewhat speculative, there is something to be said for an underlying presence of religious music in a poem driven by secular desires. The possible influence of Latin hymnody in fact renders the minstrel music at the Lady of Synadoun's enchanted castle, among other things, a far more suggestive scene.[30] The inclination toward a prescriptive morality literally underwritten by liturgical song indicates a poetic agenda aimed not merely at the production of pleasure but at the shaping of ethical behaviors.

AUTHORSHIP

Lybeaus Desconus has been attributed to Thomas Chestre, whose claim to be the "maker"[31] of *Sir Launfal* appears in one of the manuscripts in which *Lybeaus* is also found: "Thomas Chestre made thys tale / Of the noble knight Syr Launfale." Such evidence of Chestre's writing of *Launfal* is rendered credible mostly because there is an identifying signature and claim to authorship by someone named Thomas Chestre.[32] Based on what amounts to very slim evidence indeed, the claim is underwritten by an assertion that Thomas Chestre authored two other Middle English romances also found in Cotton Caligula A.ii — *Octovian Imperator* (*Southern Octavian*) and *Lybeaus Desconus*, despite the fact that neither is accompanied by an identifying comment such as that found in *Launfal*, though there are

---

[29] Purdie, *Anglicising Romance*, p. 6.

[30] Zaerr, "Music and Magic." However, as Zaerr points out, references to music and minstrelsy in the narrative come from the outside and suggest threat or evil, threat perhaps when associated with the dwarf, but danger and evil when associated with Dame Damour and the sorcerers Mabon and Igrain. See below, pp. 25–26, especially notes 90 and 91.

[31] The argument that Thomas Chestre is the author of *Sir Launfal*, *Lybeaus Desconus*, and *Octovian Imperator* (the *Southern Octavian*) has been advanced on grounds of content and meter by Sarrazin and Kaluza and on grounds of "habits of composition" by Mills (see Mills, "Composition and Style"; Mills, *Lybeaus Desconus*; see Kaluza, "Thomas Chestre, Verfasser des Launfal"). Two of the romances (*Sir Launfal* and *Octovian Imperator*) attributed to Chestre are unique to British Library, MS Cotton Caligula A.ii, and McSparran argues that the unique layout of *Sir Launfal*, *Lybeaus Desconus*, and *Octovian Imperator* in this manuscript suggests a grouping found in the copyist's exemplar, which might confirm the common authorship of Thomas Chestre for all three romances (see McSparran, "British Library Manuscript Cotton Caligula A.II," and M. Evans, *Rereading Middle English Romance*, p. 71).

[32] *Sir Launfal*, lines 1039–40, in Laskaya and Salisbury, *Middle English Breton Lays*, p. 239.

similarities in content and style.[33] Those who advocate Chestre's authorship of *Lybeaus Desconus* advance a plausible argument based on diction, dialect, meter, and "habits of composition."[34] Nonetheless, the lack of convincing external evidence, especially when added to the absence of a signature in any of the redactions of the poem, raises more concerns than it lays to rest.[35] For these reasons we have chosen to identify the poet of *Lybeaus Desconus* not as Thomas Chestre but in keeping with the way that other anonymous authors of the time have been identified, that is, as "the *Lybeaus* poet."[36]

NARRATIVE POPULARITY AND EARLY RECEPTION

The six extant manuscripts of *Lybeaus Desconus* attest to its popularity, placing *Lybeaus* in the company of *Guy of Warwick*, *Bevis of Hampton*, and *Sir Isumbras* as among the most popular of the Middle English romances.[37] In addition to Chaucer's allusion in Sir Thopas, the poem and/or its hero are cited in the anonymous *Squire of Low Degree* and in two of the Gawain romances, briefly in Malory's *Works*, and twice by John Skelton — in *Phyllyp Sparowe* and "Agenst Garnesche" — in ways that indicate a positive valuation and appreciation of the work, its protagonist, and its genre. That perception appears to change by the time Richard Hyrde translates Juan Vives's *De Institutione Feminae Christianae* (1524) as *The Instruction of a Christen Woman* (1529), and Henry Crosse pens *Vertues Common-Wealth or The High-Way to Honour* (1603). Indeed, reservations expressed about *Lybeaus* as suitable reading material for young women indicate that the genre of the poem had become suspect for a vernacular audience, especially one including women. Likewise, though for slightly different reasons, the seventeenth-century clergyman Bishop Thomas Percy expresses ambivalence in his assessments of the poem, and by the nineteenth century, even after significant efforts had been made to enfold early English poetry into a distinctively British literary tradition, the canon appears not to have included *Lybeaus Desconus*. If the remarks of Henry J. Todd in his 1812 catalogue are any indication of *Lybeaus*'s reception by English-reading audiences, then the

---

[33] As Purdie states, "The case should perhaps be reopened, although I am not sure there is enough evidence available to solve it" (*Anglicising Romance*, p. 212). The problem with this hypothesis, she notes, is that the "evident fame of *Lybeaus* (compare the reference in Chaucer and wide distribution of its manuscripts) and the very minor impact of *Launfal* (unique manuscript; lack of contemporary references)," mitigates the link between *Launfal* and *Lybeaus Desconus*. There must have been an earlier copy of *Lybeaus Desconus* by another poet in the London area.

[34] Mills, "Composition and Style," p. 89.

[35] McSparran, "British Library Manuscript Cotton Caligula A.II," pp. 55–58, summarizes the views on common authorship expressed by earlier scholars.

[36] That is, similar to the texts of another famous fourteenth-century author, the *Gawain-* / *Pearl*-poet.

[37] The popularity and therefore the centrality of *Lybeaus Desconus* in the Middle English romance tradition has largely been overlooked, despite the survival of six manuscript copies and numerous allusions to it. Recently, for example, Ivana Djordjević and Jennifer Fellow's "Introduction" in *Sir Bevis*, argues: "Although it is relatively little known today, the story of Bevis of Hampton was among the most popular narratives of the medieval and early modern periods, its only serious rival in this respect being that of Guy of Warwick" (p. 1). Furrow's *Expectations of Medieval Romance* makes no mention of *Lybeaus*.

tale seems to have enjoyed its heyday from the fourteenth to the seventeenth century, falling into the sphere of the "strangely neglected" by the early nineteenth century.[38]

While there is a lack of absolute certainty about how Chaucer came to know the tale in the late fourteenth century, it apparently intrigued him enough to invent a rivalry between the indefatigable protagonist of Sir Thopas and Sir Lybeux. Given the association of The Wife of Bath's Tale with the transformation motif so central to Fair Unknown narratives, it is also quite possible that Alisoun's tale of an unnamed knight errant may be understood to describe another variation on Lybeaus Desconus or even a disguised version of Gawain himself. Since the knight's ultimate marriage to the loathly lady who saves his life is common to a number of interrelated narratives, the Fair Unknown's presence in the *Canterbury Tales* becomes all the more plausible.[39] That The Wife of Bath's Tale evinces such a compelling kinship to the Gawain romances that form a subset of the imposing corpus of Arthurian tales known to a wide audience by Chaucer's time underwrites an intertextual affiliation that includes *The Wedding of Sir Gawain and Dame Ragnelle*, *Sir Gawain and the Carle of Carlisle*, *The Squire of Low Degree*, and to a lesser extent, Malory's "Tale of Sir Gareth."[40]

Not surprisingly, the Gawain narratives allude to Gawain's son in terms that bind the charismatic knight's progeny firmly to the English branch of the Fair Unknown family. In *Wedding*, for instance, when Gawain not only promises to marry Dame Ragnelle, the loathly lady figure in The Wife of Bath's Tale, but bequeaths her sovereignty on their wedding night, Ragnelle changes into a beautiful woman with whom Gawain begets a son subsequently named Gyngolyn: "Syr Gawen gatt on her Gyngolyn / That was a good knyght of strengthe and kynn / And of the Table Round" (lines 799–801).[41] Within the context of marriage, this characterization of Gawain's progeny is untroubled by the stigmatizing effects of illegitimacy that appear to haunt *Lybeaus Desconus*. Instead, he is a crucial signifier of a procreative nuptial ideal, the wedding of "true" love and the famously elusive knight errant, Gawain.

In *Sir Gawain and the Carle of Carlisle,* the name "Lybeaus Desconus" appears in the list of knights in Arthur's hunting entourage in an early scene that sets up the meeting of the king's men with the Carle of Carlisle, a man who, like Bertilak/Green Knight in *Sir Gawain and the Green Knight* or Sir Gromer Somer Jour in *Wedding*, challenges the Arthurian court and the veracity of its "proude" knights: "Syr Lebyus Dyskonus was thare / Wytt proude men les and mare" (lines 55–56). Lybeaus is named along with Gawain, who is described as "stwarde of the halle" (line 46) and "master of hem all" (line 47); and while Gawain's paternity of the

---

[38] See Richmond, *Popularity of Middle English Romance*, especially pp. 1–24. Richmond traces the dissemination of romances in England from manuscript culture to the advent of printing and beyond. As is well known, Caxton printed new materials to satisfy the demand of a growing vernacular audience; medieval romances were widely disseminated in the fifteenth century. This assessment comes from Todd's *Catalogue of the Archiepiscopal Manuscripts*, p. 41.

[39] There is much speculation about the relation of The Wife of Bath's Tale to the loathly lady/Gawain romances as well as to those of the Fair Unknown. See *Riverside Chaucer*, pp. 872–73.

[40] Another narrative that belongs at least tangentially to this group is *The Marriage of Sir Gawain*, which survives in the Percy Folio. The absence of the child of the union between Gawain and Dame Ragnelle as in *Wedding* suggests yet another variation on the tale. See Hahn, *Sir Gawain*. All citations are from this edition.

[41] Hahn, *Sir Gawain*, p. 69.

young man is not in evidence here, his authority as "master of hem all" makes him responsible for overseeing the less-experienced knight.

While the association of Gawain and Lybeaus Desconus is noteworthy, however vaguely that association is forged, what deserves to be addressed more explicitly in *Sir Gawain and the Carle of Carlisle* is that Lybeaus's name as cited in the lines above (Lybeaus Desconus) appears shortly before Syr Ferr Unkowthe (Sir Fair Unknown) — as if the two were completely different characters: "Syr Grandon and Syr Ferr Unkowthe / Meryly they sewyde wytt mouthe, / Wytt houndys that wer wyght" (lines 61–63).[42] Thomas Hahn's suggestion that Lybeaus's "mysterious identity seems to have led to his being presented in *Carlisle* as two different knights" is clearly the case.[43] The division of one character into two separate entities — one presumably derived from *Li Biaus Descouneüs* and the other from the translation of that name to "the Fair Unknown" — suggests that the meaning of "Lybeaus Desconus" may not be fully understood in English, though confusion and/or doubling of names is not unusual in medieval romance.

While Lybeaus seems to have found a place in this family of narratives, his presence in Malory's *Works* is less overt, perhaps even latent and embedded in other motifs. Lybeaus is mentioned ever so briefly by his other name — Gyngolyn — as the knight defeated by Tristan during his madness and later as one of the "twelve accompanying his uncles Mordred and Aggravayne in the ambush of Lancelot."[44] He is neither a crucial signifier of legitimate wedlock nor much of a signifier at all. As obscure and fleeting as these moments are, however, they register a degree of awareness of this character's presence. Many have noted the general outlines of the Fair Unknown in the "Tale of Sir Gareth," the kitchen boy whose kinship to Gawain goes unrecognized when he comes to Arthur's court to ask for a boon. Sir Kay's pejorative nickname for Gawain's brother, "Beaumains" or "Fair Hands," indicating Gareth's inexperience at manual labor and combat, as Christopher W. Bruce points out, "suggests Malory's familiarity with the *Bel Inconnu* or Fair Unknown romances, featuring Gawain's son."[45] The Fair Unknown may be known, in other words, in the figure of the disenfranchised youth who rises to a position of status and renown in Arthur's court, his covert presence accounting for the near absence of an explicit reference to him by name.

There seems to be no absence of citation of the Fair Unknown in subsequent narratives. In *The Squire of Low Degree*, for instance, the young hero is alluded to twice: first, when the Squire expresses a wish to be a king's son "Or els so bolde in eche fyght / As was Syr Lybius that gentell knyght" (lines 77–78), and second, when his lady advises him to emulate "Sir Lybyus" in order to win her hand in marriage (line 614).[46] As a poverty-stricken squire "of symple kynne," the aspiring young man has little chance of becoming a suitor to the daughter of a powerful king. Nonetheless, the lady offers him a glimmer of hope when she cites the Fair Unknown as an exemplum for his edification:

Though you be come of symple kynne.   *humble descent*
Thus my love, syr, may ye wynne,   *In the following way*

---

[42] Hahn, *Sir Gawain*, p. 86.

[43] Hahn, *Sir Gawain*, p. 106n55.

[44] Malory, *Works*, ed. Vinaver, pp. 494–95 and p. 1164.

[45] Bruce, *Arthurian Name Dictionary*, p. 60.

[46] Kooper, *Sentimental and Humorous Romances*, pp. 136, 148.

Yf ye have grace of victory,   *the good fortune*
As ever had Syre Lybyus (or Syr Guy) —   *once*
Whan the dwarfe and mayde Ely
Came to Arthoure kyng so fre
As a kyng of great renowne —
That wan the lady of Synadowne.
Lybius was graunted the batayle tho;   *then*
Therfore the dwarfe was full wo,   *upset*
And sayd: 'Arthur, thou arte to blame.
To bydde this chylde go sucke his dame
Better hym semeth, so mote I thryve,
Than for to do these batyles fyve
At the chapell of Salebraunce.'

                        (lines 611–25)

It is probably no coincidence that a redaction of *The Squire of Low Degree* is found in the seventeenth-century Percy Folio, an anthology that also contains *Lybeaus Desconus*. The very fact that these narratives pass into a new audience of "not-so-wealthy commoners, who had only just started to read and buy books," as Erik Kooper suggests, attests to their cultural capital in an increasingly literate economy.[47] But popular interest is driven as much by subject matter as by affordability, and the Squire's humble background and ultimate success are appealing narrative themes. When the proof of the Squire's eligibility for marriage to a king's daughter resides in actions modeled on those of Sir Lybeaus, an outsider and ostensible social inferior, his success offers hope that any young man can grow up to be a knight of great renown.

AUDIENCE RECEPTION IN THE LATE FIFTEENTH CENTURY AND BEYOND

The appeal of these themes may provide an explanation, at least in part, for the popularity of the Fair Unknown during the late fifteenth and early sixteenth centuries. At least that inference appears to be possible if the work of John Skelton may be taken as evidence. The first of Skelton's references to Lybeaus is in a poem called "Agenst Garnesche" in which the poet verbally eviscerates his rival "Master Garnesche" in response to an impudent challenge. In an act of what one scholar calls "poetic territorialism," Skelton defends his art at the expense of his hapless opponent, who not surprisingly loses the debate.[48] The poet casts his *flyting* in terms of a tournament, a metaphorical framework aptly chosen for its one-to-one confrontational pairing in which the combatant is characterized as a foul and fierce brawler whose disagreeable countenance exceeds only his ineptness in battle: "Ye fowle, fers, and felle, as Syr Ferumbras the ffreke, / Syr capten of Catywade, catacumbas of Cayre, / Thow ye be lusty as Syr Lybyus launces to breke, / Yet your contenons oncomly, yor face ys nat fayer, / For alle your proude prankyng, yor pride may apayere" (lines 15–19).[49] Though deemed to be as "lusty" as Lybeaus in the joust, Master Garnesche fails miserably in his attempt to overcome a more skilled rhetorician. The allusion to the Fair Unknown, the

---

[47] Kooper, *Sentimental and Humorous Romances*, p. 132.

[48] Scherb, "John Skelton's 'Agenst Garnesche,'" p. 123.

[49] Skelton, *Poetical Works*, ed. Dyce.

name that tacitly supplants the hero's other name, provides a comparative standard against which the uncouth and naive poetic novice eager for rhetorical combat and *not* very good looking is measured. Although the comparison makes the challenger worthy of combat he fails to equal the Fair Unknown. What becomes immediately apparent is that the poet's insult works only if his audience is familiar with the reputation of Lybeaus as a hero known for his physical attributes as well as for his martial prowess.

The subject of Skelton's *Phyllyp Sparowe* suggests that the early modern audience included female readers. The 1,382-line poem is a lament for a dead bird spoken by a fictional narrator named Jane Scrope from her confinement in the Benedictine nunnery at Carrow. The bird, killed by an apparently voracious convent cat, is the subject of this lengthy eulogy, one that draws heavily from the liturgical Office of the Dead found in every layperson's primer. That dimension of the work is noteworthy in itself: Skelton has provided a credible female speaker with literary skills and an impressive reading list. Not only does the list of works acknowledge and comment upon the triumvirate of early British literature — Gower, Chaucer, and Lydgate — but it also includes several works of classical literature and an ample sampling of the "matter" of France, of Rome, and of Greece. Of most interest, especially in relation to the canonical literature just noted, is Jane Scrope's citation of tail-rhyme romances such as "Gawen and Syr Guy . . . And of Syr Libious / Named Dysconius" (lines 629, 649–50). If *Phyllyp Sparowe* is "quite simply, about reading and readers," as one scholar suggests, then readers are invited to identify with this highly literate woman in the act of performing a poem of her own.[50] At the very least, both speaker and poem acknowledge women's study of literature and endorse an education that includes romances such as *Lybeaus Desconus*.

Such an inclusive approach to literary study seems not to be endorsed by Richard Hyrde or Henry Crosse. When Hyrde translated Juan Luis Vives's *De Institutione Feminae Christianae* (1524) as *The Instruction of a Christen Woman* (1529), he added a number of English narratives that young women were advised *not* to read: "Parthenope, Genarides, Hippomadon, William and Melyour [William of Palerne], Libius and Arthur, Guye, Bevis, and many other."[51] The association of this list of romances, which includes *Libius and Arthur*, with women's reading is clear — after all, Hyrde is translating a work aimed directly at their instruction. But lest we understand Hyrde's recommendation as merely another example of gender bias, it is important to point out that the censure of certain reading materials fits into a larger pattern of changing attitudes toward creative work deemed threatening to the morals of minors and other such impressionable people. Henry Crosse's early seventeenth-century *Vertues Common-Wealth or The High-way to Honour* (1603), in which the author addresses the value of education and the proper discipline of "youth," follows in this vein when it prompts such an audience to avoid those who have succumbed to vice: "The drunkard, idler, spendthrift, person with a painted face, etc." And while Crosse's primary target is the theater and everyone involved in its production and performance, he nonetheless lists medieval romances such as *Libius*

---

[50] Schibanoff, "Taking Jane's Cue." See also Daileader, "When a Sparrow Falls."

[51] Vives, *Instruction of a Christen Woman*. Vives's list of censured texts reads: "in Spain Amadise, Florisande, Tirante, Tristane, and Celestina. . . . In France Lancilot du lake, Paris and Vienna, Ponthus and Sidonia, and Melucyne. In Flanders, Flori and Whit flowre, Leonel and Canamour, Curias and Floret, Pyramus and Thysbe" (p. 25).

and Arthur as works to avoid.[52] Like other reformers of the time, Crosse suspects poets to be purveyors of pleasures deemed detrimental to the young whose "untempered affections" are so easily set ablaze.[53]

One would think that nearly a half century later (c. 1650), attitudes toward romances such as *Lybeaus* might have changed, particularly since Bishop Percy, the antiquarian responsible for assembling the Percy Folio, includes the poem in his collection of reliques.[54] Percy's prefatory remarks do indeed seem to provide an antidote to previous negative assessments of certain medieval romances when the bishop voices an affirmative opinion of early poets. As evidence of his high regard, he selects *Lybeaus* as "one specimen of their skill in distributing and conducting their fable, by which it will be seen that nature and common sense had supplied to these old simple bards the want of critical art, and taught them some of the most essential rules of Epic Poetry" (3:xxii). As positive an assessment as this seems to be — that is, even without training these "old simple bards" are able to write something of note — Percy's subsequent commentary qualifies that assessment by denying the poem epic status.[55] The bishop apparently thinks highly enough of *Lybeaus* to present it as an exemplary piece of work valued more highly as historical artifact than as a work of art to be appreciated on its own terms.[56] Like subsequent antiquarians interested in recovering lost texts and shaping a distinctive literary canon in English (John Dryden comes to mind here), Percy acknowledges Middle English romance primarily as evidence that native poetry — beyond the bounds of an evolving Chaucerian canon — might be worth knowing about, its values worth assimilating.

Such interest in the poem appears to have waned in the eighteenth and early nineteenth centuries, though it was not completely forgotten. In his preface to the 1812 *Catalogue of the Archiepiscopal Manuscripts in the Library at Lambeth Palace*, Henry J. Todd, antiquarian and

---

[52] Crosse, *Vertues Common-Wealth*, pp. 102–03. When Crosse describes the items on his list as "editions," it suggests that there is indeed another printed version of the Lybeaus narrative, one that ties him explicitly to Arthur. This edition is apparently lost. "For if a view be had of these editions, the *Court of Venus*, the *Pallace of Pleasure*, *Guy of Warwicke*, *Libius and Arthur*, *Bevis of Hampton*, the wise men of *Goatam*, *Scoggins* jeasts, *Fortunatus*, and these new delights that have succeeded these, and are now extant, too tedious to recken up: what may we thinke? but that the floudgates of all impieties are drawne up, to bring a universall deluge over all holy and godly conversation: for there can be no greater meanes to affright the mind from honestie, then these pedling bookes, which have filled such great volumes, and blotted so much paper, theyr sweete songs and wanton tales do ravish and set on fire the young untempered affections" (pp.102–03).

[53] See the discussion below on medieval conduct books and romance reading.

[54] Percy, *Reliques of Ancient English Poetry*, 3:317.

[55] "If an Epic Poem may be defined, 'a fable related by a poet, to excite admiration, and inspire virtue, by representing the action of some one hero, favoured by heaven, who executes a great design, in spite of all the obstacles that opposed him;' I know now why we should withhold the name of Epic Poem from the piece which I am about to analyse" (Percy, *Reliques of Ancient English Poetry*, 3:xxii–xxiii).

[56] Percy Folio, "Such is the fable of this ancient piece, which the reader may observe, is as regular in its conduct, as any of the finest poems of classical antiquity. If the execution, particularly as to the diction and sentiments, were but equal to the plan, it would be a capital performance; but this is such as might be expected in rude and ignorant times, and in a barbarous unpolished language" (Percy, *Reliques of Ancient English Poetry*, 3:xxvi).

keeper of the archives, describes the Lambeth manuscript as one of many volumes to be of great value to patrons interested in early literary work:

> To the lovers of our early literature the POEMS in this Collection present an abundant feast. . . . Of the ancient metrical Romance of Sir Libeaus Disconus, there is a most valuable copy, till lately unknown. And in the same volume are several poetical reliques of the olden time.[57]

Todd's implication of himself as a lover of literature is abundantly apparent and perhaps the primary reason for his statement in a subsequent description in his catalogue of the version of *Lybeaus Desconus* contained in Lambeth 306:

> This is a valuable copy of the ancient romance of Sir Libeaus Disconus; a copy hitherto unknown to the curious inquirers after our ancient literature. In the old manuscript catalogue this ROMANCE OF PRICE, as Chaucer esteemed it in his RIME OF SIRE THOPAS, has been strangely neglected.[58]

That Todd would consider the work to be valuable but "strangely neglected" and "unknown to the curious inquirers after our ancient literature" appears to contradict claims to the popularity of the work after it passed through the hands of poets, historians, education reformers, antiquarians, bibliophiles, and various others over time. Whether interest in the poem falls away due to a shift in values or as an effect of educational reform and a concomitant antimedieval sentiment remains a subject for further inquiry.[59] What can be said about Todd's observation with a measure of certainty is that he considered *Lybeaus Desconus* to be worth studying.

LAMBETH AND NAPLES

The Lambeth and Naples versions of *Lybeaus Desconus* chosen for this edition represent two traditions in the manuscript production of the text. According to Maldwyn Mills, the author's "own version of the story is reasonably well preserved in manuscripts Cotton Caligula A.II and Lambeth Palace 306 (CL), while the texts found in manuscripts Ashmole 61, Naples XIII.B.29 and the Percy Folio manuscript (ANP) must derive from a common source in which an unknown reviser had tidied up some of the contradictory material found in the original version."[60] As Mills maintains, the Lambeth version is "fundamentally the best text of those available to us,"[61] though the Naples redaction is the longest and therefore the most complete reflection of the reviser's work, one that demonstrates a connection to one

---

[57] Todd, *Catalogue of the Archiepiscopal Manuscripts*, pp. 40–41.

[58] Todd, *Catalogue of the Archiepiscopal Manuscripts*, p. 40.

[59] Sir Walter Scott viewed the Naples manuscript in 1832. He copied *Bevis of Hampton*, but it is unknown if he viewed or read the Naples *Lybeaus Desconus*.

[60] Mills, "Mediaeval Reviser," pp. 11–12. Mills dismisses the Lincoln's Inn manuscript because half of it is missing, but he claims that it stands "midway between CL and ANP" ("Mediaeval Reviser," p. 12n4).

[61] Mills, *Lybeaus Desconus*, p. 12.

of the alleged authorial manuscripts, that is, Cotton Caligula A.ii.[62] Although Mills argues that the reviser mainly corrected the errors and inconsistencies of the author, a case can be made that the reviser, rather than being a correcting "hack," creatively introduces changes in the text that reflect a fifteenth-century reception of *Lybeaus Desconus*. What emerges from this sequence is a clear illustration of manuscript production in the late medieval period where a reviser functions not merely as a scribe but rather as a co-author. The most relevant of the revised texts is the Naples version with its consistent exploration of the hero, the villains, and the heroines in the cluster containing the Ashmole, Lincoln's Inn, and Percy versions.

The texts presented together in this volume make it possible for readers to compare the two most significant threads of development in the *Lybeaus* textual tradition.[63] Both the Naples and Lambeth manuscripts were produced in the mid-fifteenth century, so that differences in certain key passages render the Lamabeth and Naples redactions particularly fruitful substrates for comparative examination. When studied together, each complements the other in ways that reveal something more significant about the Fair Unknown tradition as a whole.

BEGINNINGS AND ENDINGS

An incipit designating Gyngelain as the "bastard son" of Gawain informs the audience uniquely in Lambeth, and Lybeaus's identity as Gyngelain is made apparent to readers right from the beginning of the poem in all but the Lincoln's Inn version. Further, his "real" name — Gyngelain — is revealed to the hero and the Arthurian court as well as the audience at the end of the poem in three of the six manuscripts — Naples, Lincoln's Inn, and Ashmole, a final revelation of identity missing in Cotton Caligula, Lambeth, and the Percy Folio, which lacks an ending altogether. In Naples, Lincoln's Inn, and Ashmole, at the marriage feast of Lybeaus and the Lady of Synadoun, Gawain commands all those gathered together to call Lybeaus by the name given to him by Gawain, that is, Guinglain: "calle Libeous 'Gyngelayn'" (Naples, line 2267). Because all versions except Lincoln's Inn begin with the narratorial naming of Gyngelayn, Gawain's revelation of his son's name at the end is an expected conclusion provided by those versions that end with this scene. Moreover, in the final episode in Naples and Ashmole, Lybeaus's mother returns to the court of Arthur, and even though time has passed and her son Bewfiz has matured, she recognizes him instantly. In Naples she is afforded the opportunity to reveal the young knight's identity to Gawain in a disclosure that prompts a joyful kiss of acknowledgment from the famous knight. Gawain then explains to the Lady of Synadoun that he begat Lybeaus of "a giant's lady" ("a gentyll lady" in Ashmole). These scenes, played out in the last few stanzas in Naples, are completely absent in Lambeth.

---

[62] Mills, "Mediaeval Reviser," pp. 11–12.

[63] It is not altogether certain, however, that the shorter form (C and L in this case) indicates the more authorial version of a *Lybeaus Desconus*. Jill Mann, for example, has called into question the assumption that medieval texts that exist in two versions (or more) necessarily progress from a shorter form (closer to the original) and a rewritten expansion. There is no external evidence to support the view that the C and L shorter accounts of *Lybeaus Desconus* reflect more authoritative texts than the lengthier N, A, P, LI tradition. See "Power of the Alphabet," especially p. 24.

THE LAMBETH MANUSCRIPT

Lambeth 306 is a compendious commonplace book (or miscellany) consisting of ten "originally independent" gatherings or fascicles, many of which are dated to the second half of the fifteenth century.[64] The entire book, written on paper, measures 29.5 x 21.5 centimeters and sports a style of binding that can be dated to the Tudor era. The section of the fascicle in which *Lybeaus Desconus* is found, thought to date from around 1460, makes that particular section of the manuscript roughly contemporary with the Naples manuscript. The principal scribe writes in a distinctive fifteenth-century secretary hand, though the manuscript includes a number of items added to its contents over time. Some items are attributed to John Stowe, a well-known sixteenth-century historian, while others, written in different hands, indicate owners with interests other than history. Because of the overwhelming number of medical "recipes" and various nonliterary items scattered among didactic narratives, chronicles, historical documents, and memoranda by Stowe, Gisela Guddat-Figge surmises that "the manuscript must have passed through the hands of owners interested in science, especially biology, and medicine, who, in their turn, filled blanks with recipes, diets for a nightingale and other curiosities."[65] *Lybeaus Desconus* is located between a list of names of herbs — nomina herborum—and "The Adulterous Falmouth Squire." The text is written in single columns (fols. 73r–107r) with one marginal note (fol. 74r), where "lybeus disconius" is inserted in a later hand.[66] *Lybeaus Desconus* is the only romance in Lambeth 306.

THE NAPLES MANUSCRIPT

The Naples manuscript is a plain paper manuscript (seventy-three folios and two fly leaves), copied in the mid-fifteenth century and completed in 1457.[67] The vellum binding is modern, and the leaves have been trimmed so that pages have an average size of 28.5 x 19.5 centimeters.[68] There are catchwords but no signatures or marginal notes. Why or how it ended up in Naples or in its present location in the former Royal Library remains unknown. Although there are several opinions concerning the number of scribes responsible for copying the entire manuscript, the *Lybeaus* poem was copied by one scribe who calls himself "More."[69]

---

[64] Guddat-Figge, *Catalogue of Manuscripts Containing Middle English Romances*, p. 28. Descriptions of Lambeth Palace MS 306 also occur in James and Jenkins, *Descriptive Catalogue of the Manuscripts in the Library of Lambeth Palace*; Mills, *Lybeaus Desconus*; Jones, "Life of St. Eustace," p. 13; and Pickering and O'Mara, *Manuscripts in Lambeth Palace Library*, online at the University of Edinburgh.

[65] Guddat-Figge, *Catalogue of Manuscripts Containing Middle English Romances*, p. 28.

[66] The spelling of "disconious" in the marginal note differs from the text; in fact, it matches the spelling of the Naples title.

[67] That is, according to a scribal colophon at the end of the manuscript. As to the accuracy of this date, Manly and Rickert note that they have "no reason to doubt it" (*Text of the Canterbury Tales*, 1:376).

[68] Descriptions of the Naples manuscript can be found in Mills's introduction to *Lybeaus Desconus*, as well as in Guddat-Figge and Manly and Rickert.

[69] Without considering the medical recipes, Mills contends that two scribes copied the manuscript, one beginning *Bevis*, and the second completing the manuscript from the second half of *Bevis* (*Lybeaus Desconus*, pp. 56–79) and all the other narratives until the end (see Mills, *Lybeaus Desconus*, p. 7). Manly and Rickert perceive one scribe for the entire manuscript (*Text of the Canterbury*

The manuscript contains in the following order: medical prescriptions (the first three are gynecological recipes), *Sir Beuys of Hampton*, *Of Seint Alex of Rome*, *Libious Desconious*, *Sir Isumbras* (brief fragment, lines 1–123), and Chaucer's *Grisilde* or The Clerk's Tale (missing lines 1–91). *Libious Disconious* appears in double columns, pages 87–113, with anywhere between fifty-two and sixty lines per page. There are also scribal jottings (including lines from Lydgate's "Beware of Doubleness") as well as later sixteenth- and seventeenth-century notes and drawings. The nature of the medical recipe collection together with the concentration of romances, a saint's life, and *Grisilde* may indicate a collection intended for a female audience.[70]

Like the Ashmole version, the Naples *Lybeaus* contains a number of passages and interpretations not found in Lambeth or Cotton Caligula. In addition to what Mills cites as correcting revisions and adjustments, the most significant additions include an enhancement of the giant features of Maugis, the comparison of Dame Diamour's sorcery to the power of witches, the follow-up killing of Iran, and the arrival of Lybeaus's mother at the marriage celebrations following the wedding of Lybeaus and the Lady of Synadoun at Arthur's court. The significance of these features and their relation to other manuscript versions appear in the Explanatory Notes, but the episode of Lybeaus's mother represents an important addition to the narrative. Up until this point, Lybeaus only knows that he is in some way related to Sir Gawain: Sir Lambart and the Lady of Synadoun have both explained to him that only Sir Gawain or one of his relations could have accomplished the *fier baiser* and rescued the Lady of Synadoun from the evil enchantment of Mabon and Iran. Lybeaus's mother supplies his final identification as the son of Sir Gawain, thus providing a conclusion to Lybeaus's search for identity both personal and social, and it is this knowledge that moves Sir Gawain to embrace his son, acknowledge him publicly, and disclose his true name as Gyngelayn (N).

CHIVALRIC ROMANCE AND THE MEDIEVAL CONDUCT BOOK

In an enactment of what Stephen Knight has dubbed the "social function of Middle English romance," *Lybeaus Desconus*, perhaps more than other Arthurian narrative in the English literary canon, addresses the concerns of a variety of audiences — the problematic nature of intimate kinship relations, the resolution of troubled social and political affiliations, the perpetual quest for self-identity and place in the world, and the "proper" relationship between men and women.[71] Romances functioned to some extent like conduct books in medieval society, setting parameters for interpersonal and communal identity and action.[72] The illegitimate child relegated to the fringes of society, the stigmatization of unwed motherhood, forced separation of family members, the loss of patrimony and social status, as well as simple consent and choice of marriage partner are some of the matters addressed in narratives that encourage audiences to revel in the glamorous life of the adventurous knight while

---

Tales, 1:376–78), whereas Ralph Hanna suggests there may be three, one for the medical recipes, and the two others described by Mills (Ralph Hanna, private email correspondence with James Weldon, 27 August 2006; it should be pointed out, however, that Hanna's reading was based upon representative samples from the three contended areas of the manuscript and not the entire manuscript).

[70] See Weldon, "Naples Manuscript," pp. 139–48.

[71] Knight, "Social Function."

[72] For medieval conduct books, scholarly investigation begins with Nicholls, *Matter of Courtesy*, and Ashley, "Medieval Courtesy Books."

contemplating reconciliation and recompense for those not born into a privileged class or disenfranchised by circumstances beyond their control.[73]

Typically in chivalric romances, discipline and training prepare a novice knight to negotiate a range of obstacles designed to challenge his martial prowess as well as his adherence to strict codes of knightly behavior. Hence, many of these narratives offer situations and circumstances that test the novice at every stage of development. Such physical and intellectual training ostensibly contributes to the shaping of discernment and the young knight's ability to exercise sound judgment in difficult situations, to decide quickly and correctly when to apply force and when to offer mercy, for instance. The process, so evident in the training of renowned chevaliers such as Perceval, Tristan, Lancelot, and Gawain, explains its ubiquitous presence in the literary work of the time.

The mentorship of young knights as a component of chivalric education is particularly relevant to *Lybeaus Desconus* when it comes to the shaping of the protagonist's identity, especially since his father is Gawain, a native British knight whose reputation as "the proverbial equivalent of courtesy itself," accompanies his renown for prowess and loyalty to the king.[74] By the fifteenth century, Sir Gawain was well known not only in the late medieval literature often referred to as the "Gawain romances" but even beyond the literary world that made him a household name. Perhaps most famous in this regard is the acknowledgment written at the end of *Sir Gawain and the Green Knight*, signaling the close connection between the establishment of the Order of the Garter by Edward III, the poem, and the knight whose character is tested by a verdant outsider, his seductive wife, and Morgan le Fay.[75] Yet Gawain's training of the Fair Unknown in the English version is perfunctory compared to his more extensive guidance in *Wigalois*, for example, and omitted entirely in some English manuscripts, leaving the impression that everything Gawain's son knows about jousting, horsemanship, and the wielding of lethal weapons is somehow hardwired into his DNA, ready to be recalled by some triggering gesture or verbal cue.[76] Lybeaus at first appears to know very little about chivalry or the protocols of honor and loyalty or even the basic strategies of civil discourse; he seems to be the very antithesis of courtesy and refined courtly behavior; in other words, he is everything his father is *not*. But what Lybeaus expresses in a rather flagrant disregard for decorum — barging into Arthur's court to demand a boon, for instance — he makes up for in martial acumen, skills apparently bequeathed as much by natural law and biological determinism as by formalized discipline and training.

Akin to *Bildungsroman* and *enfances* literature, *Lybeaus Desconus* is a compelling narrative, a veritable emblem of a hero's progress from a state of ignorance and marginalization to a

---

[73] An example of a female version of the disenfranchised or foundling child is Marie de France's *Lai le Freine* and its Middle English translation *Lay le Freine*. See Laskaya and Salisbury, *Middle English Breton Lays*, pp. 61–87 and 409–14.

[74] Hahn, *Sir Gawain*, p. 3.

[75] At the end of the poem is the motto of the Order of the Garter founded in 1350, added by a copyist: *hony soyt qui mal pense* (shame be to him who thinks evil).

[76] The Lambeth manuscript omits Gawain's training of Lybeaus, and the passage is missing in Ll. C and the N, A, P manuscripts include a three-line passage: "Aftur, him taught Gaweyn, / With strenghe in the pleyn, / Poynt of knyghtis play" (N, lines 91–93).

state of experience and integration.[77] His story demonstrates the ramifications of illegitimacy and the lack of a "proper" name in a world that demands identities, genealogies, and verification at every turn. The Fair Unknown's entry into a realm from which he has been excluded or denied — equivalent perhaps to a "wild" child's introduction into polite society — makes for an attractive underdog narrative, the story of the gradual recognition of a hero's potentiality for success in the world. Like medieval male Cinderella figures such as Havelok the Dane, King Horn (or Horn Child), Bevis of Hampton, Degaré, Perceval, Lancelot, Gareth, La Cote Male Tayle, Alexander the Orphan, and even Arthur himself,[78] Lybeaus encourages an audience to identify with his unwavering determination in the face of otherwise impossible odds. With their emphasis on physical attractiveness and the prowess that complements the protagonist's good looks, male Cinderella narratives foreground the duties and responsibilities of those destined to assume governance of the land. Like their female counterparts, the heroes of these tales engage in domestic labor as a prerequisite for the public recognition of inner virtues disguised at first by humble outward appearances. Like a male Cinderella, the Fair Unknown is typically born of noble blood though he is often unaware of his patrimony until the end of the tale when he is about to marry an appropriately chosen mate.

As is also evident in chivalric literature and conduct books, training for medieval combat did not fully prepare a young man for participation in the refined discourses of the court — the recitation of poetry, the playing of musical instruments, the demonstration of exemplary table manners, carving skills, and overall civility and deference to courtly protocols. Courteous behavior and a dedication to helping those in need—widows, orphans, and disadvantaged others — were expectations for all experienced chevaliers. Since a knight was imagined not only to be a better combatant when he had a lady to impress but to be a better man vis-à-vis her influence and guidance, formidable feats of arms, as well as impressive displays of courtly refinement, were prerequisites to attaining an honorable reputation. The social function of the lady was to lend her prospective champion a patina of civility and to introduce him to the ways of women.

Medieval references to romances indicate that different readers approached these narratives in different ways, however. Male clerics would not necessarily view the genre in the same way as aristocratic women, and even within these groups one finds variations among responses.[79] In vernacular circles, romances were frequently read as courtesy or

---

[77] *Lybeaus Desconus* evinces a kinship to *enfances* narratives particularly in relation to their emphasis on chivalric training. These stories include *Enfances Garin de Monglane*, *Enfances Gauvain*, *Enfances Guillaume d'Orange*, *Enfances Hector*, *Enfances Ogier*, and *Enfances Vivien*. *Les Enfances Gauvain* is the most relevant of these, though it exists now only in a fragment. The Latin version is complete in its telling of the rise of Gawain; his illegitimate birth, and his abduction, fostering and adoption by the emperor of Rome. See *Rise of Gawain, Nephew of Arthur (De ortu Waluuanii nepotism Arturi)*.

[78] See Hoffman, "Malory's 'Cinderella Knights.'" To this list of notable protagonists Sarah Patricia Flanagan adds Sir Torrent of Portugal, Tristram, Ipomedon, Sir Isumbras, Guy of Warwick, William of Palerne, Gamelyn, Octavian, Eglamour, and Sir Gowther. See her "Male Cinderella in English Metrical Romance." See also Wilson, "'Fair Unknown' in Malory," and Salisbury "(Re)dressing Cinderella." While we recognize the fluidity of gender categories, the designation of "male" Cinderella simply acknowledges traditional scholarship on the subject and provides nomenclature that identifies the essentialist nature of this particular narrative.

[79] See Furrow, *Expectations of Romance*, pp. 1–42.

conduct books, that is, texts that taught social skills not only for young men and women of the gentry and aristocratic families but also for the children of the upwardly mobile urban middle class. Indeed, in his preface to Malory's *Morte Darthur*, William Caxton argued that stories of knightly deeds formed appropriate reading for "al noble lordes and ladyes, wyth al other estates of what estate or degree they been of," wherein they will find vice punished but also "many ioyous and playsaunt hystoryes and noble and renomed actes of humanyte, gentylness, and chyualryes."[80]

Romances also served as mirrors for young princes and engaged women readers, a practice to which later moralists objected. As noted earlier, Richard Hyrde strongly complained of women who wasted their time and endangered their morals by reading such improper narratives: "I marvayle that wyse fathers wyll suffre theyr daughters, or that husbandes wyll suffre theyr wyves, or that the maners and customes of people wyll dissemble and over loke, that women shal use to rede wantonness."[81] Hyrde stands in a long line of critics who charged medieval romances with inciting lechery ("wantonness") and promoting violence through tales of knightly combat. Henry Crosse voiced a similar opinion: "it will be demaunded how Ladies, Gentlewomen , &c. should spend the time, and busie their heads, as though idlenesse were not a vice bade inough of it self, without fire to be added, and as though there were not a Bible, and many good bookes wherein they might be virtuously exercised."[82] Margaret Tyler, who translated and published Diego Ortúñez de Calahorra's *Espejo de Príncipes y Cavalleros* in England in 1578, changed the title to *The First Part of the Mirrour of Princely Deedes and Knighthood*, suggesting not an audience of "princes and knights" but a wider audience responsive to a more universal focus on admirable behavior or "deedes."[83] And although she counters male charges that such reading is inappropriate for women and outside their proper spheres of knowledge, she also makes it clear that her edition is primarily aimed at women. As for allegations of inciting lust and violence, Tyler asserts that her defense is "by example of the best" and despite controversial subject matter such as war, she states that women "can farther wade into them to the search of a truth."[84] Hyrde, Crosse, and Tyler attest to a widely disseminated female practice in the late Middle Ages that placed romances at the center of their reading: whereas Hyrde and Crosse dismiss them as empty stories with immoral themes, Tyler defends both the genre and the practice; she suggests that discerning women "farther wade into them" and that they constitute, as her title intimates, "mirrors" of behavior, conduct books for both men and women.

Shunning bad behavior and embracing approved behavior, then, constituted a way of reading romances in the late Middle Ages and beyond. Lybeaus, with his uncouth background, frequently acts wrongly or questionably, especially in the early parts of the narrative. His impetuous and abrupt speeches in Arthur's court mirror uncourtly comportment, and his entry in the gerfalcon contest, where he coerces Elene to substitute deceptively for his lady, or his insistence on keeping the hunting dog of Otis d'Lyle, at best, seem dubious motives for generating the ensuing violence. Women guide and nurture Lybeaus: his mother

---

[80] Caxton, "Caxton's Prologue," 1:2–3.

[81] Vives, *Instruction of a Christen Woman*, p. 25.

[82] Crosse, *Vertues Common-Wealth*.

[83] Tyler, *Mirrour of Princely Deeds and Knighthood*, p. Ai (title page).

[84] Tyler, *Mirrour of Princely Deeds and Knighthood*, p. A.iiiir.

seeks to protect him from the world of male violence, but in the end (in the Naples and Ashmole versions) endorses his chivalric accomplishments and confirms his completed identity by publicly announcing Gawain's paternity before the court. Elene acts as initiator (as messenger she proclaims his defining quest, the rescue of the Lady of Synadoun), critic (she chastises and belittles Lybeaus at the beginning but ceases when she recognizes his prowess), and finally guide, especially when she stirs Lybeaus from the enchantment of Dame Amoure and sets him back on the road to Synadoun.

Various women present false alternatives to Lybeaus. Violet, whom he rescues from giants, offers the possibility of an arranged marriage, which while acceptable in many ways (she is an earl's daughter), falls below Lybeaus's destiny (he ultimately marries a queen); Elene, in her guise as his lover in the gerfalcon incident, represents a false option, as does Dame Amoure, whose sorcery and sexuality bewitch Lybeaus into temporarily abandoning his quest.[85] Even when they require rescue, women often offer positive assistance to the young knight as guides and mentors in ways that go beyond damsel-in-distress stereotypes. Violet tests his ability to obey a lady's direction and the Lady of Synadoun prepares him for political marriage and a kingship that he would not be able to attain in any other way. The functions of Elene's guidance and chastisement have already been mentioned, but the loyalty that she demonstrates toward her lady, not unlike the loyalty of any knight to his feudal lord, is exemplary. The Lady of Synadoun and Elene, her messenger and, in many ways, her surrogate, mirror strong independent women; while Elene provides guidance and counsel at every turn, the Lady of Synadoun offers the final pronouncement of Lybeaus's lineage and confirms his true identity.

There is much to admire about a poem that addresses the kinds of kinship matters so much at stake in the real lives of actual women, and it is not surprising that at least one redaction of this poem was thought to have been intended explicitly for an audience of female readers.[86] Certainly its strong female characters — Elene, the Lady of Synadoun, Violet, Dame Amoure, the hero's unnamed mother — whether cast in terms of stereotypes of victimization or unfettered from the constraints of literary convention, demonstrate ways in which women could assert a modicum of control on the world around them. The possibility of transformation by a kiss initiated not by the knight but by the lady he rescues speaks to the emotional and psychological changes brought about by contact with a force beyond the control of any individual, and offers a potentiality for transcendence that speaks provocatively not only to women but to all readers.

The literary construction of female characters, whether in supporting roles or the role of the woman in need of rescue, may be attributed in part to the literary conventions of the time and the expectations of medieval audiences who by the late Middle Ages had acquired a taste for romance. But so too may the conceptualization of "Woman" have something to do with the real-life experience of young men of the upper classes who often spent their formative years, as Ruth Mazo Karras notes, "in a military atmosphere, highly charged with knightly values . . . [wherein] the daily companionship was with other men, with whom a knight competed for the favor of a higher-status man," hence, "the young knight-to-be thus

---

[85] In C, Violet's father, "Erl Antore . . . Profrede hys doftyr hym to wyue" (lines 688–89). Although missing in all other versions, these lines, Mills in his edition maintains, are "genuine" (*Lybeaus Desconus*, p. 220n688–99).

[86] See Weldon, "Naples Manuscript."

learned that women were objects to be won, while men were comrades and rivals in the winning of honor."[87] While such childhood indoctrination may account, at least in part, for the development of fantasy stereotypes such as the unattainable courtly goddess, the transformative loathly lady, the vulnerable damsel-in-distress, and the erotic enchantress, it does not address the strength of many of the female characters in supporting roles, characters who provide narrative direction, initiate the rescue operation, and guide the knight through the perils of the quest. In the trope of rescue at the center of much chivalric romance, a knight is compelled to defeat marauding villains in whatever form they appear, to acquire the object that will prove him to be a man among men, and to restore order to the kingdom. Such constructions of the opposing other, an antagonist typically depicted as rapist giant or fire-breathing dragon, point to an amorphous fear of the unknown and otherworldly places, fears that the literary knight is expected to conquer. But when the lady is *both* damsel-in-distress *and* desiring monster (a woman deformed by sorcery and kept captive in an enchanted castle) as in *Lybeaus Desconus*, anxiety and confusion can drive the hero into momentary paralysis.[88]

FAIRY MISTRESSES, ENCHANTED WOMEN, AND THE POWER OF A KISS

Like *Li Biaus Descouneüs*, *Lybeaus Desconus* incorporates a version of the fairy mistress tale, where a knight falls in love with an otherworldly woman or an enchantress. Usually, the fairy mistress of medieval romance, such as la Pucele as Blances Mains in *Li Biaus Descouneüs*, Tryamour in *Sir Launfal*, La Fata Bianca in *Bel Gherardino*, or Ponzela Gaia in *Ponzela Gaia: Galvano e la donna serpente*, helps the knight accomplish his mission, often becoming the beloved woman who initiates the hero into true love while more malevolent sorceresses or fairies, such as Morgan le Fay, entice the knight to betray his chivalric principles and his destiny.[89] Dame Amoure (Lambeth) or Diamour (Naples) appears to be the latter sort of captivating enchantress whose function is to undermine the hero's progress and prevent him from fulfilling the conditions of his quest.[90] Despite the abbreviated nature of Lybeaus's liaison with her, as Corinne Saunders points out, "[t]he emphatic vocabulary of sorcery and

---

[87] Karras, *From Boys to Men*, p. 30.

[88] See Neal, *Masculine Self*, pp. 217–22, especially p. 219, for an interesting psychoanalytical reading of this scene.

[89] See Predelli, *Bel Gherardino*, pp. 225–39, for an analysis of the fairy mistress motif in *Lybeaus* and its analogues. The portrayal of Morgan le Fay as a malevolent enchantress is being reconsidered in the work of a new generation of scholars. See Hebert, *Morgan le Fay*.

[90] Dame Amoure's sorcery includes music, one of the clerical arts linking her to the necromancers Iran and Mabon. Part of Dame Amoure's enchantment of Lybeaus, then, is a result of her minstrelsy: "She made hym suche melodye / Of all maner mynstralsye / That any man myght discryve" (L, lines 1488–90). As Linda Marie Zaerr points out, Dame Amoure's conjunction of magic and music reappears later in the narrative in the enchanted hall of the clerics Iran and Mabon, so that one seems to be an extension of the other. In Iran and Mabon's enchanted hall, Lybeaus hears and sees minstrels: "Trumpys, hornys, sarvysse, / Right byfor that highe deys, / He herde and saughe with sight" (L, lines 1836–38). As he proceeds further into the hall, he sees minstrels in the niches of the walls and again hears their music in language, recalling Dame Amoure's sorcery, "Suche maner mynstralsye / Was never within wall" (L, lines 1855–56). The same "musical" magic victimizes Lybeaus and the Lady of Synadoun, who is transformed into "A worme . . . With a womanes face" (L, lines 2067–68).

witchcraft characterises the love of this lady as dangerous: rather than fulfilling desire, she literally corrupts vision to keep Lybeaus in her seeming paradise, a Circe figure in whom the power of Tryamour is negatively written."[91]

Perhaps the most memorable scene in *Lybeaus Desconus* comes when the eponymous hero meets the Lady of Synadoun, the damsel whose castle-under-siege distress call prompts Arthur's delegation of the mission to Lybeaus. Having been transformed by two sorcerers, the dragon lady approaches an awestruck Lybeaus, wraps her massive winged appendages around him, and plants the fiercest of dragon kisses upon his lips, an amorous act that triggers her metamorphosis from hybrid monster to fully-formed woman. Like Sleeping Beauty awakened by the kiss of her prince or a female Beast transformed by a male Beauty, the Lady is suddenly returned to her pre-enchanted state, as she appears "moder naked" before the astonished young knight. There is much to be said about a moment in which the enchanted world intimately touches the realm of the human as it does when the dragon lady kisses this impressionable young man.[92]

The fearsome audacity of such an intimate gesture clearly would challenge any knight's fortitude and restraint, but given Lybeaus's kinship to Gawain it is not surprising that such an episode emerges in a romance in which he must prove himself as stalwart in love as he is in battle. As he is the son of Gawain, whose own reputation includes the capacity to break magic spells and resist the temptation of a woman's kiss, it stands to reason that this scene would be necessary to prove Lybeaus's ability to endure this species of erotic assault, if only to provide evidence of his kinship to Gawain.[93] But perhaps what is most notable about this particular narrative moment is that Lybeaus neither attempts to slay the beast nor to defend himself from her ardent embrace. Instead, he stands immobilized and awestruck as the beastly beauty makes her move.

The transformative kiss known as the *fier baiser* has drawn so much critical attention that it has acquired a name and a genealogy of its own. The *fier baiser* is a popular medieval story in which a young man is required to kiss an enchanted woman who appears in some dormant state of inaction or repulsive physical form, typically as a serpent or dragon, in order to trigger her transformation back to her previous condition. Versions of this motif appear in medieval narratives throughout Europe, overlapping, as Roger Sherman Loomis has demonstrated, with the loathly lady tale in which a knight is tested by his willingness to kiss (or have sex with and/or marry) an enchanted woman in the shape of an ugly hag or loathly lady.[94]

---

[91] Saunders, *Magic and the Supernatural*, p. 188. Saunders sees Dame Amoure as essentially separate from the evil sorcerers; she is "a powerful enchantress whose explicitly faery magic contrasts with the 'nigromancy' of the two clerks who have enchanted the lady of Synadoun. The episode interweaves the folk motifs of the magical condition and transformation into bestial form, but these enchantments are shaped by clerical magicians" (p. 171). Dame Amoure's Circe-like enchantment perhaps figures in the animal features of Maugis, but it especially recurs in the music that characterizes her enchantment of Lybeaus and the clerks' transformation of the Lady of Synadoun.

[92] Saunders, "Subtle Crafts." See also her article "Erotic Magic."

[93] Larrington, *King Arthur's Enchantresses*, p. 215n56; Saunders, *Magic and the Supernatural*, p. 188.

[94] Loomis, "Fier Baiser in Mandeville's Travels." One such version is John Mandeville's tale of Hippocrates's daughter, who is changed into a dragon by the goddess Diana until a kiss from a daring knight turns her back into a mortal woman before she dies. Unfortunately, no knight is sufficiently courageous, and she dies having found no rescuer to lift the curse.

His willingness to grant the lady sovereignty and choice in the matter results in her trans-formation into a feminine icon and fantasy lover. Whether this transformation occurs by day or by night is typically left up to the woman to decide.[95]

While Loomis has argued for a Celtic nature myth as the source of these related tales, Madeleine Tyssens and Christine Ferlampin-Acher demonstrate that the snake-kiss is a pan-European folktale phenomenon, and not just a Celtic variation of the tale.[96] Two versions of *fier baiser* tales in Great Britain have been recorded by Francis James Child in "Kempe Owyne" and "The Laidley Worm of Spindleston Heugh."[97] Other variations are also in evidence. According to Laura A. Hibbard, in the Old French *Gui de Warewic* Guy's son Reinburn, in what seems an inverted form of the *fier baiser*, must kiss Amis in order to prevent his being turned into a serpent.[98] In some versions — *Li Biaus Descouneüs, Lybeaus Desconus, Lanzelet, Le Roman de Belris*, and *L'Hystoire de Giglan*, for example — the serpent/dragon woman takes the initiative, while in others — such as *Carduino* and *Ponzela Gaia* — the knight (sometimes with a little coaxing) initiates the disenchanting act.

FROM CHIVALRIC OPPONENT TO MARAUDING GIANT

As in the transmogrification of the enchantresses noted above, *Lybeaus Desconus* presents several of the knight's opponents in ways that transform their otherwise chivalric charac-teristics into something far more sinister and threatening. Transformations of characters such as Malgiers and Lambard indicate a shift in perceptions of otherness by late medieval audiences as well as by poets. Not only is Malgiers made into a stereotypical giant named Maugis, but he is aligned with pagan idols associated with Mohammed (Mahomet). And while it is fair to say that negative portrayals may be requisites of the genre, it is also fair to point to increasing xenophobia in England at the time.[99] Giants of Middle English romance, including Amoraunt and Colbrond in *Guy of Warwick*, Grander's brother and Ascopart in *Bevis of Hampton*, the Green Knight in *Sir Gawain and the Green Knight*, and the giant of Mont St. Michel in the *Alliterative Morte Arthure*, to name a few, provide a means by which a hero's martial skills and deliberative acuity may be tested, to be sure. But also at stake in these con-frontational moments is the validation of institutional authority, since the winner of such battles was thought to be on the side of justice. That being said, there is a discernible element of fearsomeness added to depictions of larger-than-life characters who do not subscribe to the dominant values of the land.[100] Lambard's characterization accords with other giants of romance, most notably Sir Valentine in *Sir Launfal*, but his otherness is distinctly ethnic when he is made into a Lombard. The presence of giants is clearly nothing new to Middle

---

[95] For an interesting range of possibilities see Passmore and Carter, *English "Loathly Lady" Tales*, and particularly Peck's "Folklore and Powerful Women in Gower's 'Tale of Florent.'"

[96] See Tyssens, "Les Sources de Renaut de Beaujeu," and Ferlampin-Acher, "La Fée et la Guivre," pp. xx–xxii. For a more recent survey of the fier baiser episode, see Jewers, "Slippery Custom(er)s," pp. 19–23.

[97] Child, *English and Scottish Popular Ballads*, 1:306–11 and 311–13.

[98] Hibbard, *Mediæval Romance in England*, p. 142.

[99] For an interesting reading of Lybeaus, see Cohen, *Of Giants*, especially pp. 73–76.

[100] See Cohen, *Medieval Identity Machines*, esp. pp. 188–221. Also relevant to the discourse on race and ethnicity in the Middle Ages is Heng, *Empire of Magic*.

English romance, but the shifting nature of their characterization provides a significant marker of changing perceptions of religion, race, and ethnicity.

ILLEGITIMACY, SOVEREIGNTY, AND RECONCILIATION

That marriage is considered to be a stabilizing social force in the late Middle Ages probably goes without saying. In a romance that addresses illegitimacy, however, the subject of legitimate marriage accrues greater significance, not only for the children born out of wedlock or not knowing who their parents are, but for the couple whose illicit sexual liaison produces offspring, the procreative "good" reserved for marriage.[101] According to medieval law, an illegitimate child was *filius nullius* and could not legally inherit property from either parent, a situation that places Lybeaus in a disadvantageous position from the start.[102] Even though his parents come together in the end in one version (Naples), there is no overt indication that they marry. This leaves the rather awkward dilemma of Lybeaus's status as renowned but socially disenfranchised, a dilemma resolved by his own marriage to the Lady of Synadoun. And despite the approval of this nuptial alliance by Arthur, both parties consent to an arrangement that promises to benefit each one, albeit in different ways. While the Lady of Synadoun stands to inherit a sizeable kingdom, with "Castellys fyfty and fyve" (L, line 2110), medieval law allowed such property to pass into the governing hands of a husband.[103] Lybeaus/Guinglain thus gains sovereignty over the Lady of Synadoun's land and erases his illegitimacy by the reconciliation of his parents, by their public acknowledgment of him as their son, and by his marriage to a queen.[104]

THIS EDITION

Readers will note that the editors do not identify possible scribal or spurious verses.[105] Our decision to present both the Lambeth and Naples versions of *Lybeaus Desconus* was made in an effort to provide a complementary double perspective on this important narrative rather than a compilation of all extant redactions or a single tradition of manuscripts considered to be "the two best copies."[106] An edition that attempts to blend all available redactions, to splice together stanzas and passages too often disjunctive in diction and phrasing, greatly affects the reading of the narrative as a whole. Likewise, a presentation of texts that represents a singular

---

[101] Augustine, *De bono coniugali*, p. 7.

[102] Brand, "Family and Inheritance."

[103] Because she succeeds to the kingdom, she can legally "welde all with wynne" (L, line 1787), since she operates within the same framework as male heirs; she exercises seignorial powers as well as manorial rights and later accepts the fealty of her tenant-knights.

[104] For the significance of female consent and legal arrangements, see Weldon, "'Naked as she was bore.'"

[105] It is difficult to decide with certainy authorial lines or phrases from authorial revisions, scribal corruptions of authorial revisions, and scribal interventions. For speculations on spurious lines in *Lybeaus*, see Mills, *Lybeaus Desconus*, pp. 10–13, and his articles, "Composition and Style" and "Medieval Reviser at Work."

[106] We are referring to Max Kaluza's early composite version and Maldwyn Mills's critical edition of C and L. For a comparison of the two editions, see Hunt, "Editing Arthuriana," p. 45.

component of a complex manuscript network forecloses a full appreciation of the richness of the late medieval literary environment in England. The editors of this METS edition believe that by presenting these two versions — one that represents the central editorial tradition of the text (Lambeth) — and the other that represents the most complete of the revisions (Naples) — our readers will generate more illuminating readings of a pivotal narrative in the Arthurian literary corpus and come to a more comprehensive understanding of the dissemination and development of a thriving manuscript industry in the late Middle Ages.

We have followed the editorial conventions of the Middle English Text Series:
- The Middle English letters thorn (þ) and eth (ð) have been replaced by *th*, and yogh (ȝ) by *g, gh*, or *y*.
- The use of *u* and *v* as well as *i* and *j* has been regularized in accordance with modern English practices.
- In order to avoid confusion with the definite article *the*, the second person pronoun, often spelled *the* in the manuscripts, is regularly printed as *thee*.
- Roman numerals have been replaced with their numerical equivalents in word form.
- Manuscript abbreviations have been silently expanded throughout the text.
- Punctuation is editorial and follows modern usage. Final *e*'s deemed to have syllabic value as a long vowel have been marked by an accent.
- Word division has been silently regularized in accord with modern English practice, including compound and frequently hyphenated words.
- Capitalization conforms with modern English practice.
- Double *ff*'s have been silently emended to single *f*, except for words such as *off*.

Any other deviations from the Lambeth or Naples manuscripts have been addressed in the textual notes.

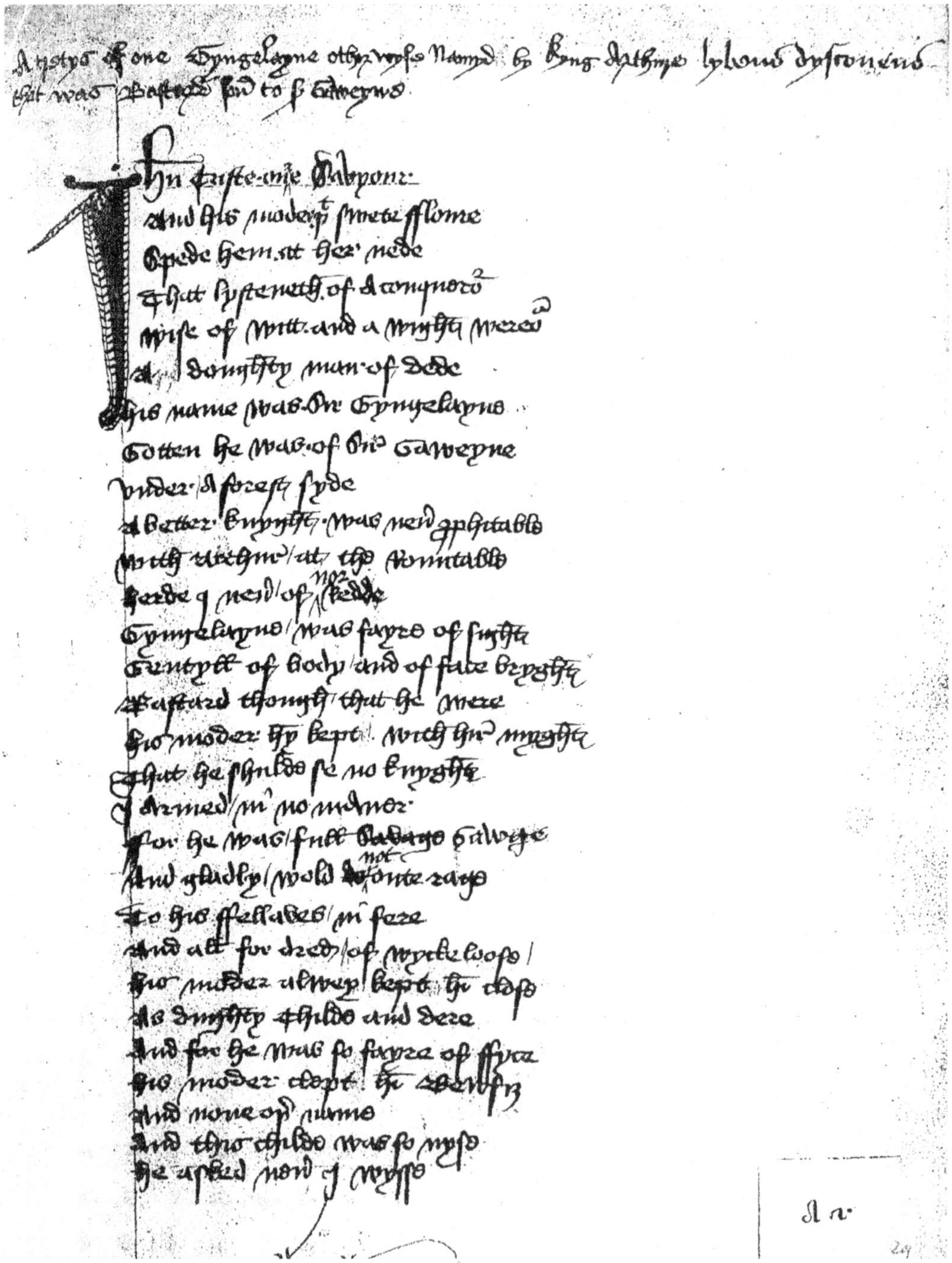

A gestys of one Gyngelayne otherwyse Namyd by kyng Arthur libeaus disconus
þat was ... for to ...

Jhu Criste oure savyour:
And his moder swete flowre
Spede hem at her nede
That herkeneth of a conquror
Wise of witt and a myghty werrer
A doughty man of dede
His name was Sir Gyngelayne
Goten he was of Sir Gaweyne
Under a forest syde
A better knyghte was neuer aphytable
With Arthur at the Rounntable
Herde I neuer of redde
Gyngelayne was fayre of sighte
Gentyll of body and of face bryghte
Bastard thoughe that he were
His moder hym kept with hir myghte
That he sholde se no knyghte
Armed in no maner
For he was full sauage halwey
And gladly wold not onte raye
To his felawes in fere
And all for dred of mykel woo
His moder alwey kept hym cloos
As dughty childe and dere
And for he was so fayre of fface
His moder clept hym sabulfis
And none oþ name
And this childe was so nyse
He asked neuer I wysse

Figure 1. Lambeth Palace, MS 306. Reproduced by permission of the Lambeth Palace Library.

LYBEAUS DESCONUS (LAMBETH PALACE, MS 306)

A tretys of one Gyngelayne othir wyse namyd by Kyng Arthure Lybeus Dysconeus that was bastard son to Sir Gaweyne.

	Jhesus Criste oure Savyour	
	And His Moder, that swete floure,	*flower*
	Spede hem at her nede	*Help them in their*
	That lysteneth of a conquerour,	*Who listen*
5	Wise of witt and wight wereour	*Intelligent; skillful warrior*
	And doughty man of dede.	*valiant; deed*
	His name was Sir Gyngelayne,	
	Gotten he was of Sir Gaweyne,	*Begotten*
	Under a forest syde;	*At the edge of the woods*
10	A better knyght was never prophitable	*[more] honorable*
	With Arthur at the Roun Table:	*Round*
	Herde I never of redde.	*tell of*
	Gyngelayne was fayre of sight,	*good-looking*
	Gentyll of body and of face bryght,	*Noble; handsome*
15	Bastard though that he were;	*illegitimate*
	His moder hym kepte with hir myght	*determination*
	That he shulde se no knyght	*see (have contact with)*
	I-armed in no maner,	
	For he was full savage	*wild*
20	And gladly wold do outerage	*violence*
	To his fellaues in fere;	*companions; together*
	And all for dred of wycke loose	*fear of a wicked reputation*
	His moder alwey kepte him close,	
	As dughty childe and dere.	*worthy; beloved*
25	And for he was so fayre of fyce,	*because; face*
	His moder clepte him Bewfiz,	*named; Beautiful Son*
	And none other name,	
	And this childe was so nyse	*naïve*
	He asked never, i-wysse,	*as far as I know*
30	Whate hight of his dame.	*What name his mother had given him*
	Tyll hit befell uppon a day,	*Until one day (At that time)*
	The childe wente him forthe to playe,	*hunt*

31

	Of dere to have som game	*deer; amusement*
	He fond a knyght there he lay,	*found; where*
35	In armes stoute and gaye,	*armor strong; beautiful*
	Slayne and made ful tame.	*Dead; fully subdued*

	He toke off that knyghtis wede;	*knight's armor*
	Hymsylffe therin well fayre can shrede,	*Dressed himself*
	All in that bryght armour.	
40	Whan he had do that in dede,	*done; in fact*
	To Glastynbury the childe him yede,	*youth took himself*
	Ther lay Kyng Arthure.	*Where lived*
	And whan he came to Arthurs hall	
	He fond him there and his lordis all;	
45	This childe knelyd downe on his kne;	
	"Kyng Arthure, Criste thee save and see.	*Christ; protect*
	I am come oute of fer contré	*from a country far away*
	My mone to make to thee.	*appeal (request)*

	I am a child unkowthe	*outlandish (ignorant)*
50	And come out of the southe	*from*
	And wolde be made a knyght;	
	Lorde, I pray thee nowthe,	*now*
	With thi mery mouthe,	*mirthful*
	To graunte me anone right."	*recognize; at once*
55	Than saide Arthure the kynge,	
	"To me childe, without dwellinge:	*Tell; delay*
	Whate is thi name aplight?	*What is your name truly*
	For never sethe I was born,	*since*
	Sawe I never me beforne	*Never saw I [anyone] in my presence*
60	So semely to my sight."	*[One] so handsome*

	Sayde Gyngelayn, "Be Seint Jame!	*By; James*
	I ne wote whate is my name;	*do not know*
	I am the more nyse;	*naive*
	But while I was at home,	
65	My moder, on hir game,	*for amusement*
	Clepped me Bewfice."	*Called; Beautiful Son*
	Than sayde Arthur the kyng,	
	"This is a wonder thinge,	*wondrous*
	Be God and Seint Denyce,	*By; Denis*
70	Whan that he wold be made a knyght	
	And wote not whate his name hyght	*knows not what he is called*
	And hathe so fayre a vice.	*visage*

	I shall yif hym a name,	*give*
	Amonge you all in same,	*gathered here together*
75	For he is fayre and fre;	*handsome; noble*

Be God and be Seint Jame,   *By*
So clepped him never his dame,   *called; mother*
Whate woman so she be.   *Whoever she is*
Clepeth him in your use,   *Call; for practical purposes*
80   Lybeus Disconeus,   *The Fair Unknown*
For the love of me;
Than mowe ye wit, on a rowe,   *more; understand in turn*
That the better ye mowe knowe
Certis so hight hee."   *Certainly might he be called*

85   Kynge Arthur anone right   *at once*
Con make him a knyght,   *Did*
In that sylffe daye,   *On; very same*
"Now Kyng Arthur hathe made me knyght,   *Now [that]*
I thanke him with all my myght;
90   Bothe by day and nyght
With my fomen I will fight   *foemen (enemies)*
Them to say with strok of myght   *test (assail)*
And to juste in feere."   *(see note)*

Whan he was a knyght made,
95   Of Arthure a bone he bade   *boon; requested*
And sayde, "My lorde fre: *noble*
In hert I were full glad   *would be; happy*
The first fyghtinge that ye hadde   *battle*
That men will aske of thee."
100 Than saide Arthure the kynge,
"I graunte thee thine askynge,   *grant; your request*
Whate batayll so it bee;
But me thinketh thou arte to yonge   *you are too young*
To do a gode fyghtynge,
105 Be ought that I can see."   *From what*

Withouten eny more reyson,   *discussion*
Duke, erle, and baron
Wesshed and went to mete.   *Washed; supper*
Volatyle and venyson,   *Wildfowl; venison*
110 As lordis of grete renon,   *lords; renown*
I-now they had to ete.   *Enough; eat*
Nade Arthure syt but a while,   *Nor had; sat*
The mountence of a myle,   *For a few minutes*
Att his tabyll sett,
115 Ther con a mayde in ryde   *[Before] there came*
And a dwerfe by hir syde,   *dwarf*
All beswett for hete.   *sweaty; heat*

	The may hight Ellene,	*maiden was called*
	Gentyll, bryght and shene,	*Noble; beautiful*
120	A lovely messengere.	
	Ther nas countes nor quene	*was neither countess; queen*
	So semely on to sene	*attractive; behold*
	That myght be hir pere.	*peer*
	She was clothed in tarse,	*exquisite fabric*
125	Rownd and nothinge scarse,	*Full cut; skimpy*
	I-pured with blawndenere;	*Edged; white fur*
	Hir sadill was overgilt	*saddle; overlaid (with gold)*
	And with diamondis fyltt:	*covered*
	Milke white was hir destere.	*destrier (riding horse)*
130	The dwerf was clothed in ynde,	*indigo*
	Byfore and eke behinde:	*In front*
	Stoute he was and pertte.	*Strong; attractive*
	Amongis all Cristyn kyng	
	Suche sholde no man fynde;	
135	His surcote was so ryche bete.	*surcoat; richly worked*
	His berde was yelewe as wax,	*beard; yellow*
	To his girdyll hange his fax:	*belt; hair*
	The sothe to say in sertenté,	*truth; certainty*
	Of gold his shone were dight	*shoes; made*
140	And coped as a knyght:	*caped*
	That signyfied no poverti.	*showed; poverty*
	Theodeley was his name:	*Theodeley*
	Wyde were spronge his fame,	*Far and wide*
	By northe and eke by southe;	*also*
145	Mekyll he couthe of game,	*Much; knew; entertainment*
	Sotill, sawtrye in same,	*Citole, psalter as well*
	Harpe, fethill, and crowthe.	*fiddle; stringed instrument*
	He was a gentill boourdour	*noble entertainer*
	Amonge ladyes in boure,	*bedchamber*
150	A mery man of mouthe.	*cheerful storyteller*
	He spake to the mayde hende,	*noble*
	"For to tell thine erende,	*Now; your errand*
	Tyme hit were nouthe."	
	The mayde knelyd in hall	*kneeled*
155	Befor the knyghtis all	
	And sayd, "My lorde Arthure,	
	A casse is nowe befall,	*cause*
	A worsse within wall	
	Was never yitt of doloure.	*sorrow*
160	Mi lady of Synadowne	*Snowdon*
	Is brought in stronge prison,	*taken into*

	That was of grete valure,	*Who; value*
	And pray you sond hir a knyght	*beseeches you send her*
	That is of wer wyse and wight,	*war*
165	To wynne hir with honoure."	*win her [release]*

	Uppe startte that yonge knyght,	
	With hert mery and light,	*heart hopeful*
	And sayde, "Arthur, my lorde,	
	I shall do that fight	*undertake*
170	And wyn that lady with myght,	*win; strength*
	If ye be trewe of worde."	
	Than sayde Arthoure, "That is sothe,	*true*
	Certeyn withouten othe,	*oath*
	Therto I bere recorde.	*witness*
175	God yf thee strenthe and myght	*give*
	To hold that ladyes right	*uphold; cause*
	With dynte of sper and swerde."	*spear; sword*

	The mayde began to chide	*object*
	And sayde, "Alas that tyde	*time*
180	That I was heder i-sentt!	*here sent*
	Thy worde shall sprynge wide:	*Your edict*
	Forlorne is thy pryde	*Lost; honor*
	And thi lose shentt,	*reputation tarnished*
	When thou wilt send a childe	
185	That is witles and wylde	*stupid; churlish*
	To dele eny doughty dent,	*blow*
	And haste knyghtis of renoun,	*When you have; renown*
	Syr Persyfal and Syr Gawyn,	*Perceval; Gawain*
	That ben abled in turment."	*proven in tournament*

190	The dwerfe with grete erroure	*anger*
	Went to Kynge Arthowre	
	And saide, "Kynde kynge:	*Rightful king*
	This childe to be weroure	*warrior*
	And to do suche labour	*hardship*
195	Is not worthe a ferthinge	*farthing*
	Or that he that lady see,	*Before; (Lady of Synadoun)*
	He shall do bataylles thre,	*battles three*
	Wythoute eny lesynge;	*doubt*
	At Poynte Perilowse,	
200	Besyde the Chapell of Awntrous,	
	Shall be his begynynge."	*fate (chance)*

	Syr Lybeus than answerde,	
	"Yett was I never aferde	*afraid*
	For dred of wordys awe.	*fear of daunting words*

205	To fyght with spere and swerde	
	Somdell have I lernede.	*A little something*
	There many man hathe be slawe,	*been slain*
	That man that fleyth by wey or strete,	*who flees*
	I wolde the devyll had broke his nek,	
210	Wherever he hym take;	
	Also I wolde he were to-drawe	*drawn and quartered*
	And with the wyne to wawe,	*wind; be tossed*
	Till the devill him take.	
	The batayll I undirtake	
215	And never none forsake,	
	As hit is londes lawe."	*it is the law of the land; (see note)*

	The kynge said anone right,	*immediately*
	"Thou gettist here none other knyght,	*You will get*
	By Him that bought me dere!	*[Christ]; redeemed*
220	If ye thinke the childe not wyght,	*worthy*
	Get thee another wher thou myght,	*wherever*
	That is of more power."	
	The mayden for ire and hete	*rage; anger*
	Wolde neyther drynke ne ete,	*drink nor eat*
225	For none that there were.	*no one*
	She sate downe dismayde	*disappointed*
	Tyll the table was raysed,	*taken away*
	She and the dwerfe in fere.	*together*

	Kyng Arthoure, in that stounde,	*very place*
230	Comaunded of the Tabill Rownde	
	Foure of the best knyghtis,	
	In armys hole and sownde,	*weapons whole; sound; (see note)*

	To arme him anone rightis;	*arm [Lybeaus] immediately*
	And sayde, "Throwe the helpe of Criste,	*Through*
235	That in the flome was baptiste,	*river [Jordan]; baptized*
	He shall holde uppe all high hightis,	*[Lybeaus]; promises*
	And be gode champyon	*good champion*
	To the Lady of Synadon	
	And fellen hir foon in fyghtis."	*defeat her foe in battle*

240	To armen him the knyghtis were fayne:	*[Lybeaus]; eager*
	The fyrst was Syr Gawayne,	*Gawain*
	That othere, Syr Persyvale,	*Perceval*
	The third was Syr Iwayne,	*Ywain*
	The fourthe highte Agfayne:	*Agravain*
245	Thus telleth the Frensshe tale.	
	They kestyn on him of sylke	*placed upon*
	A sorkett white as mylke,	*surcoat; milk*

That semely was in sale;   *handsome; hall*
Theron an haubryk bryght   *hauberk*
250 That richely was dyght   *appointed*
With mayles thik and smale.   *links thick; small*

Syr Gawyn, his owe syre,   *[Lybeaus's] own father*
Henge aboute his swyre   *Hung; neck*
A shelde with one cheferon;   *chevron (emblem)*
255 And an helme of riche atyre   *helmet elaborately made*
That was stele and none ire   *not iron*
Sir Percyvale sett on his crowne;   *head*
Lawncelett brought him a spere,
In armes him with to were,   *weapons; fight*
260 And a fell fauchone;   *fine falchion*
Iwayne brought him a stede   *Ywain; steed*
That was gode at nede   *good in battle*
And egir as eny lyoun.   *high-spirited; any lion*

The knyght to hors gan sprynge   *mounted*
265 And rode to Arthure the kynge
And sayde, "My lorde hende,   *gracious*
Yeff me thy blessynge,   *Give; your*
Withoute eny dwellynge;   *delay*
My will is nowe to wende."   *depart*
270 Arthur his honde up haffe   *hand raised*
And his blessyng him gaffe,   *gave*
As curteys kynge and kynde,   *courteous; just*
And sayde, "God yf thee grace,   *give*
Of spede and eke of space,   *aid; also*
275 To brynge that byrde oute of bonde."   *lady; bondage*

The messanger was stoute and gaye   *[Elene]; strong; spirited*
And leppte on her palfraye.   *horse*
The dwerfe rode by hir syde,
Tyll on the thirde day,   *Until*
280 On that knyght alwaye   *perpetually*
Faste he gan to chide.   *Constantly she; complain*
And saide, "Lorell, caytyfe,   *Fool, caitiff (wretch)*
Though thu were worthe suche fyve,   *Although you*
Lorne is thy pryde!   *Lost; honor*
285 This place beforne kepith a knyght   *before us keeps*
That with eche man will fight: *each*
His wordis spryngen full wyde.   *reputation is well-known*

He hat Syr William Delaraunche: *is called*
His fyght may no man staunche,   *strength; stop*
290 He is a werreour oute of wytt;   *warrior fearsome*

	Throwe herte other throwe haunche,	*Through heart or; hip*
	His spere he will throwe launche	*through*
	Whoso agayne hym sytt."	*Whoever opposes him*
	Quod Lybeous Disconeous,	*Said*
295	"Is his fyght of suche use?	*strength*
	Was he never i-hitt?	*smitten (unhorsed)*
	For ought that may betyde,	*whatever; betoken*
	Ayenes him will I ride	*Against*
	To se how he will fytte!"	*sit (remain mounted)*

300	They redyn forthe all thre	*rode on*
	Upon that fayre cause	*just purpose*
	Ryght to Chapell Auntours;	
	The knyght they con see,	*did*
	In armys bryght of blee,	*gleaming in appearance*
305	Uppon the Poynte Perylous.	
	He bare a shelde of grene	*bore a shield*
	With three lyons of gold shene,	*lions; shining*
	Well proude and precious;	
	Of sute lynnell and trappes.	*matching harness straps and saddle trappings*
310	To dele strokys and rappes	*deliver; blows*
	That knyght was evyr vyous.	*ever eager*

	Whan he sawe Lybeous with syght	
	Agayne him he rode right	
	And sayde, "Welcome bewfere!	*fair knight*
315	Whoso ridis here day or nyght	*Whosoever rides*
	He most nedys with me fight	*by necessity*
	Or leven his armes here."	*leave; weapons*
	Quod Lybeous Disconeus,	*Said*
	"For the love of Jhesus,	
320	Lette us nowe passe here:	*pass through*
	We be fer from any frende	*far; friend*
	And have wylde wey to wende,	*uncharted way; go*
	I and this mayden in fere."	*together*

	William answerd thoo,	*then*
325	"Thowe shalt not scape soo,	*escape so [in this way]*
	So God yf me rest!	*give*
	We shall bothe twoo	
	Fyght or than we goo,	*before*
	A forlonge here be weste."	*furlong to the west*
330	Quod Lybeus, "Nowe Y see	
	Hit will non other bee:	*It will be no other way*
	In haste do thi best.	
	Take thi course with thi shafte,	

	Iff thu conne thy crafte,	*prove your skill*
335	For here is myne all prest."	*ready to go*
	They wolde no lenger abyde,	*wait*
	But togeder con they ryde	*did*
	With well grete raundoun.	*energy*
	Lybeus Disconeus that tide	*instant*
340	Smote William under the syde	
	With a sper felloune;	*deadly spear*
	But William sate so faste	*firmly*
	That bothe his styropis to-brast	*stirrups broke*
	And his hynder arsoune,	*As well as the back of his saddle*
345	That he begann to stoupe	*slump*
	Over his hors crowpe,	*hind quarters*
	And in the felde fell downe.	*field*
	His stede ranne away,	
	But William nought longe laye	
350	But stertt up anone ryght	*jumped up quickly*
	And sayde, "Be my faye!	*faith*
	Nevyr afor this daye	*Never before*
	Ne fonde I none so wyght.	*Have I ever found; strong*
	My stede is nowe agoo:	*gone*
355	Sir, fyght on fote also,	*foot*
	Yff thou be a gentyll knyght."	*If; noble*
	Sayde Libeus Disconeus,	
	"By the leve of Jhesus,	*love*
	Therto I am full lyght."	*willing*
360	Togeder con they dynge	*clash*
	And fauchones oute to flynge	*falchions unsheathed*
	And faughten frely faste.	*fiercely*
	Dyntis con they dynge	*Blows they delivered*
	That fyre, withoute lesynge,	*fire, truthfully*
365	From helme and basnett oute braste;	*helmet; basinet burst out*
	But Wylliam Sellabraunche	
	To Lybeus con launche	*did thrust*
	Through his shelde on highe.	*shield high up; (see note)*
	Lybeus anone ryght	*quickly*
370	Deffended him with myght,	*himself*
	As werreor queynte and slygh;	*warrior skilled; clever*
	Barbe and crest in syght	*Barbel (chin protector)*
	He made to fle downe ryght	*slip down*
	Of Williams helme on highe;	*on top*
375	And with the poynte of the swerde	
	He shove Williams berde	*shaved; beard*

	And came the flesshe not nyghe.	*(without cutting the skin)*
	William smote to Lybeus soo	*so powerfully*
	That his swerd barst a-two,	*burst in two*
380	That many a man hit syghe.	*saw*
	Tho can William to crye,	*plead*
	"For the love of Mary,	
	On lyve now lett me passe!	
	Hit were a grete vylonye	*It; villainy*
385	To do a knyght to dye,	*cause; to die*
	Wepenles in a plasse."	*Weaponless; place*
	Quod Lybeus Disconeus,	
	"By the love of Jhesus,	
	Of lyfe gettest thu no grace	*mercy*
390	But thu swere me an othe	*Unless you; oath*
	Or than ye hense gothe	*Before you go hence*
	Righte before my face."	
	"In haste knele thu downe	
	And swere on my fauchon	*swear; falchion*
395	Thou shalt to Artor wende	*Arthur go*
	And say, 'Lord of renon,	*renown*
	As overcome person,	*a vanquished*
	A knyght me heder ganne sende,	*sent me here*
	That ye cleppen in your use	*you call; manner*
400	Lybeus Disconeus,	
	Unkothe of right and kynde.'"	*Unknown; lineage*
	William on kneis him sett	*his knees dropped*
	And swore, as he hym hett,	*as he was told*
	Her forward worde and ende.	*agreement from start to finish*
405	Thus they departed all:	
	William to Arthours hall	
	Toke the right waye.	
	A case ther can befall	*Something happened*
	Thre prynces proude in palle	*splendidly clad*
410	He met that ylke daye.	*very*
	The knyghtis all thre	
	Weren his syster sonnes free,	*sister's sons freeborn*
	That weren so stoute and gaye.	
	Whan they sawe William blede,	
415	As men that wolden wede	*who were enraged*
	They maden grete deraye.	*outcry*
	And seyde, "Eme William,	*Uncle*
	Who hathe wrought thee this shame?	*has done*
	Why bledest thou so yeren?"	*are you bleeding so much*

420	"By God and be Seint Jame,	*by*
	Of that he is nought to blame,	
	A knyght wel stoute and sterne.	
	Lybeus Disconeus he highte	*is called*
	To fell his fone in fyght	*foeman*
425	He nys nothinge to leren.	*has nothing to learn*
	A dwerfe rydis him byfore,	*rides; before*
	His squyer als he were,	*squire*
	And eke a well fayre berne.	*also a fair youth*
	But o thinge grevis me sore	*one; grieves me sorely*
430	That he hathe made me swere	*swear*
	By his fauchone bryght	
	That I shall nevermore,	
	Till I be Artour before,	
	Stynte day nor nyght.	*Never stop*
435	To hym I mot me yelde	*must present myself*
	As overcomen in felde	*defeated; field*
	Of his owne knyght;	*By his (Arthur's)*
	I shall never agenes him bere	*bear*
	Nother sheld nother spere,	*Neither shield nor spear*
440	Thus have Y him hight."	*promised*
	Than said the knyghtis free,	
	"Thou shalt awroken bee	*avenged*
	Sertys withoute fayle!	*Certainly; fail*
	Hym agayne us thre	*against; three*
445	Ys not worthe a stree	*straw*
	For to holde batayle.	*endure*
	Wende thedyr and do thine othe,	*Go yonder; keep your oath*
	And though the traytour be wrothe	*formidable*
	We shall him assayll;	*assail (attack)*
450	Or he this forest passe	*Before; passes through*
	His hambrek we will to-rasshe,	*hauberk; tear apart*
	Though hit be thike of mayle!"	*chain mail; (see note)*
	Hereof wyst no wyght	*Of this knew nothing*
	Syr Lybeus that yonge knyght,	
455	But rode forthe pase by pase.	*step by step*
	He and that mayden bright	
	Made togeder that nyght	*together*
	Gamen and grete solas.	*Sport; pleasure*
	"Mercy," she con hym crye,	*"Forgive me"*
460	For she had spoken hym vylonye;	*villainy of him*
	He foryave hir that trespas.	*forgave*
	The dwerf was hir squyer	*their squire*

And served hem bothe in fere   *together*
Of alle that worthi was.

465   On morowe, whan it was daye,   *In the morning*
       They redyn on her jornaye   *continued their journey*
       Taward Synadoune.   *Toward*
       Then met they in the way
       Thre knyghtis stoute and gaye,   *richly attired*
470   Rydynge from Carboun.   *Caerleon*
       To hym they cryed aright   *them*
       "Traytor, torne agayne and fight,   *turn around*
       Or leve here thi rennoun!   *relinquish; reputation*
       For here we westward wende
475   Thyne haubrek we shall rende   *rip to pieces (lacerate)*
       Ther to we bethe full bounde."   *To that purpose*

       Syr Lybeus to hem cryed,   *them*
       "I am redy to ride
       Agenes you all in same!"   *all of you at once*
480   As prince proude in pride,   *confident in his ability*
       He prekyd his stede on eche syde   *spurred*
       And to them stoutly con rede   *against; did ride*
       On ernest and nought in game.   *In seriousness; not in sport*
       The eldest brother can bere
485   To Sir Lybeus a spere:
       Gower was his name;
       Lybeus rode Gower so neghe   *close*
       That he to-brake Gowers thiegh,   *Gower's thigh*
       And evyr after was lame.   *ever after [Gower]*

490   The knyght gronyd for payne;   *groaned in pain*
       Lybeous, with myght and mayne,
       Held hym fast adowne.
       The dwerfe of Theodoleyn
       Toke the stede by the rayne   *rein*
495   And lepte up in the arson,   *saddle*
       And rode forthe, also skette,   *quickly*
       Ther the mayde Elyne sette   *Where*
       That faire was of fassyon;   *Who; form*
       Than loughe this mayden bright   *laughed*
500   And seide that this yonge knyght
       Is chose for champyon.   *chosen; champion*

       The medyllest brothere beheld   *middle; watched*
       How his brother in the felde   *field*
       Had lorne bothe mayne and myght.   *lost*
505   He smote, as it is tolde,

Syr Lybeous in the shelde
With his spere full right.   *directly*
The shafte a-two did brest,   *broke in two*
The hede steked faste   *lance head stuck firmly*
510   In place ther hit was pight;   *where it; driven [thrust]*
Lybeous than can ber   *carried*
With the poynte of his spere
The helme awey of the knyght.   *helmet*

The yongest brother full yerne   *eagerly*
515   Upon a stede full sterne   *strong*
As egir as eny lyon,   *fierce*
Hym thought his body can bren   *burn; (see note)*

But he myght, also yerne,
Ber Lybeous downe.   *Knock*
520   As werour oute of witt   *warrior in a battle frenzy*
Lybeous on the helme he hit
With a fell fauchon;   *deadly falchion*
So styffe a stroke he sett,   *strong; landed*
Throwe helme and basnett,   *helmet; basinet*
525   Hit clave in Lybeous crowne.   *It (his stroke) stuck; helmet*

Tho wax Lybeous agreved   *Then grew; aggrieved*
When he felte on his hede
The swerde, with egir mode;   *renewed vigor*
His bronde aboute he wende.   *sword; waved around*
530   All that he hit he shende,   *destroyed*
Alse werreour wilde and wode.   *As if [he were]; crazy*
Full fast men saide thoo,
"A man agaynes two,   *One; against*
To fyght is nothinge gode!"   *no fair*
535   Harde he hewe on him,   *slashed*
And he, with strokys gryme,   *grim*
Styfly agenes him stode.   *Staunchly against*

But throwe Godis grace,   *through God's*
That other brother he canne brace   *seized*
540   Under his right arme thoo;
He threwe him in that place
And in that selfe space   *very same*
His lyfte arme brast atwoo.   *left; burst in two*
The yongest say with sight   *with his own eyes*
545   That he ne had mayne no myght   *neither strength nor courage*
To fyght agaynes his foo;
To Lybeous up he helde

His spere and eke his shelde
And mercy cryed hym thoo.   *cried for mercy*

550   Lybeous answerd, "Naye,
Thou ascapest not so away,   *You will not escape*
By Hym that holpe mankynde!
Thou and thi bretheren tweyne   *You; brothers two*
Shull plight me your fayne   *pledge; promise*
555   Ye shullen to Artor wende,   *Arthur go*
And sey, 'Lord of renon,   *renown*
As overcome of persoune,   *[one] person*
A knyght me hedyr can sende   *sent me here*
To yelde you toure and towne   *surrender; tower*
560   And dwell in your bawndon,   *under; rule*
Ever withoute ende.'

"And but ye will so doo,   *unless*
Certis, I will you sloo,   *slay*
Longe or hit be nyght."   *Before nightfall*
565   The knyghtis sworne two   *two knights promised*
They shulde to Arthur goo,
Her trowythe ther they plight.   *Their oath; pledge*
Lybeus and that may   *maiden*
Rydden in her jornaye   *Rode on (continued) their*
570   Ther they haden tight.   *Where they had left off*
Tyll that the therd day   *Until; third*
They reden in game and playe,   *rode; leisurely conversation*
He and that mayden bryght.

They reden even weste   *[farther] west*
575   Into the wilde forest
Taward Synadoun.
They nuste whate hem was best;   *knew not; for them*
Taken they wolde fayne reste   *gladly*
And myght not come to towne.   *town*
580   In the grene greves   *groves*
Thei dight a loge of leves,   *built; lodge out of leaves*
With swerdys bryght and browne;   *strong*
Therein they dwelled al nyght,
He and that mayden bright,
585   That was of fayre fassyon.   *form*

And evyr the dwerf can wake   *all night; stayed awake*
That nothinge shulde betake
Here hors aweye with gyle.   *Their horses; stealth*
For dred he ganne quake   *fear; shake*
590   Grete fyre he sawe make,   *fire*

Thensse halfe a myle.   *Half a mile away*
"Aryse, sir," he sayde, "knyght!
To hors that ye were dight,   *may prepare yourself*
For dred of more perile;
595   Certis, I hire boste   *hear boasting*
And fele grete smylle of roste,   *smell; roasting*
Be God and be Saint Gyle!"   *Giles*

Lybeous was stoute and fayre   *hearty; bright*
And lepte upon his desteyre   *warhorse*
600   And hent shelde and spere,   *picked up*
And whan that he nyghed nere,   *drew near*
As he rode tawarde the fyre,
Two gyauntes he sawe there.   *giants*
That one was rede and lothelych,   *red; loathly*
605   That other black as eny pyche   *any pitch (i.e., tar)*
Gressly bothe of chere!   *Grisly; countenance*
The black helde in his arme
A mayde i-clypped in his barme   *clasped to; bosom*
So bryght as blossom on brere.   *briar*

610   The rede giaunte full yerne   *eagerly*
A wylde bore canne torne   *boar; did turn*
Aboute apon a spytt.   *upon; spit*
The fyre bright can bren,   *burned*
The mayde cryed yerne   *screamed ceaselessly*
615   For some man shuld it wit,   *witness*
And sayde ever, "Wayle-a-waye!
That ever I shulde bide this daye   *live through*
With two devylles to sitt!   *devils*
Helppe me, Mary mylde,
620   For love of thine childe,
That I be nought forgett!"   *forsaken*

Than Lybeous: "Be Seint Jame!
To save this maiden from shame,
Hit were enpure enprice;   *It; worthy enterprise*
625   But for to fight with bothe in same,   *at the same time*
Hit is no childes game —   *child's play*
They be so grym and gryse!"   *terrible*
He toke his course with a shafte,   *lance*
As a knyght of kynde crafte,   *natural cunning*
630   And rode be right assyse.   *just cause*
The blacke giaunte can to smert   *pierce*
Thorugh lounge and hert,   *lung; heart*
That never after can rysse.   *did rise*

Tho flye the mayden shene   *Then fled*
635   And thanked tho Heven Quene   *(the Virgin Mary)*
       That suche socoure hir sent;   *succor*
       Tho came the mayde Elene,
       She and the dwarffe bydene,   *together*
       And by the hande hir hentte,   *her took*
640   And lad hir into the greves,   *led; woods*
       Into the loge of levys,   *lodge; leaves*
       With well gode entent,   *good intentions*
       And besought swete Jhesus   *beseeched*
       Helpe Lybeus Disconeus
645   That he ner nought shent.   *never would be overcome*

       The rede gyaunte smote thore
       To Sir Lybeous withe the bore   *boar*
       As wolfe oute of wede.   *wild wolf*
       His dynnte he smote so sore   *stroke; lethally*
650   That Lybeous stede therefore   *steed*
       Downe to grownde yede.   *went (fell)*
       Lybeous was redy bounde   *reacted instantly*
       And lepte on his arson   *out of; saddle*
       As sparkyll dothe on glede;   *spark from a burning coal*
655   With hartt egyr as a lyon,   *heart fierce*
       He faught with his fauchon
       To quyte the gyaunte his mede.   *pay back; reward; (see note)*

       Ever the gyaunte faught,   *For a long time*
       But at the secunde draught   *round*
660   His spere barst evyn a-twoo;   *[The giant's]; burst; in two*
       As man that was unsawght   *enraged*
       A tronchon oute he laught   *tree; lifted*
       To fyght agaynes his foo,
       And with the hede of the tre   *top*
665   He smote Lybeous shelde in thre: *broke; into three [pieces]*
       Than was Lybeous woo.   *worried*
       As he his tronchon up haffe,   *[the giant]; tree lifted up*
       Syr Lybeous a stroke him gaffe: *gave*
       His right arme fell hym froo.   *from him*

670   The gyaunte fell to grownde:
       Syr Lybeous, in that stownde,   *place*
       Smote off his hede full right.   *head; decisively*
       In Frensshe as it is ifounde,   *found*
       He that he gave the fyrste wounde,
675   He servyd hym so aplyght.   *likewise*
       And then toke the hedis two   *heads*
       And bare the mayden thoo,   *carried them to*

For whom he made that fyght;
The mayde was glade and blythe *happy; relieved*
680 And thanked God fele sythe *many times*
That ever he was made knyght. *[Lybeaus]*

Quod Lybeous, "Gentil dame, *Noble lady*
Tell me whate is thi name
And where ye were y-bore."
685 "Syr," she sayde, "Be Seynt John, *By*
My fader is of riche fame *father; great renown*
And wonnes yonder beforne: *was once*
An erle, an olde hore knyght, *earl; gray-haired*
That hathe ben man of myght: *authority*
690 His name is Syr Anctour.
They clepen me Violet; *call*
The gyauntes had me besett *abducted*
Aboute our castell yore. *From outside; a while back*

Yesterday, in the evenynge,
695 I went on my playenge: *i.e., flower picking*
None harme Y ne thoughte.
The gyaunte, withoute lesynge, *lying (truthfully)*
Oute of the busshes con sprynge *leapt*
And to this fyre me brought; *fire*
700 Of hem I had be shent *By him; violated*
Nad God me socoure sent, *Had God not sent aid*
That all the worlde wrought.
He quyte thee thy mede, *[May] He give*
That for us canne blede
705 And with His body us bought." *redeemed*

Withoute more talkynge,
To hors con they sprynge *[Lybeaus and company]*
And reden forthe all in same, *rode; together*
And tolde the erle tydynge
710 Howe he wanne in fightynge
His doughter fro woo and shame. *sorrow*
Than were the hedis sent *heads*
To Kynge Arthour in present, *as a gift*
With mekyll glee and game; *much good cheer; celebration*
715 And tho in courte fast roose *quickly arose*
Syr Lybeous Dysconeus noble loose *reputation*
And all his gentill fame. *noble; (see note)*

The Erle, for his gode dede, *[Lybeaus's] good deed*
Yave him full riche mede: *Gave; reward*
720 Shelde and armes bryght, *armor*

And also a noble stede
That was gode at nede
In turnament and in fyght.
Lybeus and that maye   *maiden*
725   Redyn in her jurnaye,   *Confer; their*
Ther they logen tyght.   *Where; lodge secure*
Thanne sawe thei in a parke
A castell store and starke
That richely was ydight.   *built*

730   Fayre walled hit was with stone: *Beautifully; it*
Suche sawe he never none,
With cornyllus styff and stoute.   *crenellated towers*
Sayd Lybeous, "Be Seynt John!   *By*
This were a worthy wone,   *man*
735   Who had hit wonne with dyntt."   *conquered; force of arms*
Than lough that byrd bryght   *laughed; lady*
And sayde, "Alwey a knyght,   *Call for*
The best here all aboute,
Whoso will with him fyght,
740   By day or by nyght,
Lowe he maketh him loute.   *grovel*

"For love of his leman,   *lady*
That is so fayre a woman,
He hathe done crye and grede   *declared*
745   Whoso bryngeth a fayrer on,   *Whoever brings; one*
A gerfawkon, white as swanne,   *gerfalcon; swan*
He shall have to his mede.   *reward*
And yf she is not so bright,   *as beautiful*
With Jeffron he most fight;   *(see note 768)*
750   And yf he may not spede,   *win*
His hede shall him be rafte   *cut off*
And sett upon a shafte
To seen in lenthe and brede.   *far and wide*

The sothe to se wele   *(see note)*

755   An hede or two up-right."
Saide Lybeous als snelle,   *quickly*
"By God and Saint Michelle!   *Michael*
With Jeffran Y will fyght
And chalaunge that faukon   *lay claim to; falcon*
760   And sey I have in towne
A lemman two so bright;   *lady twice as beautiful*
And when he will hir a-see,   *gaze upon*

I shalle shewe him thee,
By day other by nyghte!"   *or*

765   The dwerfe said, "By Jhesus!
       Gentill Lybeous Disconyous,   *Noble*
       Thou puttist thee in grete perille.   *yourself; danger*
       Jeffron le Freudous   *(see note)*
       In syght hathe a queynte use   *secret stratagem*
770   Knyghtis to begylle."   *beguile*
       Lybeous answerd ther,
       "Therof have I no care,
       Be God and be Seint Gile!   *By*
       I shall see his face,
775   Or Y esteward passe   *Before; eastward*
       From this cité a myle."   *city; mile*

       Wythoute more renowen   *reason*
       They dwellyd still in towne
       All that nyght in pease.
780   On morowe Lybeous was bowne   *ready*
       To wyne him renon   *win himself renown*
       And rose, withoute leese;   *delay*
       And armed him right sever   *himself; completely*
       In that noble armwre   *armor*
785   That Er Aunctours was.   *Earl*
       His stede ganne to stride,   *began*
       The dwarfe rode him beside
       Taward the proude palleys.   *formidable palace*

       Jeffrond le Frendys,
790   He rose and was with us,
       In that morowe tide   *morning*
       To honoure swete Jhesus
       And ses Lybeus Disconyous,   *sees*
       Come prickande with pryde!   *galloping*
795   Withoute any abode,   *hesitation*
       Agayne Libeous he rode   *[Jeffron]*
       And lowde to hym can crye   *loud; did cry*
       With vaise sharpe and shille: *voice; shrill*
       "Comest thu for gode or ille?   *you; good*
800   Tell me anone in highe!"   *at once*

       Quod Lybeous also tite,   *Said; immediately*
       "I have grete delyte
       With thee for to fighte.
       Thou seyste a foule dispite,   *false thing*
805   Ther is no woman so white   *pure*

As thy leman be lighte,   *lady by daylight*
And I have one in towne
Well fayre of fassyon,   *form*
In clothis when she is dight.   *dressed up*
810   Therfor the gerfaukon   *gerfalcon*
To Arthur kynge with crowne
Bringe I shall with right."   *rightfully*

Quod Jeffrey, "Gentyll knyght,
We shull proven aright   *shall prove rightfully*
815   Whether the fayrer be."   *Who; fairer*
Quod Lybeous anone right,   *soon*
"In Cordile cité with sight,
That eche man may hir see,
And amyddis the market   *in the midst of*
820   Bothe thei shull be sette,   *they (the ladies)*
To loke on, bonde and free.   *[by those] bound; freeborn*
Yff my leman is browne,   *i.e., beautiful enough*
To wyn the jerfaukon   *gerfalcon*
Juste Y will with thee."   *Joust*

825   Quod Jeffrounse also snell,   *quickly*
"Forsothe, I graunte it wele;
This daye at undertide,   *noon*
By God and by Seint Michell!   *Michael*
Oute atte this castell   *From*
830   To Cardyle we shull ride!"   *Carlisle*
Her glovis up they helde   *Their gauntlets*
Ther right in the felde,   *right there*
As prynce proude in pryde.   *princes*
Lybeus also snelle   *quickly*
835   Rode home to his ostell: *hostel (guest quarters)*
He nolde no lenger abide,   *would no longer stay*

And hit the mayde Elyne,   *it [told]*
That semely was to sene,   *comely*
To buske and make hir bownde;   *dress; herself presentable*
840   And seyde, "By Heven Quene,
Geffrouns lemman, the shene   *Jeffron's lady; beautiful*
Today shall come to towne;
Amydward the cité   *To the middle of*
That all men shall you see,
845   Of wede and fassyon;   *clothes; comportment*
Yff thu arte not so bryght,   *If you are; as beautiful*
With Jeffround I mot fight   *must*
To wynne the jerfaukon."   *win; gerfalcon*

	The dwerf answerd and seid,	
850	"Thow doste a savage dede,	*You are doing; uncouth act*
	For any man i-borne!	
	Thow wilt not do be rede	*You refuse counsel*
	But faryst with thi madd hede	*follow; irrational impulses*
	As lorde that will be lorne.	*lost*
855	For His love, forthe we wende,	*go*
	That died for all mankynde	
	And in Bedlem was borne!"	*Bethlehem*
	Lybeous said, "That were shame:	
	I hadd levyr, be Seint Jeme,	*rather, by; James*
860	With wilde hors to be torne!"	*torn apart*
	The mayde Ellyne, also tighth,	*immediately*
	In a robe of samyte	*samite*
	Gaylie ganne hir atyre	*did she dress herself*
	To do Lybeous prophite,	*profit*
865	In kerchevys fayre and white	*head coverings*
	Aryved with gold wyre.	*Decorated*
	A velvet mantill gaye	*cloak*
	Purfild with gryce and graye	*Edged; gray squirrel fur*
	She did aboute hir swyre;	*neck*
870	The serkell upon hir moolde	*circle (crown); head*
	Of precious stones and goolde:	
	The best of that empire.	
	Lebeous sate that daye	
	Upon a gode palfraye,	*good saddle horse*
875	And reden forthe all three.	
	Eche man to other ganne saye,	
	"Here cometh a lady gaye:	*beautiful to look at*
	Is semely unto see!"	
	Into the markete thei rode	*marketplace*
880	And boldly ther abode,	*stopped*
	Amydward the citee;	*In the middle of*
	Then sawe thei Jeffron com ryde	*they saw*
	And two squyers by his syde	
	And no more mayne.	*companions*
885	He bare the shelde of gowlys,	*He (Jeffron) bore; red (gules)*
	Of sylver thre white owlys,	*owls*
	And of gold the bordure;	
	And of that same colours	*color scheme*
	And of that other floures	*flowers*
890	Was fyne golde and trappure.	*trappings (decorations)*
	The squiers that by him rode	
	That one bare shaftis gode,	*carried lances*

	Thre shaftis gode and sewre;	*sure*
	That other lade redy bownde	*lady; carried*
895	The joly gentill jerfaukowne:	*noble gerfalcon*
	The two ladyes were there.	

	And aftir hym come ryde	
	A lady proude in pryde,	
	Iclothed in purpyll palle.	*Dressed; cloth*
900	The folke came fer and wide	
	To se them back and syde:	*see*
	Howe gent she was and smalle.	*refined*
	Hir mantill was ryght fyne,	*cloak; exquisite*
	Ipowderd with ermyne,	*Interspersed; ermine*
905	Well riche and ryalle.	*royal*
	The sercle on hir molde	*crown; head*
	Of stones and of goolde	
	And many a ryche amayle.	*enamel figure*

	As rose hir rudde was rede;	*complexion; red*
910	The here shone on hir hede	*hair*
	As gold wyre shynynge bryght.	*thread (wire) shining*
	Hir browes also blacke as sylke threde	*silk thread*
	Ibent in leynthe and brede;	*Curved; length; breadth*
	Hir nose was streght and right.	*in proportion*
915	Hir eyen gray as glasse,	*eyes*
	Milke white was hir face:	
	So seid they that sawee that syght.	*who saw*
	Hir swyre longe and smale;	*neck; thin*
	Hir bewté to tellen alle	*beauty*
920	No man with mowthe myght.	*describes*

	But tho men did hem brynge	*those*
	Two cheyers into the chepyng,	*chairs; marketplace*
	Her bewtees to discryve.	*Their beauties; display*
	Then seid bothe olde and yonge,	
925	Forthewithe withoute lesynge,	*Immediately; doubt*
	"Betwene hem was partye:	*Among them; agreement*
	Geffroune leman is clere,	*Jeffron's lady; beautiful*
	As rose on rise or in erbere,	*stem; arbor*
	Forsothe and nought to lye!	*I am not kidding*
930	Ellyne the messangere	
	Ne were but a lawnder:	*Nothing but a laundress*
	Of hir no loose make I."	*praise*

	Quod Geffrounde ly Froundes,	*Declared*
	"Sir knyght, by swete Jhesus,	
935	This hauk thou haste lore!"	*hawk; lost*

Quod Lybeous Disconeous,
"Suche was never myne use;   *intent*
Juste I will therfore.   *Joust*
Yf thowe berest me downe,   *bring*
940   Take my hede and the faukon,   *head; falcon*
As forwarde was thore;   *agreed upon*
And yf I ber downe thee,   *defeat you*
The hauk shall wend with me,   *go*
Magré thyne hede, hore."   *In spite of you, old man*

945   Withoute more tale to telle,   *With nothing more to say*
They redyn downe in the felde   *rode*
And with hem grete partye;   *party [of knights]*
With cornellus styff and shelde   *steel-tipped lances*
Eythir agayne othir in the felde   *Each against*
950   With well grete envye.   *hatred*
Her shaftis brosten asondre,   *Their lances burst asunder*
Her dyntis ferden as thonder   *Their blows sounded like*
That cometh oute of the skey;
Tabowres and trompours,   *Drummers; trumpeters*
955   Heroudes and dissoures,   *Heralds; raconteurs*
Her strokys con discrye.   *Their; did describe*

Tho can Geffroune to lepe
And said, "Gyve me that will not breke: *[a lance]*
A shaffte withoute cornall!   *a head*
960   This yonge frely freke   *noble man-at-arms*
Sytteth in his sadyll sete   *as firmly*
As stone in castell wall;
I shall do him stoupe   *cause; to slump*
Ovyr his hors crowpe   *horse's rump*
965   And gyve hym an evill falle:
Though he be as wise wereour
As Alysaunder or Kyng Arthur,   *Alexander [the Great]*
Lawncelot or Syr Percevalle."

The knyghtis bothe twoo
970   Redyn togeder thoo,   *then*
With well grete rawndon;   *energy*
Lybeos smote Jeffroun soo   *so [forcefully]*
That his shelde smote him froo   *shield knocked away*
Into the felde adowne.
975   Then lowe all that ther was   *laughed all who were there*
And sayde, withoute lees,   *lying*
Dukes, erle and baron,   *earls; barons*
That never yette they seye   *had they seen*

	A man that myght durye	*endure*
980	A cours of Syr Jeffroune.	*joust with*

	Geffoun toke his cours outeryght	*started on his way at once*
	And was nyghe oute of his witte	*nearly; mind*
	For he myghte not spede,	*That; succeed*
	And rode agene als tighte	
985	And Lebeous on the helme he hitte,	
	As wolfe that wolde at wede.	*in a state of madness*
	But Libeous sate so faste	*sat so firmly [in his saddle]*
	That Jeffroune downe caste	*fell down*
	Bothe hym and his stede:	*with his horse*
990	Geffrounes backe to-brake	*back broke [so loudly]*
	That men herd the crake	*crack*
	Aboute in leynthe and brede.	*far and wide*

	Than sayde all that ther weren	*who were there*
	That Jeffroun had ilorne	*lost*
995	The gentill jerfaukon;	
	To Lybeous they hym bare	*him [the gerfalcon] carried*
	And went, bothe lesse and more,	
	With hym into the towne.	
	Geffroun oute of the felde	
1000	Was borne home on his shelde	*shield*
	With care and reuthefull rowne;	*joyless lamentation*
	The gerfaukon isent was	
	By a knyght that hight Cadas	*named*
	To Arthur, kynge with crowne.	

1005	And wretyn alle the dede	
	With him he can to lede	
	The hauk tho Lybeous wan.	*that; won*
	Tho Arthure hard hit redde,	*heard it (the story) recounted*
	To his knyghtis he sayde,	
1010	"Lybeous well wer can!	*war (battle)*
	He hathe sent me with honour	
	Of foure fightis the floure,	*prize*
	Sethen he fyrst byganne.	*Since*
	I will him send tresoure	*treasure*
1015	To spend with honour,	
	As falleth for suche a man."	

	An hondered pounde honeste	*hundred pounds*
	Of floreyns with the best	*florins*
	He sent to Kardill towne.	*Carlisle*
1020	Ther Lybeous made a feste	*feast*
	That forty dayes it leste,	*lasted*

As lord of grete renowne;
And at the six wokis ende   *end of six weeks*
They toke her leve to wende: *their permission; go*
1025 Duke, erle, and baroune.
Syr Lybeous and that may   *maiden*
Tokyn her right waye   *Took up their former path*
Tawarde Synadowne.   *Toward*

As they redyn by a lowe,   *rode; hill*
1030 Hornes herd they blowe.
And huntynge grete of gile.   *craft*
The dwerf saide, in a thorowe,   *quickly*
"That horne wele I knowe,
For youre frely sale: *noble hall*
1035 Hit blowis motis jolelye,   *hunting calls*
That servid sometyme my lady,
Semely in hir sale.   *castle*
When she was takyn with gile,   *beguiled*
He fled for grete perile
1040 West into Wyralle."   *Wirral*

As they redyn talkynge   *rode [while] talking*
They sawe a rache com renynge   *hunting dog; running*
Overthwerte the waye.   *Across*
Than said olde and yonge,
1045 From her first begynynge,   *i.e., since they were born*
Thay sawe never none so gaye:
He was of all coloures
That man may se of floures   *flowers*
Bytwene Mydsomer and Maye.   *Midsummer; May*
1050 The mayde saide, alse snell,   *instantly*
"Sawe I never no jowell   *jewel*
So lykinge to my paye,   *pleasure*

"So that I hit aught!"   *should have it*
Lybeous as tight it caught   *quickly*
1055 And toke hit the mayden clene.   *bore it to*
Thay ridden forthe all softe   *leisurely*
And tolde howe knyghtis faught   *talked about*
For birdes bryght and shene.   *ladies; beautiful*
Ne had they redyn but a while,
1060 The mountence of a myle,   *distance*
In that forest grene,
They sawe an hynde come strike   *[When]; doe; running*
And two grewndis like   *greyhounds*
The racche that I of mene.   *hunting dog; spoke*

1065	They hovyd under a lyne	*waited; linden tree*
	And sawe the course of the hynde,	*path; doe*
	Lybeous that was so fre.	*noble*
	Then sawe they com behynde	*following*
	A knyght iclothed in jende	*indigo*
1070	Uppon a baye destré;	*bay destrier*
	His bugill canne he to blowe	*bugle; began*
	For houndis shulde him knowe	*so that hounds*
	In whate stede that he were.	*where he was*
	He seide to hem that throwe,	
1075	"That racche do I owee,	*greyhound; own*
	Agone is eight yere.	*Gone for; years*

	Frendis, lettes him goo!"	
	Lybeous answerd thoo,	
	"That shall never betide:	*No! That shall never happen!*
1080	With myn hondis two	
	I gave it the mayden me froo	
	That hovith me bysyde."	*Who sits beside me*
	Quod Sir Otis de Lile,	
	"Thou puttist thee in grete perile,	*yourself*
1085	To bycker and thou abide."	*bicker when you [should be] patient*
	Lybeous sayde, "Be Seint Gile,	*By*
	I ne gyf nought of thi gile,	*care nothing of your guile*
	Chorle, though thou chide!"	*Churl; complain*

	Quod Sir Otys de Lyle,	
1090	"Syr, thi wordis ar wile,	*your; are rash*
	Chorle was never my name.	
	My fader an erle was awhile,	*earl for a long time*
	And the countesse of Carlehille,	*Carlisle*
	Forsothe, was my dame.	*mother*
1095	Yf I were armed nowe,	
	Redy as arte thowe,	*Prepared; you are*
	We shulden fight in same.	*right now (together)*
	But yf thow the racche levyn,	*Unless; leave the hound*
	Thowe pleyest, longe or evyn,	*before evening*
1100	A wondyr wilde game!"	*reckless*

	Quod Lybeous, also prest,	*stance*
	"Therof, sir, do thy beste:	
	The rache with me shall wende."	*go*
	Thay token her way evyn west	*They; their*
1105	Into that faire forest,	
	As the dwerf hem kende.	*dwarf led them*
	Syr Otis, with grete errour,	*anger*
	Rode home to his toure	*tower*

	And after his frendis did send;	
1110	And tolde hem anone rightis	
	Howe one of Arthur is knyghtis	*Arthur's*
	So shamefully canne him shende;	*defy*
	And his racche was inome.	*taken away*
	Than sware they, all and some,	*swore [Otis's friends]*
1115	That traytur shulde ben itake	*traitor should be*
	And never agene home come,	
	Though he were the grymmer grome	*more fearsome young man*
	Than Launcelet de Lake.	
	They dighten hem to armes	*armed themselves*
1120	With swerdys and giyarnes,	*battle-axes*
	As werre that shulde awake.	*As if they were going to war*
	Knyghtis and squyers	*squires*
	Leppyn on her desters,	*their warhorses*
	For her lordis sake.	*their lord's*
1125	Upon an hill full hie	*high*
	Syr Lybeous ther he seye,	*they (Otis's men) saw*
	Rydinge forthe pase by pase.	*slowly*
	To hym they con crye,	
	"Traytor, thou shalt die,	
1130	Todaye for thye trespace!"	*trespass*
	Lybeus ayene behelde	*again*
	Howe full was the felde,	*field*
	So mekyll folke that ther was.	*many*
	He sayde, "Mayde Ellyne,	
1135	For this racche, Y wene,	*Because of; hound*
	Me cometh a carefull case.	*serious problem*
	I rede ye you withdrawe	*strongly advise that*
	To the wode shawe,	*edge of the forest*
	Youre hedis for to hide;	*heads*
1140	For Y am frely fayne,	
	Though Y shulde be slayne,	
	Bekyr with hem to abyde."	*Engage them in battle*
	Into the forest he rode	
	And ther he boldly abode.	*there; waited*
1145	As avauntors proude in pryde,	*adventurers*
	With bowes and arblast,	*crossbows*
	They shotten to him faste	
	And made hym woundis wyde.	
	Syr Lybeous stede ranne	*charged*
1150	And bare downe hors and man,	*bore; horse*
	For nothinge wolde he spare.	

All men sayde than,
"This is the devyll Satan,
That mankynde will forfare."   *Who; betray*
1155   For whomso Lybeous araught   *whomever; struck*
       At his fyrst drawght,   *blow*
       He slepte for evermore.   *i.e., was dead*
       But sone he was besette,   *trapped*
       As dere is in the nette,   *[a] deer*
1160   With grymly woundis sore.   *serious injuries*

       For twelve knyghtis, all prest,   *ready for battle*
       He sawe come oute of the west,
       In armys bryght and clere.
       Alday thay haden yrest   *All day; waited*
1165   And thoughtyn in that forest   *plotted*
       To slee Lybeous that knyght.   *slay*
       Of sewte they weren all twelve,   *Dressed in matching garb*
       That one was the lorde himselve,   *[Otis de Lyle]*
       In ryme to redyn aright.   *rhyme*
1170   They smotyn to hym at onys   *once*
       And thoughten to breke his bonys   *intended*
       And to fellyn hym in fyght.

       Tho myght men hire dynge   *hear*
       And rounde rappis rynge,   *hard blows*
1175   Amonges hem all in feere: *together*
       The sparkylles conne to sprynge   *sparks began to fly*
       Forthe, witheoute lesynge,   *truly*
       From sheld and helmes clere.
       Lybeous slowe of hem three,   *slew; three of them*
1180   The fourthe begon to flee   *fourth began*
       And durste nought neye him nere.   *stay near*
       The lorde lefte in the stoure   *abandoned; conflict*
       And his sonnes foure,
       To syllen her lyves dere.   *sell their lives dearly*

1185   Tho runne rappes ryffe: *i.e., mayhem ensued*
       He one agaynes fyve   *alone against*
       Faughte as he were wode.   *crazed*
       Nye downe they con hym dryve;   *Nearly overcame him*
       So watyr dothe off the skythe,   *As water does; scythe*
1190   Off hym ranne the bloode.
       Whan Lybeous was ney spilte,   *nearly done for*
       His swerde barst in the hilte: *broke; hilt*
       Than was he madde of mode.   *enraged*
       The lord a stroke he sete

1195	Throwe helme and basnett,	*helmet with visor*
	That in the skolle hit stode.	*skull it stuck*
	In swounynge he fel downe	*swooning*
	Upon his ferther arsoune,	*front of his saddle*
	As man that was all mate.	*done for*
1200	His fone weren full bownde	*enemies; fully intending*
	To persyne his aketowne,	*pierce; armor*
	Bothe mayle and plate.	*chain mail; steel breastplate*
	When he ganne sore to smerte,	*began; hurt*
	He pulled up his herte	*i.e., mustered his courage*
1205	And sterryd up his state;	*stirred; spirit*
	An ax he hente him nyghe,	*had at hand*
	That henge by his thighe:	*was hanging*
	Almost him thought to late.	*it seemed to him too*
	Tho he steryd him as a knyght:	*Then; aroused himself*
1210	Thre stedis adowne right	*Three horses*
	He slowe at strokys three.	*slew in three strokes*
	The lorde sawe that in sight	
	And of his stede he alyght:	*dismounted*
	Away he began to flee.	
1215	Lybeous no lenger abode	*waited*
	But aftyr hym he rode.	
	Under a chesteyne tree	*chestnut*
	Ther he hadde him qwelled,	*would have killed*
	But that the lorde hym yelde	*Except; yielded himself*
1220	At his will for to bee,	*[Lybeaus's] mercy*
	And, by certeyne stente,	*prescribed amount*
	Tresure, londe and rentte,	
	Castell, hall and boure,	
	Lybeous therto assente,	*assented*
1225	By forward so that he wente	*sworn contract*
	Unto Kynge Arthure	
	And sayde, "Lorde of renowne,	
	As overcome and prisowne,	*defeated; taken prisoner*
	I am to thine honowre."	*(i.e., subject myself)*
1230	The lorde graunted his wille,	
	Bothe lowde and stylle,	*aloud; silently*
	And ladde him to his toure.	*led; tower*
	Anone the mayden Ellyne	*Soon*
	With gentillmen fyftene	*noblemen fifteen*
1235	Was ifett to the castell.	*led*
	She and the dwerffe bydene	*together*
	Tolden all the dedis kene	*Told; mighty deeds*

Of Lybeous, howe it befell,
And whiche persones foure
1240　He sent to Kynge Arthure,
That he wanne fayre and wele.   *won fairly*
The lord was well blythe   *i.e., Arthur; grateful*
And thanked fele sythe   *many times*
God and Seint Michell

1245　That swyche a nobyll knyght   *such*
Shulde with werre in fyght
Wynne his lady free.
To covere with mayne and myght,   *recover; strength*
Lybeous a fourtenyght   *fortnight*
1250　Ther with him canne lende.   *stay*
He did helen his wounde   *heal*
And made hym hole and sownde   *whole; sound*
By the fowrtenyght ende;   *end of the fortnight*
Than Lybeous and that maye   *maiden*
1255　Toke her right waye   *Resumed their*
To Synadon to wende.   *Snowdon*

The lorde, withoute dwellynge,   *[Otis]; delay*
Went to Arthur the kynge
And for presowne hym yelde,   *as a prisoner surrendered himself*
1260　And tolde him the begynnynge
Howe suche a knyght in fyghtyng
Wan hym in the felde.   *Conquered*
Kynge Arthur had gode game,   *amusement*
And so had alle in same,   *everyone there*
1265　That herde that tale ytolde.
And chosyn hym prophytable,   *[Arthur] Who; honorably*
By knyght of the Rounde Table,   *As*
To fyght with spere and shelde.

Nowe rest we here a while
1270　Of Sir Otys de Lyle   *Before*
And tell we forthe oure talis,   *other stories*
Howe Lybeous rode many a myle
And sey awntours the while   *took part in adventures*
And Irlande and in Walys.   *In Ireland; Wales*
1275　Hytt befell in June, Y wene,   *It happened; I think*
Whan fenell hangeth al grene   *fennel*
Abowte in semely saale;   *sign of the season*
The somerys day is longe,   *summer's*
Mery is the fowlis songe   *Merry; birds' song*
1280　And notis of the nyghtyngale.   *notes*

That tyme Lybeous canne ryde
Be a reveres syde   *river's*
And sawe a fayre cité
With palys prowde in pryde   *palace splendidly built*
1285   And castelles high and wyde   *castles*
And gates grete plenté.   *plentiful*
He axed whate hit hight;   *asked what it was called*
The mayden sayde anone right,   *immediately*
"Syr, I will telle thee: *you*
1290   Men clepeth this Il de Ore,   *call; Isle of Gold*
Here be fightis more;   *battles*
Ther is werr in every countré.   *war*

For a lady of price,   *Because of; great excellence*
Roddy as rose on rice,   *Ruddy (red); stem*
1295   This contré is in dowte;   *trouble*
A gyaunt that heght Maugys,   *called*
Nowhere his pere is,   *equal*
Hir hathe besett aboute.   *blocked passage*
He is as blacke as pyche,   *pitch*
1300   Nowher is none suche   *[like him]*
Of dedis sterne and stowte;
Whate knyght so passyth the bryge   *Whichever; bridge*
His armys he moste downe legge   *lay down his weapons*
And to the gyaunte alowte.   *bow (pay homage)*

1305   He is thirty fote on leynthe   *feet tall*
And myche more of strenthe   *stronger*
Than other knyghtis fyve;
Syr Lybeous woll bethynke thee   *think carefully about*
That thou with him ne macched bee: *Whether; matched*
1310   He is gryme to discryve.
He berreth on every browe   *each eyebrow*
As it were brystillus of a sowe;   *bristles; sow*
His hede grete as an hyve,   *a beehive*
His armys the lenthe of an elle,   *i.e., forty-five inches*
1315   His fystis arne full felle   *fists are powerful*
Dyntys with to dryve."   *Blows*

Quod Lybeous, "Mayden hynde,   *Maiden gracious; (see note)*
My way nowe will Y wende   *proceed*
For alle his strokys ylle.   *Despite; strokes ill (evil)*
1320   If God will me grace sende,
Or this day come to ende   *Before*
With fight Y hoppe hym fell.   *hope to slay him*
I have sene grete okys   *oaks*
Fallyn with wyndes and strokys,   *winds; lightning*

1325	And the lytell stande full stille.	*little [trees] prevail*
	Thoughe that Y be litell,	
	To hym will I smyte,	
	Let God do his wylle!"	
	They roden forthe all three	
1330	Tawarde that fayre cité	*Toward*
	That men calleth Ile Dolour.	*Isle of Sorrow*
	Maugys they con see	
	Upon a bryge of tree,	*wooden bridge*
	Bolde as a wilde bore.	*boar*
1335	His shelde was blacke as pycche,	*pitch*
	And all his armour suche:	*too*
	Thre mawmentis therin wes,	*pagan idols*
	Of gold gayly gilte;	*brightly gilded*
	A spere in honde he helde	
1340	And his childe him before.	*shield in front of him*
	He kryede to hym in spyte,	*shouted; anger*
	"Sey, thou fellaue in white,	*Hey you!*
	Tell me whate arte thowe!	*what you are*
	Torne home agene tite,	*Turn; immediately*
1345	For thyne owne prophite,	*safety*
	Yf thow lovyst thy prowe."	*your well-being*
	Lybeous sayde anone right,	
	"Kynge Arthure made me knyght,	
	To hym Y made avowe	*a pledge*
1350	That I shulde never turne my backe;	*i.e., run away*
	Therfor, thow devyll black,	*you devil*
	Make thee redy nowe!"	*Prepare yourself now*
	Syr Lybeus and Maugis	
	On stedis proude in prise	*splendidly arrayed*
1355	Togeder redyn full ryght.	*rode purposefully*
	Bothe lordis and ladyes	
	Laynen in her toures	*are positioned; their towers*
	For to se that syght;	
	And praied to God bothe lowde and stille,	*aloud; silently*
1360	Yf it were His swete wille,	
	Save that Crysten knyght,	
	And that fyl gyawnte	*vile giant*
	That levyd on Turmagaunte	*worshiped*
	This day to dye in fighte.	
1365	Her shaftes borsten on sonder,	*Their lances burst*
	Her dyntis ferd as thonder:	*Their blows seemed like; thunder*
	The pecis canne of sprynge.	*pieces; fly off*

Euche man had wonder   *Each spectator*
That Lybeous ne had gon under   *had not been killed*
1370   At the fyrste begynnynge.   *very start*
They drewe swerdis bothe
As men that were wrothe   *angry*
And gonne togedir dynge;   *to strike*
Sir Lybeous smote Maugis soo   *so [hard]*
1375   That his shelde fell him froo   *from*
And in the felde canne flynge.   *did fly*

Maugis was qweynt and qwede   *cunning; cruel*
And smote Lybeous stede on the hede   *horse; head*
And dasshid oute the brayne;   *brain*
1380   The stede fell downe dede,   *dead*
Syr Lybeous nought sayde   *said nothing*
But stertt hym up agayne,
And an ax hent ybowne   *seized quickly*
That henge by his arsowne   *hung; saddle*
1385   And stroke to hym with mayne   *i.e., strongly*
Through Maugis stede swyre: *horse's neck*
He forkarve bone and lyre   *severed bone and flesh*
That the hede fell in the playne.   *head; field*

On fote bothe they fyghte,
1390   Discryven no man myght   *Describe*
The strokys betwis hem two;
Bothe woundes they laughte,   *Both scoffed at their wounds*
For they were unsaught   *undaunted*
And either other is foo.   *each is the other's foe*
1395   From the oure of pryme   *hour of prime (sunrise)*
Tyll hit were evensonge tyme,   *evensong (vespers)*
To fyghtyn they were throo.   *relentless*
Sir Lybeous thrested soore   *thirsted sorely*
And sayde, "Maugis, thine ore!   *have mercy*
1400   To drinke thou lett me goo.   *Let me take a drink*

"And Y shall graunte thee   *grant*
Whate bone thowe aske of me,   *Whatever boon you ask*
Swiche case if thee betide;   *should the need arise*
For grete shame hit wolde be   *it would*
1405   A knyght for thurste to slee,   *thirst; slay*
And no maner parfyte."   *acceptable*
Maugis graunted his will
To drynke all his fille,
Withoute more dispite.   *assault*
1410   As he lay on the banke   *[Lybeaus]; riverbank*

And throw his helme dranke,   *through (by means of)*
Maugis smertly hym smytte   *sharply; whacked*

That in the rever he flye fylle: *river [Lybeaus] fell*
His armoure every dele   *everywhere*
1415 Was wette and evill ydight;   *in bad shape*
But up he sterte as snelle   *quickly*
And seyd, "Be Seint Michell,   *Michael*
Nowe am Y two so light!   *twice as eager*
Weneste thou, fendys fere,   *Did you think, devil's companion*
1420 Uncristened that Y were
Tylle Y sawe thee with sight?
I shall for this baptyse   *baptism*
Quyte well thi service,   *Repay*
Thorough grace of God almyght!"

1425 Then newe fyght byganne:
Eyther to other ranne   *Each at the other*
And deltyn dyntes strange;   *delivered hard blows*
Well many a gentilman
And ladyes as white as swanne
1430 For Lybeous her hondys wrange;   *their hands wrung*
For Maugis in the felde
Forkarfe Lybeous' shelde   *Sliced through; shield*
Thorough dynte of armes longe.   *By strokes*
Than Lybeous ranne awaye   *ran to*
1435 There Maugis shelde laye   *Where*
And up he gan hit fange.   *it seized*

And ran agayne to hym;   *[Lybeaus to Maugis]*
With strokys sharpe and gryme
Eyther other ganne assayle.   *Each the other began*
1440 Till the day was dymme   *i.e., until dusk*
Upon the watir brym   *water's edge*
Bytwene hem was bataylle.
Lybeous was werreour wight   *[a] strong warrior*
And smote a stroke of myght   *great strength*
1445 Thorowe jepowne, plate, and mayle,   *emblazoned surcoat*
Thorowe the shulderbone   *shoulder bone*
That his right arme anone   *[Maugis's]*
Fell in the fled, saunce fayle.   *field; I kid you not*

The gyaunte this ganne see,   *began to realize*
1450 That he shulde slayne bee: *should be slain*
He fledde with myght and mayne.   *fled*
Syr Lybeous after ganne tee   *ran after him*
With sterne stroky thre   *three hearty strokes*

	He smote his backe on twayne.	*in two*
1455	The gyaunte ther belevyde;	*remained*
	Syr Lybeous smote off his heved:	*head*
	Thereof he was fayne.	*satisfied*
	He bare the hede into the towne;	*carried*
	With a fayre processyoune	
1460	The folke come hym agayne.	*came to greet him*

	A lady bright as floure,	
	That men calleth la Dame Amoure,	
	Resseyved him wele and fayre	*with pomp and ceremony*
	And thanked hym with honour	
1465	That he was hir socoure	*her champion*
	Agayne that giaunte file.	*Against that vile giant*
	To chambyr she him ledys	*led*
	And did off all his wedis	*took off; armor*
	And clothed hym in palle,	*beautiful clothes*
1470	And profirde him with worde	*asked*
	For to be hir lorde	*her*
	Of cité and castell.	

	Lybeous graunted hir in haste	*acceded to her wishes*
	And love to hir ganne caste,	
1475	For she was bright and shene.	*radiant; lovely*
	Alas, she hadde be chaaste!	*Would that; had been chaste*
	For ever at the laste	
	She dyde hym traye and tene.	*treachery; harm*
	For twelve monthes and more	
1480	As Lybeous dwelled thore	*there*
	He forgate mayde Elyne,	*forgot*
	That never he myght outebreke	*break away*
	For to helpe to awreke	*avenge*
	Of Synadowne the qwene.	*queen*

1485	For the faire lady	*[Dame Amoure]*
	Cowthe more of sorcerye	*Knew*
	Than other suche fyve;	*five others [like her]*
	She made hym suche melodye	
	Of all maner mynstralsye	*minstrelsy*
1490	That any man myght discryve.	*describe*
	Whan he sawe hir face	*gazed at*
	Hym thought that he was	
	In paradice on lyve;	*paradise on earth*
	With false lies and fayre	
1495	Thus she blered his eye:	*blurred; vision*
	Evill mote she thryve!	*May misfortune befall her*

	Till it befell upon a daye	*Until*
	He mete Elyne that may	*maid*
	Beside that castell toure;	
1500	To hym than ganne she saye,	*began*
	"Knyght, thou arte false in thi laye	*promise*
	Ageynes Kynge Arthure!	*To*
	For the love of o woman	*one*
	That mekyll of sorcery canne	*Who can do great sorcery*
1505	Thow doste thee grete dissehonour:	*yourself; dishonor*
	My lady of Synadowne	
	May longe lye in preson,	*for a long time; prison*
	And that is grete doloure!"	*sorrow*

	Syr Lybeus herde hir speke;	
1510	Hym thought his hert gan breke	*It seemed to him; heart would*
	For sorowe and for shame.	
	At a postsren isteke	*locked gate*
	There he ganne outebreke	*break away*
	Fro that gentyll dame,	*From; noble woman*
1515	And toke with hym his stede,	
	His shelde, his iren wede,	*iron clothes (armor)*
	And reden forthe all in same.	*rode away*
	Hir stywarde stoute and fayre	*Her steward*
	He made his squyer:	*[Lybeaus's] squire*
1520	Jurflete was his name.	

	They rodyn faste as they maye	
	Forthe on her jornaye	*their journey*
	On stedis baye and browne;	*light brown*
	Till on the third daye	
1525	They sawe a cité gaye:	
	Men clepen hit Synadowne;	*called it*
	With castelles high and wide	
	And palysed proude in pryde,	
	Worke of fayre facion;	*finely crafted*
1530	But Lybeous Disconyous	
	Had wonder of that use	*what activity*
	That he saye men do in towne.	*saw*

	Cor and fenne full faste,	*Carnage (corpses); filth (see note)*
	That men hade ere oute caste,	
1535	They gadered ynne iwysse,	*took back inside*
	Syr Lybeous axid in haste,	*asked*
	"Tell me, mayden chaste,	
	Whate betokeneth this?	*does this mean*
	They taken in the goore	*bring in; waste*
1540	That ar was oute yboore:	*taken out before*

Me thynketh they do amysse."   *mistakenly*
Than seyd mayde Ellyne,
"Syr knyght, withoute wene,   *doubt*
I tell thee whate hit is.

1545   "No knyght, for nesshe ne harde,   *whether weak or hardy*
Though he shulde be forfarde,   *exhausted by travel*
Getteth here none ostell,   *hospitality*
For doute of the stywarde   *suspicion*
That hight Syr Lanwarde,   *Who is called*
1550   Constable of that castelle.   *Guardian*
Go ryde into the castell gate
And axe thine inne theratte,   *ask yourself*
Bothe fayre and wele;
And ere he do thi nede,   *before; tends to your needs*
1555   Of justis he will thee bede,   *jousts; demand*
Be God and be Seint Michell!

And yf he beryth thee downe   *defeats you*
His trumpetis shall be bowne
Her bemes high to blowe;   *Their blasts loudly*
1560   Then over all Synadowne
Bothe mayde and garson   *maiden; boy*
This fen on thee to thorowe.   *garbage*
To whiche lond that yowe wende,   *whichever; go*
Ever to youre lyves ende,
1565   For kowarde thou worthe knowe;   *coward; become known*
And thus may Kynge Arthure
Lesyn his honoure   *Lose*
For thyn dedis slowe."

Quod Lybeous als tite,   *quickly*
1570   "That were a foule disspyte   *shameful disgrace*
For any knyght on lyve!
To do Arthure prophyte   *honor*
And maketh that lady quyte   *free that lady*
Thedyr will Y dryve.
1575   Syr Gyrflete, make thee yare,   *prepare yourself*
To juste with thee will not spare,   *joust*
Hastely and blyve."
They reden forthe at the gate   *rode forth to*
Right to the castell yate,
1580   With faire shaftis fyve.   *five lances*

And axed ther ostell   *asked [for] their hospitality*
At that fayre castell   *In*
For auntors knyghtis   *adventurous*

	The porter faire and wele	
1585	Lete hym yn full snell	*immediately*
	And axed him anone rightis	*asked; very soon*
	Who was here governours;	*their lord*
	And they seid, "Kynge Arthure,	
	Man of moste myghtis;	
1590	Well of curtaysie	
	And flloure of chevalyre	*flower; chivalry*
	To fellen his fone in fightis."	*defeat; foes; battle*

	The porter prophitable	*honorable*
	To his lorde the constable	*overseer*
1595	Sone this tale tolde;	*Soon*
	And sayde, "Withoute fable,	*No kidding*
	Syre, of the Rowne Table	*Sir*
	Ar comen two knyghtis bolde;	
	That one is armyd full severe	*impressively*
1600	In roose rede armoure	*rose-red*
	With thre lyons of goolde."	
	The lord was glad and blythe	
	And sayde, also swythe,	*just as quickly*
	Justyn with hym he wolde.	*Joust; them*

	And bade hem make hem yare	*prepare themselves*
1605	Into the felde to fare,	*field; go*
	Withoute the castell gate.	*Outside*
	The porter wolde not spare:	
	As a greyhounde dothe to an hare	*does*
1610	To hem ranne to the gate	
	And sayde anone rightis,	
	"Ye auntrous knyghtis,	*adventurous*
	For nothinge ye latte:	*forebear*
	Looke your sheldis be stronge	
1615	And your shaftis longe,	
	Soketys and vaumplate,	*Spear guards; hand guard*

	And rydeth into the felde:	
	My lord, with shafte and shelde,	*lance; shield*
	Will with you playe."	*i.e., joust*
1620	Sir Lybeous spake wordis bolde:	
	"That is a tale ytolde	*That is what I want to hear*
	Lykyng to my paye!"	*pleasure*
	Into the felde they rode,	
	And boldly ther abode	*waited*
1625	As bestis brought to baye.	*beasts; bay (cornered)*
	Lambard sent his stede,	*sent for*

His shelde, his iren wede: *armor*
Hir tire was stoute and gaye. *attire; formidable*

His shelde was asure fyne, *azure*
1630 Thre beer hedis therinne *Three bear heads*
As blacke as bronde ybrent; *burnt coal*
The bordure of ermyne: *ermine (see note)*
Was none so quaynte a gynne *clever; device*
Fro Carlile into Kentt; *From Carlisle to Kent*
1635 And of that silfe peyntoure *very same design*
Was surcott and trappoure,
In worlde wherso he went.
Thre squiers by hym ryde, *Three squires*
Thre shaftis thei bare him myde *lances; carried*
1640 To dele with doughty dynte. *deliver strong strokes*

Tho that stoute stywarde *hearty steward*
That hight Sir Lancharde, *called Sir Lambert*
Was armed to the ryghtis,
He rode to the feldewarde
1645 As it were a lebarde, *As if he; leopard*
And ther abode thes knyghtis. *waited*
He sette his shelde in grate: *lance rest*
Almoste hym thought to late *too*
When he hym seigh with sightis.
1650 Lybeous rode to hym thare
With a shafte all square, *sharp*
As man of moste myghtis.

Ayther smote other in the shelde *Either struck the other*
That the peces flowen in the felde, *flew*
1655 Sothe, withoute wene; *Truly, without doubt*
Euche man to other tolde,
Bothe yonge and olde,
"This yonge knyght is kene!" *fierce*
Lambarte his cours outeright *changed course*
1660 As werour oute of wytte,
Fro ire and herte tene, *anger; hardened heart*
And sayde, "Brynge me a shafte:
Yf this knyght con his crafte, *knows*
Right sone hit shall be sene!" *it; demonstrated*

1665 Tho toke they shaftis rownde *Then*
With cornelys sharpe ygrownde *points sharply honed*
And reden with grete raundon. *rode; energy*
Eyther provyd that stownde *strove*
To gyve other dethes wounde,

1670	With herte eger as a lyon.	*fierce*
	Lambarte smote Lybeous soo	*so [hard]*
	That his shylde fell him froo	*from*
	And in the felde fell adowne:	
	So harde he hym hitte	
1675	That unnethis hy myght sytte	*scarcely*
	Upryght in his arsoune	*saddle*
	His schafte brake with power;	
	Lybeous smote hym in the laynore	*[Lambert]; chin strap*
	On his helme so bryght:	
1680	Pesawe, ventayle, and gorger	*Collar, lower helmet; neckpiece*
	Fly forthe withe the helme so clere,	*excellent*
	And Sir Lambarde upright	
	Sate and rocked in his sadylle	
	As a childe in his cradill,	*child; cradle*
1685	Withouten mayne and myght.	*strength*
	Every man toke othir by the lappe	*[those watching]; sleeve*
	And lowghen and couthe her handis clappe:	*laughed; their; clapped*
	Barowne, burgeys, and knyght.	*Barons, burgesses*
	Syr Lambartt thought to juste bett:	*joust better*
1690	Another helme hym was yfett	*fetched*
	And a shafte unmete,	*unequaled*
	And wan they togeder mette	
	Eythir to other his shelde sette	*Each*
	Strokys grysly and grete.	
1695	Syr Lambartis shafte to-braste,	*lance shattered*
	And Lybeous shoved soo faste,	
	In sadylles ther they sete,	*where*
	That the constable, Sir Lambertt,	
	Felte over his hors backwarde,	*Fell*
1700	Withoute more beyete.	*benefit*
	Syr Lamberd was ashamed sore;	
	Quod Sir Lybeous, "Wilt thou more?"	*you have*
	And he answerd, "Naye!	
	Sethe the tyme that Y was borne	
1705	Sawe I never me beforne	*I never saw*
	So rydynge to my paye.	*Such riding; pleasure*
	Be my trouthe my herte is thine:	
	Thowe arte of Sir Gawynes kynne,	*You are; Gawain's kin*
	That is so stoute and gaye.	*Who*
1710	Yf thou shalt for my lady fyght,	
	Welcome to me this nyght	
	In sekyr and trouthe in faye!"	*security; faith*

Lybeous sayd, "Sekerlye,   *Certainly*
Fyght Y shall for thy ladye,
1715   By heste of Kynge Arthure;   *promise (behest)*
But Y ne wote wherfor ne whye,   *know neither where nor why*
Ne who dothe hyr that tormentrye,   *Nor who does her; torment*
To brynge hir in dolour;   *cause her sorrow*
A mayde that was hir messanger
1720   And a dwerf brought me here,
Her to socoure."   *aid*
Lambarde sayde at that stownde,   *place*
"Welcome, knyght of the Table Rownde,
Be God and Seint Saveour!"   *By*

1725   And the mayden Elyne
Was sen for with knyghtis kene   *sent*
By-for Sir Lambarde.   *Before*
She and the dwarfe bydene   *together*
Tolde of the dedis kene   *deeds brave*
1730   That he did thedirwarde,   *beforehand*
And how that Sir Lybeous
Faught with fele shrewes   *many villains*
And hem nothinge spared.   *did not refrain from assailing*
Tho were they all blythe   *Then; happy*
1735   And thanked God fele sythe,   *repeatedly*
God and Seint Leonarde.

Anone with mylde chere   *Soon; uplifted spirit*
They sett hym to sopere   *invited; supper*
With mekell gle and game.   *much joy; entertainment*
1740   Lybeous and Lambard yfere   *together*
Of aventours that ther were
Talkeden bothe in same.   *Talked to each other*
Lybeous, withoute fable,   *lie*
Seyd, "Sir constable,
1745   Whate is the knyghtis name   *knight's*
That holdeth in prisoune   *Who holds*
That lady of Synadon,
That is gentyll a dame?"   *noblewoman*

Quod Lambert, "Be Seint John!
1750   Knyght, sir, is ther none
That durste hir away lede: *Who dares to lead her away*
Twoo clerkys ben hir foone,   *Two clerics; foe*
Fekyll of bloode and bone,   *False*
That havyth ydoo this dede.   *done; deed*
1755   They ar men of mynstrye,   *ministry*
Clyrkys of nigermansye,   *Masters of necromancy*

	Here arte for to rede.	Their; counsel
	Irayne ys that o brother	one
	And Mabon is that other	
1760	For whome we are in dred.	fear

	"Iran and that Mabon	
	Have made in this towne	
	A paleys queynte of gynne:	fortress cleverly engineered
	Ther nys erle nor baroun	neither earl
1765	That bereth hert as a lyon,	i.e., courage
	That durst come therin.	dares
	Hit is by nygrymauncye	It; necromancy
	Iwrought with fayreye,	Built; fairy (enchantment)
	That wondir hit is to wynne;	extraordinarily difficult it
1770	Therin lyeth in presowne	lies; prison
	My lady of Synadon,	
	That is of knyghtis kynne.	Who; knight's kin

	"Oftyn we hire hir crye:	hear her
	To sene hir withe none eye,	Though we cannot see her
1775	Therto have we no myght.	power
	They do hir tormentyre	torment
	And all the velenye	villainy
	And dreche hir day and nyght.	afflict (torture)
	This Mabon and Yrayne	
1780	Have sworne her othe certayne	their oath
	To dethe they will hir dight,	death; bring
	But she graunte hem tyll	Unless
	To do Mabones will	
	And geven him hir right.	grant; birthright

1785	Of all this kyngdome fayre	kingdom fair
	Than is my lady ayre,	heir
	To welde all with wynne.	oversee with honor (joy)
	She is meke and bonoure,	meek; good
	Therfor we ar in spere	fear
1790	Luste they done hir synne."	Lest; do her sin (rape her)
	Quod Lybeous Disconyous,	
	"By the love of Jhesus,	
	That lady shall Y wynne:	set free
	Bothe Mabon and Irayne	
1795	I shall hewen in the playne	cut down
	The hedys by the chynne."	heads; chin

	Tho was no more tale	Then [there]; serious talk
	In the castell, grete and smale,	
	But souped and made hym blythe.	Instead [they] supped; merry

1800	Baronys and burgeyses fale	*many*
	Comyn to that semely sale	*noble dwelling*
	For to listen and lithe	*learn*
	Howe Sir Lambert had wrought	*fared*
	And yf the knyght were oughte,	
1805	His crafte for to kythe.	*skill; make known*
	They fownden hem sette in fere	*sitting together*
	And talkynge at her sopere	*their supper*
	Of knyghtis stoute and stythe.	*hardy*
	Tho toke they ease and reste	*their*
1810	And lykynges of the beste	*desires*
	In the castell that nyght.	
	On morowe was Lybeous prest	*prepared*
	Of armes of the best:	*With weapons*
	Full fresshe he was to fight.	*Fully rested*
1815	Lambarde lad him that gate	
	To the castell yate	
	And fonde it full upright.	*open*
	Further durste hym none brynge,	*no others bring*
	Forsothe, withoute lesynge,	*lying*
1820	Barowne, burgeys, ne knyght.	*Baron, burgess, nor*
	But turned home agayne,	
	Save Sir Jerflete his swayne	*Except; servant*
	Wolde with hym ryde.	
	Lybeous swore, certayne,	
1825	That he wolde see his brayne	*i.e., dash his brains out*
	Yf he wolde lenger abyde.	*stay any longer*
	To the castell he rode	
	And with Lambard abode,	
	To Jhesus than they cryed	*prayed*
1830	He shulde hem send tidyngis glad	
	Of hem that longe hadde	*them who*
	Distroyed ther welthes wide.	*happiness*
	Syr Lybeaus, knyght curtays,	*Sir; courteous*
	Rode into the paleys	*embattled city*
1835	And at the hall he alight;	*dismounted*
	Trumpys, hornys, sarvysse,	*service at table*
	Right byfor that highe deys,	*in front of; high dais*
	He herde and saughe with sight,	*his own eyes*
	And amydd the hall floore	*in the middle of*
1840	A fyre well starke and store	*fire; powerful; intense*
	That tente and brende bright.	*gave out light*
	Ferther in he yede	*went*

And toke with hym his stede,
That halpe him in his fyght.

1845 Lybeous inner ganne passe   *inward proceeded*
To beholde that place: *look around*
The halys in the halle;   *remote corners*
Of men more nor lasse
Ne sawe he body nor face   *he saw no one*
1850 Butt mynstralis cladde in palle.   *Except; fine clothes*
With harpe, lute, and roote   *viol*
And orgone noyse of note,   *organ noise*
Grete gle they maden all;
With sotill and sawtery,   *dulcimer (citole)*
1855 Suche maner mynstralsye
Was never within wall.

Byfor euche mynstrale stode   *In front of each*
A torche bothe fayre and gode
Itende and brente bright.   *Ignited; burning*
1860 Sir Lybeous inner yode   *proceeded*
To witten with egir mode   *learn; great anticipation*
Who shulde with hym fight.
He yede into the corners   *went*
To beholde the pilleres   *pillars*
1865 That semely was of sight,   *were beautiful to see*
Of jasper and of fyne cristale,   *crystal*
Iflorysshed with amyall,   *Decorated; enamel*
That was of moche myght.   *a mighty work*

The dores weren of brasse,
1870 The wondowes all of glasse,
Wrought with imagerye;   *images*
The halle ypeynted was: *painted*
Nowher none fayrer nas   *none fairer was*
That he hade seyne withe eye.
1875 He sett hym on the deys: *sat himself; dais*
The mynstrales weryn in pees,   *silent*
That were so tryste and trye;   *reliable; excellent*
The torchis that brent bright   *burned brightly*
They queynte anone right: *suddenly went out*
1880 The mynstrellys weren awaye.   *disappeared*

The dorres and wyndowes all
They betten in the hall   *pounded*
As hit were dynte of thonder;   *[if] it; a thunder blast*
The stones of the walle
1885 On hym conne they falle,

And therof had he wonder. — *amazement*
The deys began to shake, — *dais*
The erthe began to quake;
As he sate therunder,
1890 The halle roofe unlyke — *to split open*
And the vasure eke, — *vaulting*
As it wolde all in sonder. — *(see note)*

As he sate thus dismayed,
He holde hymselfe dysseyved,
1895 Sertis, herde he nyghe;
Thoo he was better apayde — *pleased*
And to hymselfe sayde,
"Yett Y hope to playe!" — *Still; fight*
He loked into the felde
1900 And sawe, with spere and shelde,
Men in armes twayne, — *two men*
In pured pure armoure — *refined unalloyed*
Was lyngell and trappure, — *straps and trappings*
Wyth golde gaylye dight. — *adorned*

1905 That one rode into the hall
And byganne for to call,
"Syr knyght auntours! — *adventurous*
Suche case is nowe befall,
They thou be knyght in palle — *Although; in fine clothing*
1910 Fyght thou moste with us! — *must*
I holde thee qwaynte of gynne — *clever; ingenuity*
And thou that lady wynne — *If you [should]*
That is so precious."
Quod Lybeous anone ryght,
1915 "Fresshe Y am to fight, — *Ready*
By the helpe of Jhesus!"

Syr Lybeous with gode will
And into his sadyll gan skylle, — *did leap*
A launce in honde he hente, — *seized*
1920 And titely rode hem tyll, — *quickly rode to them*
His fomen for to felle, — *foeman*
Suche was his talent. — *intent*
Whanne thaye togeder smete, — *clashed*
Upon her shelde hit sette, — *their shields*
1925 With sperys doughtely of dynte; — *hearty; blow*
Mabounes launce to-braste, — *Mabon's; shattered*
Tho was he sore agaste — *astonished*
And held hym shamely shent. — *thought himself shamefully humiliated*

	And with that stroke fellowne	*felonious*
1930	Syr Lybeous bare Maboune	*forced*
	Overe his hors tayle;	*horse's tail*
	For his hynder arson	*back of his saddle*
	Brake and fell adawne	*down*
	Into the felde saunce fayle;	*without*
1935	And neygh he had him slayne,	*before*
	But there come Sir Irayne,	
	In helme, hawbrek of mayle;	
	So fresshe he was to fight,	*eager*
	He thought anone righte	*immediately*
1940	Syr Lybeous to assaylle.	

	Sir Lybeous was of hym ware,	*aware*
	A spere to hym he bare	
	And lefte his brother stille;	*[Mabon] lying inert*
	Suche a dynte he yave thare	*gave*
1945	That his haumbryk to-tare:	*hauberk tore*
	That liked bi Irayne ylle.	*Iran did not like that*
	Her lawnses they borsten a-two,	*Their lances; in two*
	Her swerdys they drewen thoo,	*Their swords; drew though*
	With hert grym and grylle;	*grim; fierce*
1950	They con togeder fight,	
	Eyther provid with right	
	Other for to spyll.	*defeat*

	As they togedyr gan hewe,	*began to strike blows*
	Maboune, the more shrewe,	*villainous [of the two]*
1955	In felde up aroos;	
	He herde and well knewe	
	That Irayne yave dyntis fewe:	*strokes*
	Therof hym sore agroos.	*was very terrified*
	To hym he went full right	
1960	To helpe to fellen in fight	*[Iran]; defeat*
	Lybeous of noble loose.	*fame*
	But Lybeous faught with bothe,	
	Though they weren wrothe,	*frenzied*
	And kepte hymselfe close.	*secure (protected)*

	Tho Yran sawe Maboune	*When*
1965	He smote strokys fellon	*murderous*
	To Sir Lybeous withe ire.	
	That evyn he karfe a-downe,	
	Byfor his forther arsowne,	*The front of the saddle*
1970	Lybeous stedys swyre.	*horse's neck*
	Lybeous was werreour slyghe	*a skillful warrior*
	And smote evyn to his thighe:	

	He karfe bone and lyre;	*shoulder bone; flesh*
	Ne halpe hym not his armour,	*Neither did his armor help*
1975	His chawntementis ne his chambur:	*nor enchantments; charms (see note)*
	Downe fell that sory syre.	

	Lybeous of his hors alight	*dismounted*
	With Mabone for to fight,	
	In felde bothe in feere.	*together*
1980	Swyche strokys they dight	*delivered*
	That sparkelys sprongen downe right	*sparks*
	From shelde and helmes clere;	*shining*
	As they bothe togeder smytte,	
	Her bothe swerdys mette:	*Their*
1985	As ye may se hem bere.	
	Mabon, the more shreweos,	*villainous*
	Forkarfe the swerde of Sir Lybeous	*Utterly broke*
	Attweyne quyte and skere.	*In two; cleanly*

	Tho was Lybeous asshamed	*Then*
1990	And in his harte sore agramed,	*sorely enraged*
	For he had lorne his swerde,	*lost*
	And his stede was lamed	*injured*
	And he shulde be defamed	
	To Arthur kynge his lorde.	
1995	To Yrayne swythe he ranne	*fast*
	And hente his swerde up thanne:	*seized*
	Was sharpe on eche a syde;	
	And ranne to Maboune right	
	And faste they gonne to fight:	
2000	Of love was ther no woorde!	*(i.e., an understatement!)*

	But evyr faught Maboune	
	As hit were a lyoune	*As if [he]; lion*
	Sir Lybeous for to sloo;	*slay*
	But Lybeous karfe adowne	*carved*
2005	His shilde with his fawchon,	*falchion*
	That he toke Irayne froo.	*from*
	In the right tale ytolde	
	The lyfte arme with the shelde	*left*
	Awaye he smote alsoo;	
2010	Than cryed Mabon hym tyll:	
	"Thi strokys arne full ylle;	*These*
	Gentill knyght nowe hoo!	*stop!*

	Ay will yelde me to thee,	*I will surrender loyally*
	In love and grete laughté,	
2015	At thine owne wille,	

	And that lady fre	*noble*
	That is in my powsté	*power*
	Takyn Y will thee tille.	
	For thorough the swerdis dynt	*through*
2020	My honde Y have itynte:	*lost*
	The venym will me spille;	*venom; kill*
	I venymed hem bothe,	*poisoned them*
	Certeyn, withouten othe,	*Certainly; oath*
	Therwith oure fone to felle."	*enemies; defeat*

2025	Quod Lybeous, "Be my thryfte,	
	I will nought of thi yefte,	*your offer*
	For all this worlde to wynne;	
	But lay on strokys swyfte:	*swift*
	One of us shall other lefte	*cut off*
2030	The hede by the chynne!"	*head; chin*
	Tho Mabon and Lybeous	
	Faste togeder hewes	*slashed at each other*
	And slaked not for no synne;	*consideration*
	Lybeous was more of myght:	*strength*
2035	He clove his helme downe right	*[Mabon's] helmet*
	And his hede a-twynne.	*in two*

2035	Tho Mabon was slayne	*When*
	He ranne ther was Yrayne	*where*
	With a fawchoune in his fiste;	*falchion*
2040	For to cleve his brayne:	*cleave; brainpan*
	I tell you for certayne,	
	To fight more hym lyste!	*wanted*
	But whan he come there,	
	Away he was ybore:	
2045	Into whate stede he nuste.	*place he did not know*
	Tho sought he hym, for the nonys,	*for a long time*
	Wyde in all the wonys:	*dwelling places*
	In trewthe well he truste.	

2050	And whan he fonde him noughte	*did not find [Iran]*
	He helde himselfe bekaughte	*thought; to be deceived*
	And byganne to syke sore,	
	And seide, in worde and thought,	
	"This will be dere bought	
	That he is fro me fare!	*from me fled*
2055	He will with sorcerye	
	Do me tormentrye:	*harm*
	That is my moste care."	
	Sore he sate and sighte,	

	He nuste whate do he myght,	*knew not*
2060	He was of blysse all bare.	*bereft of happiness; (see note)*

	As he sate thus in halle,	
	Oute at a stone walle	
	A wyndowe fayre unfelde:	*uncovered*
	Grete wondyr, withall,	
2065	In his herte ganne falle	*arose*
	And he sate and behelde.	
	A worme ther ganne oute pas	*dragon therewithin emerged*
	With a womanes face:	*woman's*
	"Yonge Y am and nothinge olde."	
2070	Hir body and hir wyngis	*wings*
	Shone in all thynchis,	*Shimmered; ways*
	As amell gaye and gilte.	*enamel; gleaming*

	Hir tayle was mekyll unnethe,	*mighty underneath*
	Hir peynis gryme and grete,	*wings hideous; terrifying*
2075	As ye may listen and lere.	*learn*
	Syr Lybeous swelt for swete	*sweltered; sweat*
	There he sate in his sete,	*seat*
	As alle had ben in fyre;	*on fire*
	So sore he was agaste	*astonished*
2080	Hym thought his herte tobraste	*would burst*
	As she neyhid hym nere.	*approached; near*
	And ere that Lybeous wiste,	*before; knew it*
	The worme with mouth him kyste	*dragon; kissed*
	And clypped aboute the swyre.	*grasped him; neck*

2085	And aftyr this kyssynge	
	Off the worme tayle and wynge	*dragon's tail*
	Swyftly fell hir froo:	*from her*
	So fayre, of all thinke,	*things*
	Woman, withoute lesynge,	
2090	Sawe he never ere thoo;	*before like that*
	But she was moder naked,	*mother naked (see note)*
	As God had hir maked:	
	Therfor was Lybeous woo.	*distressed*
	She sayde, "Knyght gentyll,	
2095	God yelde thee thi will	*rewarded your*
	My foon thou woldest sloo!	*enemies; would have slain*

	Thowe haste slayne nowthe	*You have defeated*
	Two clerkys kowthe,	*renowned*
	That wroughten by the fende.	*conjured; fiend*
2100	Este, west, northe and sowthe,	
	With maystres of her mouthe,	*mastery; their words (magic, spell)*

	Many man con they shende.	*did; destroy*
	Thorowe ther chauntement	*Through; enchantment*
	To a worme they had me went,	*dragon; transformed*
2105	In wo to leven and lende,	*sorrow; live; remain*
	Tyll I had kyssed Gaweyne,	*Until; kissed Gawain*
	That is doughti knyght, certayne,	*valiant*
	Or some of his kynde.	*some [member]; kin*

	Syr, for thou savyst my lyfe,	*because you have saved*
2110	Castellys fyfty and fyve	
	Take Y will thee till,	*Give; to*
	And mysylfe to be thy wyfe,	*your wife*
	Styll witheoute any stryfe,	*Meekly; hesitation*
	And hit be Arthures will."	*If it is Arthur's*
2115	Lybeous was glad and blythe	
	And lepte to hors als swythe	*swiftly*
	And that lady stille;	*as well*
	But sore he dradded Irayne	*dreaded*
	For he was nought islayne,	*not slain*
2120	With speche lyste he do him spylle.	*might he cause him [Lybeaus] to die; (see note)*

	To the castell Lybeous rode,	
	Therfor the folke abode	*Where; people waited*
	And beganne to crye.	
	Syr Lybeous to Lambard tolde	
2125	And to other knyghtis bolde	
	Howe he hem thre ganne gye,	*dealt with*
	And how Mabon was slayne	
	And wounded was Irayne,	
	Thorowe myght of Marye.	
2130	And howe her lady bright	*i.e., the Lady of Synadoun*
	To a dragon was ydight,	*changed*
	Thorowe her chawnterye,	*their enchantment*

	And thorow the cosse of a knyght	*kiss*
	Woman she was aplight,	*[Into]; changed*
2135	A comly creature:	
	"But she stode before,	
	As naked as she was bore,	
	And sayde, 'Nowe am Y sure	
	My fone thou haste slayne,	*enemies*
2140	Mabon and Yrayne:	
	In pees thou dost me brynge.'"	*peace*
	When Lybeous Disconyous	
	Had tolde the stywarde thus,	
	Bothe worde and endeng,	

2145	A robe of purpyll riche,	*priceless cloth*
	Pillured with pure grice,	*Trimmed; gray fur*
	He sent hir on hyenge;	*haste*
	Kerchewes and garlandis ryche	*Headdresses; garlands*
	He sent hir preveliche,	*privately*
2150	A byrd hit ganne hir bringe;	*lady-in-waiting*
	Whan she was redy dight	*prepared*
	She went with many a knyght	
	To hir owne wonnynge.	*their; dwelling*
	All the folke of Synadowne	
2155	With a well fayre procession	
	Her lady conne home brynge.	*Their*
	When she was comen to towne,	
	Of gold and stonys a crowne	*gemstones*
	Upon hir hede was sett,	
2160	And were gladde and blythe	
	And thanked God fele sythe	*many times*
	That hir balys were bett.	*their sorrows; relieved*
	Than all the lordis of dignité	
	Did hir homage and fewté,	*fealty*
2165	As hit was dewe dette.	*it; due to her*
	And euche lord in his degré	*each; according to; rank*
	Gave hir yeftis grete plenté,	*gifts aplenty*
	When they with hir mett.	
	Sevyn dayes they dide sojoure	*sojourn*
2170	With Sir Lambert in the towre	
	And all the peeple in same;	*together*
	Tho went thei with honour	
	Taward Kynge Arthoure	*To*
	With mekyll gle and game;	*joy; happiness*
2175	They thanked God with al His myghtis,	
	Arthur and all his knyghtis,	
	That he hade no shame.	
	Arthur gave als blyve	*eagerly*
	Lybeous that lady to wyfe,	
2180	That was so gentill a dame.	*noble woman*
	The myrrour of that brydale	*description*
	No man myght tell with tale,	
	In ryme nor in geste:	*rhyme; chronicle*
	In that semely saale	*splendid hall*
2185	Were lordys many and fale	*numerous*
	And ladies full honeste.	*honorable*
	There was riche service	
	Bothe to lorde and ladyes	

	To leste and eke to moste;	*least; also the greatest*
2190	Thare were gevyn riche giftis	
	Euche mynstrale her thriftis,	*Each minstrel; earnings*
	And some that were unbrest.	*gratuitous (unpromised); (see note)*

	Fourty dayes thei dwelden	*dwelled [there]*
	And ther here feste helden	*there held their feast*
2195	With Arthur the kynge.	
	As the Frensshe tale us tolde,	*romance*
	Arthur kyng with his knyghtis bolde	
	Home he gonne hem brynge.	*brought them*
	Sevyn yere they levid same	*Seven years; lived together*
2200	With mekyll joye and game,	
	He and that swete thynge.	*i.e., the Lady of Synadoun*
	Nowe Jhesu Criste, oure Savioure	
	And his moder, that swete floure,	
	Grawnte us gode endynge. Amen.	

Explicit *Lybious Disconyas*.   *Here ends Lybeaus Desconus*

Figure 2. Eve and the Dragon-Serpent in Eden. The enscrolled Lady of Sinadoun appears as "A worme . . . With a womanes face" (2067–8), a description that evokes images of Eve and the Dragon-Serpent, such as found in *Speculum humanæ salvationis*, Chapter 1. Bibliothèque Nationale, Paris, Ms. lat. 9854, fol. 5 recto, reproduced in Adrian Wilson and Joyce Lancaster Wilson, *A Medieval Mirror*. Berkeley: University of California Press, c.1984. P. 30. http://ark.cdlib.org/ark:/13030/ft7v19p1w6.

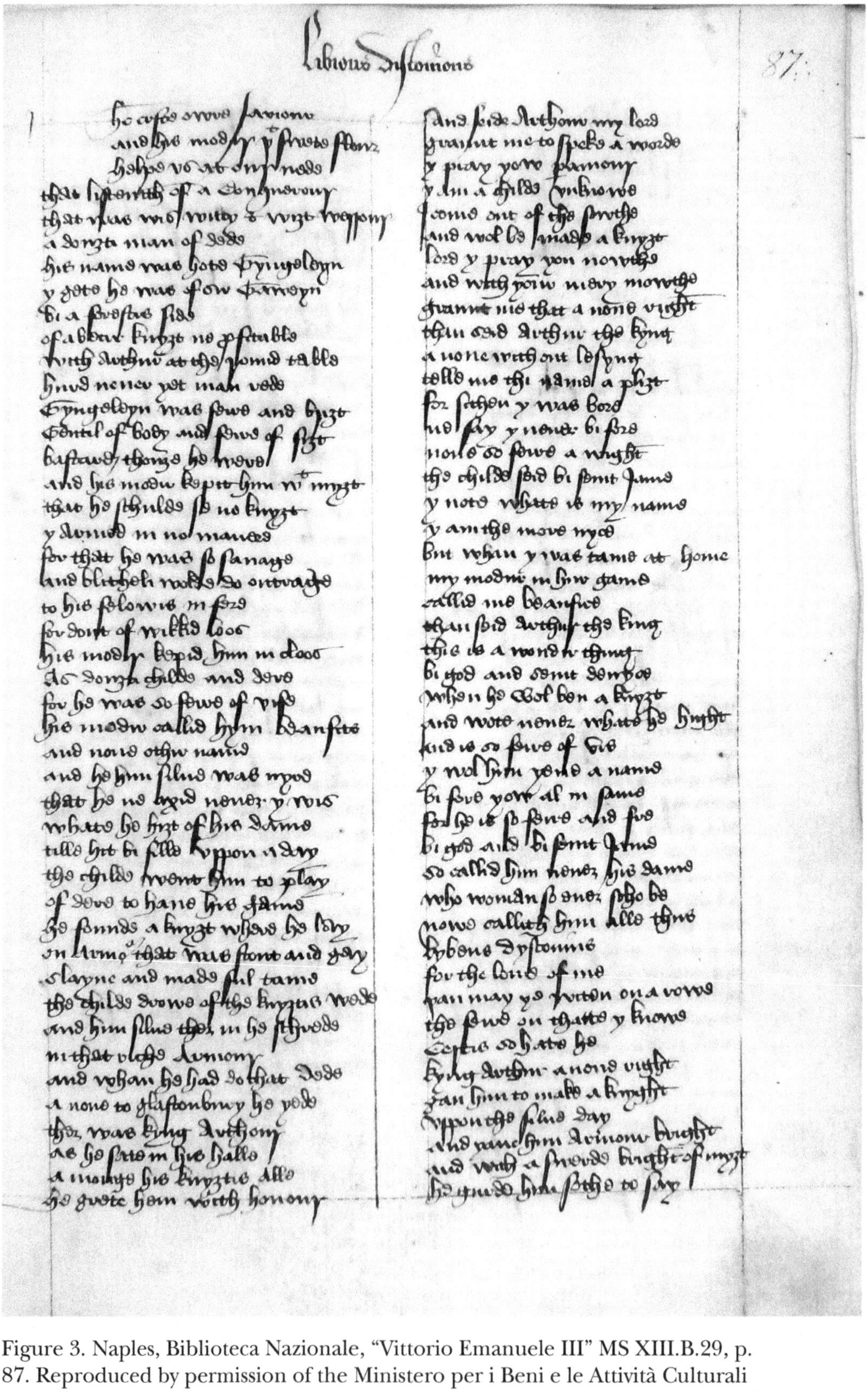

Libeaus Desconus 87.

He cryst oure saviour
And his moder y^t swete flour
Helpe us at oure nede
Thes listenith of a conquerour
That was wis wity & wyzt werrour
A dozty man of dede
His name was hote Gyngelyn
Y gete he was of Sir Gawyn
Bi a forster side
Of a better knyzt ne stable
With Arthur at the rounde table
Hurd never yet man rede
Gyngelyn was fare and bryzt
Gentil of body and fare of sizt
Bastard though he were
And his moder kepte him w^t myzt
That he shulde se no knyzt
Y armed in no manere
For that he was so savage
And blithely wolde do outrage
To his felowis in fere
For doute of wikked loos
His moder keped him in cloos
As dozty childe and dere
For he was so fare of vis
His moder callid hym Beaufits
And none other name
And he him silue was nyce
That he ne asked never y wis
Whatte he hizt of his dame
Tille hit bi fille uppon a day
The childe wente him to play
Of dere to have his game
He founde a knyzt where he lay
In armo^s that was stout and gay
Slayne and made ful tame
The childe dede of the knyztis wede
And him silue ther in he schrede
In that riche armoure
And whan he had do that dede
Anone to Glastonbury he yede
Ther was king Arthoure
As he sate in his halle
Amonge his knyztis alle
He grete hem with honoure

And seide Arthour my lord
Graunt me to speke a worde
Y pray youre favoure
Y am a childe unknowe
Come out of the forthe
And wol be made a knyzt
Lord y pray you nowthe
And with youre mery mowthe
Graunt me that anone rizt
Than sede Arthur the kyng
Anone without lesyng
Telle me thi name a plizt
For sithen y was bore
Ne say y never bifore
None so fare a wizt
The childe seid bi seint Jame
Y note whatte is my name
Y am the more nyce
But whan y was at home
My moder in hire game
Callid me Beaufice
Than seid Arthur the king
This is a wonder thing
Bi god and seint Denys
When he wol ben a knyzt
And wote never whatte he hizt
And is so fare of vis
Y wol him yeve a name
Bi fore you al in same
For he is so fare and free
Bi god and bi seint Jame
So callid him never his dame
Who womman so ever she be
Nowe calleth him alle thus
Lybeus Dyscouus
For the love of me
Than may ye witen on a rowe
The fare unknowe
Certis so hatte he
Kyng Arthur anone right
Gan him to make a knyzt
Uppon the silue day
And yaue him armoure bright
And with a swerde bright of myzt
He gurde him sothe to say

Figure 3. Naples, Biblioteca Nazionale, "Vittorio Emanuele III" MS XIII.B.29, p. 87. Reproduced by permission of the Ministero per i Beni e le Attività Culturali

LIBIOUS DISCONIOUS
(NAPLES, BIBLIOTECA NAZIONALE, MS XIII.B.29)

    Jhesu Criste owre Saviour,
    And his modir, that swete flour,
    Helpe us at our nede,
    That listenith of a conquerour   *Who*
5   That was wis, witty, and wight werrour,   *wise; discerning; valiant*
    A doughti man of dede.
    His name was hote Gyngeleyn;   *called*
    Ygete he was of Sir Gaweyn   *Begotten*
    Bi a forestis side;
10 Of a betir knyght ne profitable,   *worthy*
    With Arthur at the Round Table,
    Hurd never yet man rede.   *No one has heard tell of yet*

    Gyngeleyn was feire and bright,
    Gentil of body and feire of sight,
15 Bastard thoughe he were;
    And his modir kepit him with myght   *kept him protected*
    That he schulde se no knyght
    Yarmed in no manere,   *Armed in any way*
    For that he was so savage,   *he was so uncivilized*
20 And blitheli wolde do outrage   *without hesitation*
    To his felowis in fere.   *companions*
    For dout of wikkid loos,   *fear of his bad reputation*
    His modir kepid him in cloos   *seclusion*
    As doughti childe and dere.   *[her] strong and beloved child*

25 For he was so feire of vise   *fair of face (i.e., handsome)*
    His modir callid him Beaufits,   *Beautiful Son*
    And none othir name.
    And he him silve was nyse   *himself was innocent (naive)*
    That he ne axid never, ywis,   *asked; truly*
30 Whate he hight of his dame.   *was named by*
    Tille hit bifille uppon a day
    The childe went him to play,   *went to play (went hunting)*
    Of dere to have his game.   *deer*
    He founde a knyght where he lay
35 On armour that was stout and gay,   *In armor; sturdy and splendid*
    Slayne and made ful tame.   *rendered harmless*

	The childe drowe off the knyghtis wede	*took off*
	And himsilve therin he schrede	*himself dressed*
	In that riche armour.	
40	And whan he had do that dede,	*when he had done that*
	Anone to Glastonbury he yede,	*Immediately; went*
	Ther was Kyng Arthour,	
	As he sate in his halle,	
	Amonge his knyghtis alle.	
45	He grete hem with honour	
	And seide: "Arthour, my lord,	
	Graunt me to speke a worde.	
	Y pray yow, par amour.	

	"Y am a childe unknowe.	*youth unknown*
50	I come out of the sowthe	*south*
	And wol be made a knyght.	
	Lord, Y pray you nowthe,	*now*
	And with your mery mowthe	
	Graunt me that anone right."	*directly*
55	Than seid Arthur the kyng:	
	"Anone, without lesyng,	*lying (truthfully)*
	Telle me thi name aplight,	*truly*
	For sithen Y was bore,	*since I was born*
	Ne say Y never bifore	*I have never before seen*
60	None so feire a wight."	*so handsome a man*

	The childe seid: "Bi Seint Jame,	*youth*
	Y note whate is my name,	*I know not*
	Y am the more nyce.	*I am all the more naïve [for it]*
	But whan Y was tame at home,	*meek*
65	My modur, in hur game,	*playfully*
	Callid me Beaufice."	*Beautiful Son*
	Than seid Arthur the king:	
	"This is a wondir thing,	
	Bi God and Seint Denyce,	*Saint Denis*
70	When he wol ben a knyght	*wishes to become a knight*
	And wote never whate he hight,	*Yet knows not what he is named*
	And is so feire of vis.	*fair of face*

	"Y wol him yeve a name,	
	Bifore yow al in same,	*all together*
75	For he is so feire and fre;	*fair and noble*
	Bi God and bi Seint Jame,	*James*
	So callid him never his dame,	
	Who woman so ever scho be.	*Whatever woman she might be*
	Nowe callith him alle thus,	
80	Lybeus Dysconius,	*Fair Unknown*

For the love of me.
Than may ye witen on a rowe *know in an orderly fashion*
The feire on thatte Y knowe, *fair one that I acknowledge*
Certis, so hate he." *Certainly, that is what he is to be called*

85 Kyng Arthur, anone right, *right away*
Gan him to make a knyght
Uppon the silve day, *that very day*
And yave him armour bright, *gave*
And with a swerde bright of myght
90 He gurde him, sothe to say. *truth*
Aftur, him taught Gaweyn,
With strenghe in the pleyn, *in the plain*
Poynt of knyghtis play. *Techniques; i.e., jousting*
He hongid on him a schilde
95 With grefons overgilde, *griffons overlaid with gold*
Ipeyntid of lengthe ful gay.

Whan he was knyght ymade,
Anone a bone he bade, *request*
And seid: "My lord fre, *generous*
100 In hert were Y glad
The first fighting yef Y had *If I might have the first combat*
That men axen of thee." *ask*
Than seid Arthur the kyng:
"I graunt thee thin asking, *your request*
105 Whate bone so hit be. *Whatever the request*
But ever me thinkith thee ful yong
For to do a good fighting,
For any thing that Y can se."

Without eny more resoun, *further debate*
110 Duke, erle, and baroun,
Thei weschid and went to mete. *washed; dinner*
Of wilde fowlis and vensoune, *venison*
As lordis of gret renoune, *noblemen greatly esteemed*
Inowe thei had to ete. *Enough they had to eat*
115 Nad thei ysate but a while, *They had not been seated for long*
The montenys of a myle, *time it takes to ride a mile*
At hare tabul ysete, *their*
Ther come a maid in ride.
A dwarfe rode bi hur side,
120 Al biswat for hete. *All covered in sweat from the heat*

The maid was yhote Elyne, *was called*
Gentil, bright, and schene, *fair*
A ladyis mesynger. *lady's*

	Ther was never cuntas ne quene	*countess nor queen*
125	So semely on to sene,	*beautiful to look upon*
	Ther myght none be hur pere.	*peer*
	The maiden was clothid in tarsis,	*(see note)*
	Round and no thing skars,	*Of ample abundance, and in no way skimpy*
	With pelour blandere.	*ermine trim*
130	Hur sadul was overgilde,	*inlaid with gold*
	With diamoundis fulfillid.	*completely covered*
	Mylke white was hur desture.	*destrier (riding horse)*

	The dwarf was clothid in ynd,	*indigo*
	Bifore and eke bihinde,	
135	For he was stout and pert.	*fashionably dressed (see note)*
	Among al Cristen kynde	
	Suche on schulde no man fynde.	*Such [a] one*
	His sircote was overte;	*a sleeveless surcoat*
	His berde was as yelow as wax,	
140	To his gurdul henge the plax,	*hair*
	For sothe, to se with sight.	
	With golde his schone were dight,	*His shoes were decorated with gold*
	And kopid as a knyght —	*in a knightly mantle (cope)*
	Tho semyth of no poverte!	*He did not seem impoverished*

145	Deodelyne was his name.	
	Wide spronge his fame,	
	Bothe northe and eke bi sowthe.	
	Moche couthe he of game:	*He was skilled in courtly entertainments*
	Sotil, sawtre in same,	*Citole, psaltery*
150	Of harpe, fethil, and crowthe.	*harp, fiddle; stringed instrument*
	He spake to that maide hynde:	*gentle maid*
	"Damesel, telle thyne erande.	*declare your message to me*
	Tyme it were nowthe."	*Now the time has come*

	The maide knelid in halle	
155	Among the lordis and lordlingis all	
	And seid, "My lord Arthour,	
	A caas ther is bifalle,	
	Wors within the walle,	*The worst imaginable*
	Y note nought suche of dolour.	*I do not know of a more grievous case*
160	My lady of Synadowne	
	Is brought in stronge prisoun,	
	That was of grete honour,	*Who*
	And praid you send hur a knyght	
	In warra that were wyse and wight,	*protection; wise and courageous (see note)*
165	To wyn hur with honour."	

Than stert up a yong knyght,
In hert that was lefe and wight,   *eager and courageous*
And seid: "My lord Arthour!
I schall do that fight
170   And wynne that lady bright,
Yef ye be trewe of worde!"
Than seid Arthoure: "That is sothe,
Certis, withouten othe,
Therto Y bere recorde."   *record*
175   And seid: "God yeve thee strength and myght
To wynne the lady bright
With dynt of sper and swerde."

Than gan Elyne to chide.   *scold*
"Alas," scho seide, "that tide
180   That Y was hedir ysende!
This wordis schalle springe wide;   *story will spread*
Kynge, loste is thi pride,
And thy loce yschende,   *your reputation damaged*
Now thou woldist sende a childe
185   That is wiltes and wilde
To dele doughti dynt,   *To deliver powerful sword strokes*
Whan thow hast knyghtis of mayne,   *powerful knights*
Persavale and Sir Gaweyne,
That bene price in every turment."   *worthy in every tournament*

190   The dwarf with gret errour   *in great anger*
Stert to Kynge Arthour   *Turned*
And seid: "Thou gentil kyng,
This childe to bene a werrour,
To done a good labour,   *To accomplish a worthy task*
195   He is worthe nought a ferthing.   *a quarter of a penny (i.e., worthless)*
Er that ever he that lady se,   *Before*
Bataile five othir thre   *Five or three battles*
He dothe, withoute lesynge.   *He must do*
At Poynt Perillous,
200   Biside the Chapel of Aventours,
Ther schalle he bigynne."

Sir Lybeus than answerid:
"Yit was Y never aferd
For drede of mannys sawe.   *fear of [any] man's words*
205   Sumwhate have Y lerid,
Bothe with spere and with schild.
Ther men have ben yslawe,
The man that fleith for drede,
Bi wey othir bi strete,

210 Y wolde he were todrawe!   *drawn and quartered*
    This bataile Y undirtake
    And never one forsake,   *once*
    For suche is Arthouris lawe."

    The may answerid fulle snelle: *maiden; immediately*
215 "That semyth thee right welle,   *Your words certainly inspire confidence*
    Who so lokith on thee!   *[To] whoever beholds you*
    Thou ne durst for alle this world   *You dare not*
    Abide the wynde of a swerd,   *Endure even the wind of a sword [stroke]*
    For ought that Y can se."
220 Than seid the dwarf that stound   *at that time*
    That, "Dede men on the ground   *Dead*
    Of thee aferde may be.   *May be afraid of you*
    Nowe Y rede thee in game:
    Go home and sowke thi dame   *nurse at your mother's breast*
225 And wynne ther thi degré."   *earn your status there*

    The kyng seide, anone right:
    "Here getist thou no nothir knyght,
    Bi Him that bought me dere!   *i.e., Christ*
    Yef thow thinke him noght wight,   *capable (fit for the task)*
230 Gete thee anothir wher thou myght
    That is of more powere."
    The maide for noye and hete   *annoyance and anger*
    Wolde nought drinke ne ete,
    For alle that thei myght do,
235 But sate hur downe as careful maide   *full of care*
    Til the tabul was unleide,   *removed*
    Sho and the dworf in fere.   *together*

    Kyng Arthur in that stound
    Commaundid of that Tabul Rounde
240 Four of the best knyghtis
    To army him hole and sound   *arm him*
    Of the best armour that myght be found
    To army the childe at rightis.   *youth; fittingly*
    He seide: "Throwe the grace of Crist,
245 That in the flem Jourdan was baptist,   *the river Jordan; baptized*
    That he schulde have myght,
    And bicome a good champiowne
    To the lady of Synadowne,
    To sle hur fo in fight."

250 To army him the knyghtis were fayn,   *eager*
    Sir Percevale and Sir Gawayn,
    In that semely sale.   *majestic hall*

The third was Sir Ewayn.   *Ywain*
The fourth was Sir Griffayn,   *(see note)*
255   Thus tellith the Frensche tale.
The thei cast on him of sylke
A gippon as white as mylke,   *tunic*
In a semely sale,
And an hawberk bright,   *shining coat of mail*
260   That ful riche was ydight,   *richly constructed*
With maile grete and smale.   *both large and small rings*

Gaweyn, his owne sire,
Hynge abowte his swire   *Hung about his neck*
A schilde with on griffoun,   *with one griffon*
265   And an helme of riche atyre   *richly wrought*
Was stele and none yre.   *not iron*
Sir Persevale set on his croun
A griffon he brought with him,   *(see note L: 257)*
In werre him with to werre,   *To protect him in war*
270   And a fel fouchone.   *falchion (deadly sword)*
Ewayn brought with him a stede
That was good in every nede,
As eger as eny lyon.   *fierce*

The yong knyght to hors gan spring,
275   And rode to Arthour the kyng,
And seid: "My lord so hynde,   *gracious*
Yeve me thi blessyng.
Without eny lettyng,   *delay*
My wille is to wynde."   *to depart*
280   Arthour his hond up hafe,   *raised*
And his blessyng he him yafe,
As curteis kyng and kynde,
And seid: "God yeve thee grace,
And yeve thee spede and space,   *fortune and opportunity*
285   To bring that birde out of bond."   *liberate that maiden from her bondage*

The maide was stout and gay,   *proud and noble*
And lepe to hur palfray;   *leapt into [the saddle of] her palfrey*
The dworfe rode bi hur side.
Until the thrid day
290   Uppon the knyght alway,   *constantly*
Ever sho gan to chide,
And seid: "Thou wrecche, thou caitife,   *You wretch, you lowborn slave*
Though thou were so stife,   *sturdily built*
Sone lost is thi pride!
295   This place kepith a knyght;

With everi man he wol fight.
His name springith ful wide,   *reputation*

William Celabronche.
His fighting may no man stonche;   *overcome*
300   He is werrour out of witte.   *deranged*
But throw hart and honche,   *heart; lower ribcage*
With his spere he wol lonche   *penetrate*
Al that ayens him mete."
Quod Libeous Disconious: *Said*
305   "Ys his fighting of suche use   *Is that his customary practice*
And was he never yhitte?"
Tide so whate bitide,   *Let befall what shall befall*
To him schalle Y ride,
And loke how fast he sitte!"   *how secure he sits in his saddle*

310   Than rede thei furthe al thre   *rode*
Uppon that feire cause.
Biside the Chapel of Aventours
That knyght thei can se,
In armour bright of ble   *bright of hue (shining)*
315   Uppon the Poynt Perilous.
He bare a schilde of grene
With three lions of golde schene,   *bright gold*
Proute and precious,   *Nobly and artfully wrought*
To suche lengels and trappis.   *horse's harness and trappings*
320   To dele men rappis   *blows*
Ever hath bene his use.

Whan he had of Libeous a sight,
He rode to him fulle right
And seid, "Welcome, Beaupere!   *i.e., fair knight*
325   Whate man that here furth rides,   *Whatsoever man rides forth here*
He mote with me fight,   *must*
Othir leve his armour here."
Than seid Libeous Disconious:
"For the love of swete Jhesus,
330   Lete us pas, nowe, here,
For we have fer to wynde   *far to travel*
And bene fer fro our frende,   *far from our friends*
This may and ich in fere."   *This maiden and I together*

Than seid William tho:
335   "Thou schalt nought ascape so,   *escape*
So God yeve me rest!
For we shal bothe two
Fight ar that we go   *before*

	A furlong here bi west!"	*[As much as] one-eighth of a mile west from here*
340	Than seid Libeus: "Nowe Y se	
	That may no betir be,	*There can be no better resolution*
	In hast do thi best.	*Do your best quickly*
	Take thi cours with thi scheft,	*Prepare your lance*
	Yef thowe be connyng of craft,	*If you have any skill*
345	For her is myne al prest."	*here; all ready*
	No lengir wolde thei abide,	
	But togadir gan thei ride	
	With grete renowne.	*power*
	Sir Libeous in that tide	*at that moment*
350	Smote William in the side	
	With a spere feloun.	*deadly spear*
	But William sate so fast	*so securely*
	That his stiropis tobarst	*burst*
	And his arsoun.	*the raised back of his saddle*
355	William gan to stoupe,	
	And over his hors crowpe	*crupper*
	In that he felle adowne.	*So that*
	His stede ranne away,	
	But William nought long lay,	
360	But stert up anone right,	
	And seide, "By my fay!	*faith*
	Bi this ilke day	
	Y founde never none so wight.	*powerful*
	But nowe my stede is go,	*gone*
365	Fight ye on fote also,	
	As ye be a gentil knyght."	
	Than seide Libeous Disconious:	
	"Bi the love of swete Jhesus,	
	Therto Y am right light!"	*eager*
370	Swerdis thei drowe bothe,	
	As men that were wrothe,	*furious*
	And fought furthe fast.	*ever more vigorously*
	So fast thei gan dinge,	*vigorously did they deliver blows*
	The fire, withoute lesing,	*lying (truly)*
375	Out of hare helme barst.	*Burst (sparked) from their helmets*
	But Sir William Celabronche	
	To Libeous gan lonche	*struck*
	Throwe his schilde in hast.	
	A quarter fille to ground;	
380	Sir Libeous in that stound	*at that moment*
	In hart he was agast.	*startled*

Sir Libeous al with myght   *with all his strength*
He defendid him anone right,   *defended himself valiantly*
As werrour good and slygh.   *skillful; cunning*
385   Vesour and crest doun right,   *[William's] visor; lowered*
He lete fle with myght,   *He struck; forcefully*
Of Williamis helme in highe,   *At the top of William's helmet*
Than the poynt of the swerd   *So that*
Schave Williamis berde   *Shaved*
390   And come the flesche to nye.   *too close [for comfort]*
William smote Libeous tho,
That his swerde brake atwo,
That many men it sye.   *saw*

Than gan William mercy to cry:
395   "For the love of Seint Marie,
Lete me on lyve pas!   *Let me pass alive (keep on living)*
It were gret vilonye   *villainy*
To do a knyght to dye,   *cause*
Weponles in a place."   *Weaponless in some locale*
400   Thanne seid Libious Disconius:
"Bi the love of swete Jhesus,
Thou getist of me no grace
But thowe swere me an othe,   *Unless*
Ar that we asondir goth   *Before we separate and depart*
405   Here bifore my face.

In hast thowe knely adoun,   *kneel down at once*
And swere apon my swerd broun,   *bright sword*
Thou schalt to Arthour wynde   *travel*
And sei: 'Lord of renoun,
410   I am come to your prisoun.   *as your prisoner*
A knyght me hidir gan synde   *send*
That men clepith, in your use,   *according to your custom*
Libeous Disconious,
Unkouth of kynde and kithe.'"   *Whose lineage is unknown*
415   William on kneis him sette   *on his knees*
And sware as he him hette.   *promised*
Furthe gan he wynde.   *Then he departed*

Thus partid thei alle.
William to Arthouris halle
420   Toke the right way.
A caas ther gan bifalle;   *Something happened then*
Thre knyghtis proude in palle   *splendidly arrayed*
Met he the same day.
His sustir sones he mette there,   *sister's sons*
425   Feire knyghtis and fre,   *noble*

That were stout and gay.   *proud and noble*
Whan thei say William blede,   *saw*
As wolfe that wolde awede,   *a raging wolf*
Thei mede of grete deray.   *cried out in dismay*

430   And seid to William:
"Who hath do thee this schame?
Whi bledist thow so yorne?"   *copiously*
He seid: "Bi God and bi Seint Jame,
Of on that is nought to blame,   *[Because] of one who is faultless*
435   A knyght that is ful stout and sterne.   *fierce and formidable*
Libious Disconious he hight.   *is called*
To falle his foo in fight,   *overcome*
He is nought to lerne.   *has little to learn*
A dwarf ridith him bifore,
440   His squyar as he were,
And eke a wel faire schene.   *a very beautiful bright [lady]*

"But on thing grevith me more,   *one*
That he hath made me swore
Uppon his bronde bright   *On his bright sword*
445   That Y schal never more,
Til Y come Arthour bifore,
Stynt day ne nyght.   *cease [my journey]*
To him Y must me yelde
As overcome in fielde,
450   Bi power of his knyght,
And never agayne him bere   *against*
Nothir schilde ne spere,
And thus Y have him bihight."   *promised*

Than seid the knyghtis thre:
455   "Thow schalt wel ywreke be,   *well avenged*
Certis, without faile!   *Assuredly*
He alone ayene thre —   *against*
He is nought worthe a stre   *a straw*
To bide bataile.   *endure*
460   Go furthe, William, and do thi othe,
And though the traitour be wrothe,
We schulle him asaile,
Ar he this forest pas;   *before*
We schul his hauberk of bras,   *crush*
465   Though it be thik of maile."

Hereof wist no wight   *None [of Lybeaus's party] knew about this*
Ne Libeous, the gentil knyght,
But rode furthe paas bi pace.   *pace by pace*

He and that maide bright
470   Maden togadir that nyght
Game and grete solas.
"Merci," scho gan him crye,
For sho spake him vilonye,   *speak villainy of him*
And he forgave hir hur trespas.
475   The dwarfe was hur squyour,
And servid hem fur and nere   *far and near (i.e., continuously)*
Of alle that worthi was.

On morow, whan it was day,
Thei rod on hare journay   *their*
480   Toward Synadoun.
Than sawe thei in way
Thre knyghtis stout and gay
Come ridyng fro Karlioun.
To him thei cried anone right:
485   "Traitour, turne thowe and fight
Or els lete thi renoune,   *yield your reputation*
And that maide bright,
That is so feire of sight,
Lede we wolle to toune!"   *We will lead [her] back to town*

490   Sir Libeous to ham cried:
"Y ame redy to ride
Agayne yow al in same,   *Against all of you together*
As princis proude in pride!"   *in splendid array*
He prekid his stede that tide,   *at that moment*
495   Al in ernyst and nought in game.
The eldist brothir than bere
To Sir Libious a spere,
Sir Gawer was his name.
Sir Libious rode to him anone,
500   And brake his rigge bone,   *backbone*
And lete him ligge lame.   *left him lying crippled*

The knyght merci gan crye.
Sir Libious than sicurlye
Hilde him fast adoun.
505   The dwarfe, Deodolyne,
Toke the stede bi the rayne,
And lepe up in to the arssoune.   *saddle*
He rode than with that
To the maide ther scho sate
510   Of so feire face.
Than louge that maide bright   *laughed*

And seid: "This yong knyght
Was wel ychose champioun."

The myddil brothir stode and bihilde.
515 His brothir in the filde
Had lorne mayne and myght.   *lost both his strength and might*
He smote so, hit is tolde,
Into Sir Libiousis schilde
With a spere anone right.
520 Sir Libious awey gan bere
With the poynt of a spere
The helme awey of the knyght.
The yongist brothir gan furth ride
And prekid his stede that tide,   *spurred*
525 Egir as lioun wight.   *Fierce as a vicious lion*

He seide to Sir Libious anone:
"Sir knyght, bi Seint John,
Thou art a fel champioun and light.   *a deadly and powerful*
Bi God that deide on tre,   *died on the cross (i.e., Christ)*
530 Fight Y schalle with thee,
Y trowe, and bere thee doun."
As werrour out of witte,   *in furor*
Sir Libious gan he hitte
With a felle fauchon;   *deadly sword*
535 So stif his stroke he sette
Throwe helm and basnet   *outer helmet and basinet (inner helmet)*
He carve Libious croun.   *struck Lybeaus's skull*

Than was Libious agrevyd,
Whan he frede on his hede   *felt*
540 A swerde of egir mode.   *fierce hostility*
His swerde aboute him wend.   *drew*
Al that him toke he clevyd,   *Everything he struck he cut through*
As werrour wilde and wode.   *enraged and furious*
Than seide Libious tho: *Then said*
545 "One ayeyne two   *against*
To fight it is nought good."
Fast he hewe on him
With grete strokis and grym,
And stife agenst hem stode.   *stood against them courageously*

550 But throwe Godis grace,
He smote the myddelist in the place
Uppon the right arme tho.
He fledde in that caas,   *at that time*
And in that ilke spaas,

555   The right arme fille him fro.   *fell from him*
        The yongist sy that sight;   *witnessed that sight*
        He had no mayne ne myght   *strength or courage*
        To fight ayen his fo.
        Tho up he yelde
560   Bothe his spere and his schilde,
        And mercy he cried tho.

        Sir Libious answerid, "Nay!
        Thou schalt nought so go away,
        Bi Him that bought us bothe.
565   Thowe and thi brotherne tway,
        Ye schulle sicour me your fay: *secure me your faith (i.e., make an oath)*
        Ye schulle to Arthour wynde   *go*
        And sey, 'Lordis of renoune,
        As overcome presone   *prisoners*
570   A knyght us hedir gan send
        To yelde you towre and towne,
        And be undir your bandowne   *governance*
        To oure lyvys ende.'

        "And but ye wol do so,
575   Certis Y schalle sle you two
        Longe ar it be nyght."   *Long before it is night*
        The knyghtis sware to him tho
        That thei schulde to Arthour go,
        And trewthe to him thei plight.   *fealty; pledged*
580   Libious and that may   *i.e., to Synadoun*
        Went in hare way   *as they had [originally] vowed*
        As thei had yheght,
        Til the third day
        Thei rode in game and play,
585   He and that birde bright.   *beautiful maiden*

        Thei rode ever west
        Into a grene forest,
        And myght not come to toun.
        Thei ne wist whate was best;
590   Nedis thei must rest,
        And ther they lighte adoun.
        In the grene grevys,   *groves*
        Thei made a logge of levys   *lodge of leaves*
        With swerdis bright and broun.   *bright; polished*
595   Therin thei dwellid al nyght,
        He and that birde bright,
        So feire of facion.   *fair of face [and form]*

And ever the dwarfe gan wake.   *kept awake*
A fire he sey make,
600   Fro him nought halfe a myle.
"Arise," he seide, "Sir Knyght!
To hors that thou were dight,   *Get you to horse; prepared*
For drede of more perile!
Certis, Y hire grete bost;
605   Y have a smylle of rost,   *scent; roast*
By God and by Seint Gile."

Sir Libious was stout and gay,
And lepe on his palfray;
He hent schilde and spere.   *seized*
610   As he went furthe fast,
Two jeyauntis he founde at the last,   *giants*
Whan that he come there.
That one was blak as picche,
That othir rede and lotheliche;   *red; loathsome*
615   Ful fowle thei were of chere.   *Very ugly; expression*
The blake gan holde in barme   *The black [giant]; in his arms*
A feire maide bi the arme,
Bright so rose in brere.   *As beautiful as a rose on the briar*

The rede geaunte so yorne   *eagerly*
620   On a spitte a bore gan turne.   *boar*
For sum man schulde it wete,   *So that someone might hear*
Sho seide, "Welaway!   *Alas!*
That ever Y abode this day   *experienced this day*
Bitwene two develis to sytte!
625   Helpe me, Marie mylde,
For the love of thi childe   *i.e., Christ*
That Y be nought forgit!"   *not be forgotten*

Quod Libeous: "Bi Seint Jame,
To bring this maide out of schame
630   Hit were a feire empris!"   *worthy undertaking*
He toke his cours with his scheft,   *prepared his lance for combat*
As man that cowthe his craft,   *skilled in his craft [the art of war]*
And rode at the right asise.   *in the right manner [toward his foes]*
To fight with ham bothe in same,   *them together*
635   It is no childis game;
Thei bith fulle grymme and grise.   *grim; terrible*
The blake he smote smert   *sharply (aggressively)*
Throwe lyver, longen, and hert,   *liver, lungs; heart*
That never he myghte arise.

640	And than fleygh that maide schene,	*fled*
	And thonkid heven quene.	
	That socour hur sent.	*rescue*
	That came maide Elyne,	
	Sho and the dwarf bidene,	*together*
645	And bi the honde hur hent.	*seized her by the hand*
	Thei went to the grevys	*grove*
	Into the logge of grene levys	
	With welle goode entent,	*cheerfully*
	And bisoughte Jhesus,	
650	That he wolde helpe Libeus Disconyous,	
	That he be nought yschent.	*defeated*

	The rede geaunt smote thore	*vigorously*
	To Libeous, with the wilde bore,	
	As wolfe that wolde of wede.	*an enraged wolf*
655	His dynt he sette sore,	
	That Sir Libeous stede therfore	
	Doune to grounde he yode.	*fell to the ground*
	Sir Libeous than ful smert	
	Out of his sadille stert,	
660	As sparkil dothe of glede.	*As a spark flies from the coal*
	As egir as eny lioun,	
	He faught with his swerde broun	*bright sword*
	To yelde the geaunt his mede.	*reward*

	The giaunt with the spit gave a stroke	
665	With the butte of a yong oke	
	That he had on the bore.	*with the wild boar on it*
	He leide on Libeous fast,	
	While the spit wolde last,	
	Ever more and more.	
670	The bore was ful hote than;	
	On Sir Libeous the grece ran,	
	Swithe fast thore.	*copiously*
	The giaunt was stife and strong;	
	Fifteen fote he was longe,	
675	And smote Libeous sore.	

	And ever the giaunt	*giant [continuously attacked]*
	To Libeous, wel Y wote,	
	Tille his spit brake on two.	
	As a man that was unsaught,	*enraged*
680	A tronchon up he caught,	
	To fight ayens his fo.	
	With the ende of a tre	
	He smot Libeous schilde a-thre.	*in three pieces*

Than waxid Libeous ful wo.   *became distressed*
685   Er he the tre up hafe,   *Before [the giant] could raise the tree up*
Sir Libeous a stroke him yafe,
That the right arme fil him fro.

The giaunt fille to ground,
And Libeous in that stound   *quickly*
690   Smote of his hed ful right,   *off*
In Frensche tale as it is found.
Tille that othir he went that stound   *Immediately*
And servid him aplight.   *in the same way*
Tho he toke hedis tway
695   And bare ham to that may
That he wan in fight.
The may was glad and blithe,
And thonkid God fele sithe   *many times*
That ever he was made knyght.

700   Tho seid Libeous: "Gentil dame,
Telle me, whate is your name,
And where ye were ybore."
Sho seide: "Bi Seint Jame,
My fadir is of riche fame,
705   And wonyth here biforne.
An erle, ykidde a noble knyght,   *born*
That is a man of moche myght,
His name is furre ytolde.   *spoken of far and wide*
Mi name is Violette,
710   That the giaunt had bisette
Undir our castelle ful yore.   *many times in the past*

"Yustirday, in the mornynge,
As Y went in my playnge,   *to amuse myself*
None eville Y thought.
715   The giaunt, without lesinge,
Out of a busche gan sprynge,
And to his fere me brought.   *his companion*
Of him Y had bene yschent,   *would have been ruined*
Ne God had socoure ysent,   *Had not God sent help*
720   That alle the worlde wrought.   *[He] who made the entire world*
He yilde thee thi mede,   *May He reward you*
That for us gan blede,   *[He] who bled for us (i.e., Christ)*
And with his blode us bought."   *redeemed us with his blood*

Withoute more talkynge,
725   To hors gan thei sprynge
And rede furthe alle in same,   *rode; all together*

And tolde the erle tithinge   *tidings*
Howe he wanne in fightynge,
His doughtir fro wo and schame.
730   Than were the hedis ysent
To Kinge Arthour, in present,   *as a present*
With moche gle and game.
Thanne in Arthouris court arose   *i.e., was made known publicly*
Libeous Disconiousis noble lose   *noble reputation*
735   And his gentil fame.

The erle, for his good dede,
Gave Sir Libeous to mede   *as a reward*
Shilde and armour bright,
And also a noble stede
740   That was good at nede
In travaile and in fight.
Sir Libeous and that may
Rode in hare journay   *their*
Thedir as thei had yhight.   *as they had promised*
745   Than thei sawe in a park
A castelle stife and stark,   *formidable and imposing*
That wondir wel was dight,   *wondrously well constructed*

Ywallid was with stone —
Suche sawe he never none —
750   With towris stif and stout.   *solid; powerful*
Quod Libeous: "Bi Seint John,   *Said*
Hit were a feire wone,   *fair dwelling place*
Whoso had grete dout."   *Should anyone have any doubts*
Than lought the maiden bright   *laughed*
755   And seide: "This owith a knyght,   *belongs to*
The beste here about.
Whoso wol with him fight,
Be he baron, be he knyght,
He dothe him lowe to lowte.   *defeats and humiliates him*

760   "For the love of his lemmon,   *lover*
That is feire a womon,   *beautiful woman*
He had do crye and grede.   *cry; proclaim*
Whoso bringith a feirer ane,   *fairer one*
A jerefawken as white as swane   *gerfalcon as white as a swan*
765   He schalle have to his mede.   *as his reward*
Yef sho be nought so feire in sight,
With Greffroun he must fight.
And yef he may nought spede,   *if he is unsuccessful*
His hedde schalle him be reft,   *cut off*

770   And ysette apon a sheft,
       To seyn longe and brode.   *far and wide*

       "The sothe thowe may se welle.   *truth*
       Ther stont on every cornelle   *There stands; every angle [of the building]*
       An hede or two up right."
775   Quod Libeous also snelle:
       "Bi God and bi Seint Mighelle,   *Michael*
       With Geffroun Y mote fight
       And chalange the jerefawcoune
       And sey I have in towne
780   A lemman two so bright,   *twice as beautiful*
       And yef he will hur se,
       Forsothe, Y bringe thee,   *Truly, I will bring you*
       Be it day othir nyght."

       The dwarf seide: "Bi Jhesus,
785   Gentil Libeous Disconious,
       Thou puttist thee in grete perile.   *yourself*
       Geffron le Frediens
       In his fighting he hath defens   *a special defense*
       Knyghtis to bigile!"
790   Libeous answerid thare:
       "Therfore have thou no care.
       Bi God and bi Seint Gile,
       Y schalle se his face,
       Or Y hens pace   *Before I pass hence*
795   Fro this stede a myle."   *From this place*

       Withouten more resoune,   *ado (further discussion)*
       Thei dwellid stille in the toune
       Alle that nyght in pees.
       On the morowe Libeous was boune   *prepared himself*
800   To wynne him renoune,
       Certis, withouten les.   *Truly, without lies*
       He armyd him fulle sure
       In that ilke armour   *same*
       That the erle of Auntouris was.
805   A stede gan he bistride;
       The dworfe rode bi his side
       To that prowde place.

       Geffron le Frediens
       Rose as it was his use   *custom*
810   In the morowe tide
       For to honour swete Jhesus.
       Ther come Libeous Disconious,

Come prikyng as prins in pride.
Without more abode,   *any more delay*
815   Ayens Libeous he rode,
And lowde to him he cried,
With vois scharp and schrille:
"Comyst thowe for good othir ille?
Tel me and nought ne hide."

820   Quod Libeous also tide: *just as quickly*
"Y have grete delyte
With thee for to fight!
Thowe seiest in dispite
That woman is none so white   *beautiful*
825   And as thyne is bi day and nyghte,
And Y have in towne
Fairer of faciowne,   *presence*
In clothis and scho were dight.   *clothes as if she were properly dressed*
Therfore the jerfawcoune
830   To Arthour, kyng of crowne,
Brynge Y wolle with right!"

Quod Geffrron: "Gentil knyght,
Where schulle we preve aplight?   *where shall our contest take place*

Ther nowe men mowe se.
835   In the myddille of the market
Ther thei schulle be set,
To loke on, bonde and fre,   *[both] bond (serfs) and free (i.e., everybody)*
And my lemman be broun.   *If my beloved is the less beautiful*
To wynne the jerfaucoun,
840   Justi Y wolle with thee."   *Joust*

Quod Geffron also snelle: *quickly*
"Alle thus graunt Y welle,
This day bi undirtide,   *noon*
Bi God and bi Seint Michel.
845   Out of this castelle
To Karlylle wolle Y ride!"   *Carlisle*
Hare glovys up thay yolde   *They lifted up their gloves*
That foreward for to holde,   *To ratify their agreement*
As prins prout in pride.
850   Sir Libeous er he wolde blynne,   *cease (i.e., rest)*
He rode in to his inne,
And wolde no lengir abide,

And seide to maide Elyne,
That bright was and schene: *beautiful; fair*

855   "Loke that thou make thee bowne."   *ready*
       And seide: "Bi Heven Queen,   *i.e., the Virgin Mary*
       Gefferonis lemmon, Y wene,
       Today schalle come to towne.
       In the myddis of the cité
860   Ther men schulle you se,
       Faire of facioune,   *Beautiful in every way*
       And yef thowe be nought so bright,   *Yet even if you were not so radiant*
       With Geffron Y wol fight
       To wynne the jerfaucoune!"

865   The dwarfe answerid and seide:
       "Nowe is this a wondir dede,
       For eny manne ybore!
       Thou doste bi no manis rede,   *You will not act according; counsel*
       But first in thi childehede,   *But instead you act as a child*
870   As man that wolde be ylore.   *someone who would be destroyed*
       Therfore Y thee pray,
       Wandir we furthe in our way   *Let us depart on our way*
       That we ne come him bifore."   *do not confront him*
       Libeous seide: "That were schame!
875   Y had lever, bi Seint Jame,
       With wilde hors be ytore!"   *Be torn apart by wild horses*

       That maide feire and fre
       Hied hur, certeyne, to be   *Hastened herself*
       Fast to hur atyre,
880   For to do his profite:
       In kerchevys feire and white,
       Araied with golde wire;
       Of felwet a mantel ful gay,   *velvet*
       Yfurrid with grys ful gray,   *gray fur*
885   Scho cast abowte hur swire.   *neck*
       Stonys abowte hur molde   *the crown of her head*
       Were precious endentid with golde,   *mounted in gold*
       The best of that empire.   *in the realm*

       Sir Libeous sette that may   *maiden*
890   Uppon a good palfray.
       Thei rode furthe, alle thre.
       Ilke a man to othir gan say: *Each man [in the crowd] said to the other*
       "Here comyth a lady gay   *an elegant lady*
       And semely on to se!"   *So beautiful to look upon*
895   In to the market thei rode,
       And boldely ther abode,   *waited there*
       In myddis of that ilke cité.
       Than thei say Gefferon come ride,   *they saw*

900	Two squyars bi his side, And no more maigne.	*attendants*

He bare a schilde of grene,
That dight was wel, Y wene,   *sumptuously ornate, I imagine*
Of golde was the border, ryngid with floris,   *The gold border was ringed with flowers*
And of the same colour,
905   Ydighte with othir flowris,   *Decorated*
Was gayer than any cromponis.   *setting for jewelry*
Two squyars with him rede,   *rode*
Thre speris bare bi his side,
That good were and sure.
910   That othir bare redy boune   *at hand*
The gentil jerfaucoune,
That leide was the wagure.   *Upon which was laid the wager*

That aftur gan ride
A lady ful of pride,
915   Yclothid in purpul palle.   *in purple attire*
The folke were come ful wide
To se hur, bakke and side;   *from the back and side (i.e., get a good look at her)*
Sho was so gent and smale.
Hur mantelle was ruffyne,   *reddish*
920   Yfurrid wel with ermyne   *Decorated with ermine fur*
Ryche and rially,   *Rich; royally*
And a bende about hur molde,   *band; head*
Of precious stones of golde,
With many a riche amayle.   *enamel*

925   As rose hur rode was rede;   *red as the rose; complexion*
Hur here schyned on hur hede   *hair shone*
As golde wire schyning bright;   *shining bright*
Hur browys as silken threde   *brows as silk thread*
Ybent in lengthe and brede;   *curved in length; width*
930   Sho was ful feire in sight.
Hur ien were grey so glas;   *eyes were gray as glass*
Mylke white were hur face;
Hur nose was straight and right;   *true*
Hur swire was long and smale.   *neck*
935   Hur beauté, to telle alle,
No man with mowthe ne myght.   *might [describe fully]*

Than sho made to brynge
Tway cheiris in to cheping,   *Two chairs; the marketplace*
Hur beauté to discryve.   *On which to display their beauty*
940   Than seide olde and yonge,
Forsothe, withoute lesynge: *Truly, without lying*

"Bitwene ham was grete part.   *There was a great difference between them*
Geffronis lemman is clere   *lady (beloved); beautiful*
As rose in one erbere,   *a rose in a garden*
945 Forsothe, and nought to lye;
Elyne the mesynger
Nas but a lavender   *No more than a washerwoman*
In hur lavendrye."   *In her laundry*

Quod Geffron le Fredus:
950 "By the love of swete Jhesus,
That hawke thow hast forlore!"   *You have lost the hawk (the wager)*
Quod Libeous Disconious:
"That was never myne use!   *my custom [to lose]*
Justy Y wolle therfore,   *I will joust*
955 And yef ye falle me doune,   *unhorse me*
Take my hedde and that foukone   *head; that falcon*
As covenaunt was bifore;   *According to our agreement*
And yef iche fille downe thee,
The fawkon schalle wynde with me,
960 Though thow be wrothe therfore."   *Although you may be angry*

No more talis thei tolde.   *There was no further discussion*
Thei went into the fielde
With welle gret partye,   *ready in opposition*
With strokis stife in schilde;
965 Every ayens othir hilde   *Each fought with the other*
With wel grete envye.   *great hostility*
Here schaftis brake in sondir,
Hare dyntis fyrde as dondir   *clash of arms fared as thunder*
That comyth out of the sky.
970 Mynstrals and trompours,
Harpours and gestours,
Hare strokis gan discry.   *their; proclaimed*

Than gan Geffron speke:
"Bryng me a scheft that wol not breke,
975 A schefte good with alle!
So this yonge freke   *warrior*
Sittith in sadulle ysteke   *lodged*
As stone in castelle walle.
I schalle make him stoupe,   *bow (stoop)*
980 And over his hors croupe   *over the back of his horse*
And yeve him an eville falle,
Though he were as wight werrour   *hardy a warrior*
As Alexaundre or Kyng Arthour,   *Alexander [the Great]*
Launselake or Persevale!"   *Lancelot du Lac*

985 The knyghtis bothe two
   Reden togadir tho   *then*
   With fulle grete renoune.   *powerful determination (valor)*
   Sir Libeous smote Geffron tho
   That his schilde fille him fro
990 Into the filde a doune.
   Than loughe alle that ther was,
   And seide bothe more and las,   *both of high rank and low*
   Duke, erle, and baroun,
   That never thei ne sy   *did they see*
995 A man that myght dury   *might endure*
   A stroke of Sir Geffroun.

   Geffron rode to him swithe,   *quickly*
   Forsothe, fele sithe,   *Truly, many times*
   And yit myght not spede.   *might not succeed against him*
1000 He rode ayen ful tite,   *swiftly*
   And Libeous on the helme he hite,
   As a man that wolde of wede.   *was out of his mind*
   But Libeous smote so fast
   That Gefferon doune he cast
1005 Bothe him and his stede,
   That Geffronis rigge tobrake.   *backbone*
   Men myght hire the crake   *crack*
   Fer of lengthe and brede.   *i.e., far and wide*

   Alle seide, that ther were,
1010 That Geffron had forlore
   The gentille joly faukon;   *beautiful*
   To Libeous was he ybore.
   Al wend, las and more, *went [with him], lesser [of rank]; greater*
   With him in to the toun.
1015 Geffron in his schilde
   Was ybore out of the filde,
   With many bolde baroune.
   The gentil faukon ybore was,
   Bi a knyght that hight Clewdas,
1020 To Arthour, kynge of crowne.

   The knyght him furthe yede.   *went*
   With him he gan lede
   The faukon that Libeous wan.
   To Arthour he him bare,
1025 That the kynge sware
   That Libeous welle warre can: *can battle well*
   "He hath sende me with honour
   Of faire bataile foure,

Sithe he furst bigan.
1030 I wolle him sende tresour
For to spende with honour,
As fallith for suche a man."

An hundrid pound honest,
Of floreynes of the best,
1035 He sent to Karlille toune.   *Carlisle*
Sir Libeous made a fest:
That furtenyght it lest   *fortnight*
With grete renowne.   *festivity*
At the sixt wokes ende,   *sixth week's*
1040 He toke leve to wynde   *depart*
Of duke, erle, and baroun.
Sir Libeous and that may   *maiden*
Rode on hare way
Toward Synadowne.

1045 As he rode bi a lowe,   *by a hill*
Hornes he hurd blowe
And houndis make rebound.   *answer in reply*
The dwarfe seide in a throwe: *within a short space*
"This hornys right wel Y knowe,   *I recognize*
1050 Fer yere ferly falle!   *For many years [occurring] often*
Sir Otis hit blewe, de la Ile,
That servith my ladi sum while,   *served my lady [of Synadoun] for a period*
So semely in hur sale.   *beautiful in her hall*
Whan scho was taken with gile,
1055 He flyghe, for drede of perile,   *fled, for fear of danger*
West into Wirale."   *an area in northwest England*

As thei rode on hare talkyng,
Ther come a rache rennyng   *hunting dog*
Overthwart the way.   *Across their path*
1060 Thei seide, without lesyng,
Sith hare first bigynnynge,
None say thei never so gay,   *saw; colorful*
For he was of alle colours gay   *(see note)*

Bitwene Midsomer and May.
1065 That may seide ful sone:
"Y say never none   *I never saw [a dog]*
So welle likynge to my pay!   *So appealing to my pleasure*

Wolde Crist that ich it aught."   *By Christ, I wish that I owned it*
Sir Libeous hit caught
1070 And gave it maide Elyne.

Thei reden furthe, alle soft,   *slowly*
And tolde howe knyghtis fought
For birdis brighte and schene.   *maidens bright and beautiful*
Thei rode but a while,
1075   The space of a myle,
In that forest grene.
Thei sawe an hynde come rennyng,   *doe*
And two greyhoundis hir folowyng;
The racche bigan to mene.   *hound began to moan*

1080   Thei hovyd undir a lynde   *waited; linden tree*
And sawe the cours of the hynde,
Sir Libeous and sho in fere.   *[as well as] she together*
Than came ther aftir bihynde
A knyght yclothid in ynde,   *indigo*
1085   Apon a bay destrere.   *destrier*
His bugille gan he blowe
That his men schulde him knowe
In whate stede that he were,   *whatever location*
And seid: "By Seint Martyne,
1090   The racche was onys myne,
Nought fully gone a yere!

Good frende, lete it go."
Sir Libeous answerid tho:
"That schalle it never betide!   *That shall never happen*
1095   For with my hondis two
Y yave it the damesel me fro,
That hovys here biside."   *Who sits beside me*
Quod Sir Otis de la Ile:
"Thowe puttist thee in perile,   *You are placing yourself in great danger*
1100   Petur!, and thowe abide!"   *[By Saint] Peter, if you persist*
Sir Libeous answerid: "Bi Seint Gile,
Y yeve nought of thi wile,   *care nothing for your cunning [words (or desire)]*
Chourle, though thou chide."   *churl; complain*

Quod Sir Otis de la Ile:
1105   "Sir, thi wordis bith right file!   *are very vile*
Churle nas Y never none!
An erle my fadir was sum while;
The Cuntas of Karlyle,   *countess; Carlisle*
Certis, scho was my dame.   *mother*
1110   Yef Y were armyd nowe,
Redy as art thowe,
Forsothe, we schulde fight in same!   *together*
But thow that racche bileve,   *Unless you give up that hound*

1115	Thow pleiest, ar it be eve,	*You [are about to] play before evening*
	A wondir wilde game!"	*unpredictable (i.e., threatening to yourself)*

Quod Libeous: "Do thi best!
Here Y am alle prest!   *ready for whatever happens*
This racche schall with us wynde, than."   *go, then*
Thei toke the wey west,
1120 Into the wilde forest,
As the dwarfe hem kende.   *guided them*
Sir Otus, with grete errour,   *in great anger*
Rode home in that schoure,   *quickly*
And aftir his frendis gan sende,
1125 And tolde ham, anone rightis,   *told them at once*
One of Arthouris knyghtis
Shameliche gan him schende,   *Shamelessly insulted him*

And his racche had nome.   *his hunting dog had seized*
Than seide alle asomme: *all together (i.e., in one voice)*
1130 "That traitour shal be ytake!"
Thei seid he schulde be honge,
Though he were also stronge   *[Even] though he were as strong*
As Launcelet de Lake.
Thei dighte ham wele,   *armed themselves well*
1135 Bothe in iren and in stele,
As werre shulde ther wake.   *arise*
Bothe knyghtis and squyars
Lepe on hare palfrais,   *palfreys*
For hare lordis sake.   *their lord's*

1140 Fer on an hille fulle hye
Sir Libeous sone thei sye,   *They soon spied Lybeaus*
Ridinge pace for pace.   *at a slow pace*
To him gan thei ride:
"Traitour! Thow schalt abide,   *pay (do battle)*
1145 Today, for this trespace!"   *trespass*
Libeous stode and bihilde
Howe fulfillid was the filde,   *crowded*
So moche folke ther was.
He seide to maide Elyne:
1150 "For thi racche, Y wyne,   *I understand*
Me is come a carefulle cas!   *[To] me; a serious situation*

Y rede yow withdrawe   *I advise you to withdraw*
Undir the wode schawe,   *Under cover of the forest*
Your hede for to hide.
1155 Forsothe, for to sayne,
Though Y schulde be slayne,

Ham alle Y schalle abide."   *I shall face them all*
Into the forest he rode
And boldely ther abode,
1160   Sir Libeous rode in pride.
With bowis and with areblast   *crossbows*
To him thei schote fast
And made him woundis wide.

Sir Libeous' stede so ranne   *charged so forcefully*
1165   He bare downe hors and man;
For no thing wolde he spare!
Al the folke seide than:
"Here comyth the devil Satan,
That makith wilde fire fare!"   *makes a destructive conflagration*
1170   Whoso Libeous raught,   *Whomever; struck*
He clevith with his draught,   *clove with his blow*
And slowe for evermore.   *slew*
And sone he was bisette,   *besieged*
As fischis in a nette,
1175   With grevely woundis sore.   *grave wounds*

Twelve knyghtis prest   *knights suddenly*
Ther come out of the forest,
In armour cler and bright.
Al that day thei had yrest
1180   And abode in the forest,
To sle Libeous that knyght.
In armour ther were twelve,
That one was Otys himsilve,
In ryme to rede aright,   *In rhyme to read*
1185   That smote to him at onys.   *at once*
Thei thoughten to breken his bonys
And sle him in that fight.

Then men myght se aright
Strokis sadly plight   *Strokes seriously applied*
1190   Amonge alle ham in fere.   *all together*
Forsothe, without lesyng,
The sparklis out gan spryng
Throwe helme and basnet there

And four awey gan fle;   *fled away; (see note)*
1195   Thei durst come him no nere.
The lord faught in that stoure,
And his sonnys fowre,
To sille hare lyvys dere.   *sell their lives dearly*

	Thei leide on stroks ryve,	*abundantly*
1200	He alone ayenst fyve;	
	He fought as he were wode.	*as though he were mad*
	Togadir gan thei dryve,	*Together they began to assault [him]*
	As bene abowte an hyve.	*bees about a hive*
	Of ham ranne the blode.	*From them blood ran down*
1205	Whan Sir Libeous was nere spillid,	*exhausted*
	His swarde brake bi the hilt;	
	Than was he mad of mode.	*furiously angry*
	The lord a stroke him sette	
	Throwe helme and basnet,	
1210	That at the skulle withstode.	*stopped just before the skull*

	In sownynge he fille downe	*swooning he fell down*
	Over his hors cropoune,	*the back of his horse*
	As man that was mate.	*vanquished (checkmated)*
	His fomen were bowne	*ready*
1215	To perische his actowne,	*pierce his armor*
	Throwe helme and basnet plate.	
	Whan he gan sore smert,	*When he felt the pain*
	He plukkid up his hart,	
	And coverid his state;	*recovered his strength*
1220	And hent an ax that was him nye	*seized*
	That hynge downe bi his thye:	*by his thigh*
	Almost, he thought, to late!	*too late*

	He sterith him as a knyghte.	*stirs himself as a knight*
	Hare stedis downe right	*Their horses*
1225	He slowe at dyntis thre.	*With three strokes he killed*
	The lord say that sight,	*saw*
	And off his hors alight,	*from*
	And aweyward gan he fle.	
	Sir Libeous no lengir abode,	*longer delayed*
1230	But aftir him rode.	
	Undir a chesteyne tre	*Under a chestnut tree*
	Ther he had him yquelde,	*he would have killed him*
	But as the lord him yilde	*Except the lord yielded himself*
	At his wille to be.	*to be entirely within his power*

1235	And bi a certeyne stent,	*according to an agreed-upon assessment*
	Tresoure, londe, and rent,	*Treasure, land, and rent [from land]*
	Castelle, halle, and bowre	*Castle, hall, and mansion*
	Ther to Libeous assent,	
	In forward that he went	*pledge that he go*
1240	On to Kynge Arthour,	
	And sey: "Lord of renoune,	
	As overcome presoune	*prisoner*

Y am to thyne honour."
The lord graunt it at his wille,
1245 Bothe lowde and stille,   *aloud; silently*
And lad him home to his towre.

The dworfe and maide Elyne
Went with Sir Libeous, Y wene,   *I think*
To Sir Otys' castelle.
1250 Sho and the dworfe bidene   *together*
Tolde of the dedis kene
Of Libeous, howe hit bifelle,
And of the presentis fowre
That he sende to Kynge Arthoure
1255 That he wanne so welle.

That suche a doughti knyght   *(see note)*
His ladi schulde wyn in fight,
His ladi feire and hynde.   *noble*
To covery mayne and myght,   *recover strength and health*
1260 Furti daies with the knyght   *Forty days*
Ther than gan he lende,   *dwell*
And did him hele his wound,
That he was hole and sound.   *Until*
Bi that day six wokis ende,
1265 Than Libeous and the may   *maiden*
Toke the right way
To Synadowne to wynde.   *travel to Synadoun*

That lord, without lettyng,   *without delay*
Went to Arthour the kynge,
1270 And for prisoner him yelde,   *himself*
And tolde to the kyng
Howe aventours knyght yonge   *adventurous*
Wanne him in filde.   *Defeated him in the field*
Kyng Arthour had good game,   *was greatly amused*
1275 And the knyghtis in same,   *all together*
That hurd that tale ytolde,
And thei chose for profitable   *they acclaimed [Lybeaus] accomplished*
The knyght of the Rounde Table,
To fight with spere and schilde.

1280 Rest we nowe a while   *i.e., meanwhile*
Of Sir Otis de la Ile,
And telle we of othir talis.   *we will tell of other adventures*
Sir Libeous rode many a myle,
In aventuris and in perile,
1285 In Cornewaile and in Walis.

Hit bifille in the monethe of June,
Whan levys and buskis ben grene   *bushes*
And flowris in semely sale.   *decorate beautiful halls*
The someris day is longe;
1290   Mery is thanne the songe
Of the nyghtingale.

Than that tyme gan Libeous ride
Bi a ryveris side,
He sie a feire cité   *saw*
1295   With a palice proude in pride,   *palace splendidly constructed*
A castelle hie and wide,   *castle high*
And gatis grete plenté.   *many gates*
He askid whate hit hight.
The maide seide, anone right: *immediately*
1300   "Y wol tel to thee.
Men clepith hit Il d'Ore.
Ther hathe ybe fighting more
Than ever was in eny contré.

"For a ladi ful of pris —   *nobility (worth)*
1305   Hir rode is rede as rose on rice —   *Her complexion; red as a rose on the stem*
This contrey is al in dowt: *in fear*
A giaunt that hat Maugus,
His pere nought yfounde is,
He hath bisette hur abowt.   *blocked all passage to her*
1310   He is blakke so eny picche;   *pitch, tar*
In al this worlde is him none liche   *none like him*
Of dedis so sterne and stout.
Whate knyght that passith this brig,   *bridge*
His armys must he leg   *He must surrender his arms*
1315   And to him alowty.   *bow down to him*

He is furti fote longe,   *forty feet in length*
And also swithe stronge
As othir knyghtis fifté.   *fifty other knights*
Sir Libeous, bithinke thee   *reconsider what you are doing*
1320   With suche one to melle.   *meddle*
He is wondir grisly;
Eche here of his browyn   *hair; eyebrows*
Is liche the here of a swyn.   *hair; swine*
For it is sothe, wittirly,   *true indeed*
1325   His armys bith wondir long,
And him silve also strong,
He sleith al that comyth him by.

"And so is he grymly,
As Y telle thee, wittirly.   *truly*
1330 He is also grete
As is an ox or a kowe,
For sothe, as Y sey nowe,
Or as grete as eny nete.   *ox*
A carte stife and good,
1335 Unnethe, bi the rode,   *Scarcely, by the cross*
May hir gere lede.   *carry his equipment*
He is ful stife and stronge,
Ther may no man his dynt dure,   *endure*
For sothe, so bith thei grete."

1340 Quod Libeous: "Maide hynde,   *Gracious maiden*
My wey wolle Y wynde,
For alle his strokis ille.   *Despite*
Yif God wol grace sende,
Er this day come to ende
1345 With fighte Y schalle him spille.   *kill*
Y have ysey grete okys   *seen; oak trees*
Falle with wynde strokis,   *blasts of wind*
In litille stounde fulle stille;   *In a short time [they] lay low*
Though Y be yonge and lite,   *[relatively] little*
1350 To him schalle Y smyte.
Lete God do his wille!"

Thei rode furthe al thre
To that feire cité
That men clepith Il d'Ore.   *the Golden Isle*
1355 Maugus gan thei se,
Uppon a brigge of tre,   *On a wooden bridge*
Lokid as a wilde bore,   *wild boar*
His schilde was blak as picche —
Libeous say never none suche —
1360 Four mawmetts therin was.   *pagan idols*
For no while he stode,
But to Libeous yode
And seid to him with wowe: *malevolently*

"Turne agayne as tite,   *at once*
1365 For thin owne profite,
Yif thowe love thi prowe!"   *care for well-being*
Whan he say Libeous with fight,   *ready to fight*
He seide anone right: *quickly*
"Telle me whate art thowe!"
1370 Sir Libeous seid aplight: *truly*
"Kynge Arthour made me knyght.

To him Y made myne avowe
That Y ne schulde turne my bak.
Therfor, thowe devil so blak,
1375   Make thee redy nowe!"

Maugus on fote yode,
And Libeous rode to him with his stede,
For sothe, than, ful right.   *then*
Lordis and ladies bright,
1380   Lay in hare korvelle   *towers with ornamental ledges*
To biholde that fight.
Thei praid to God of His wille,
Bothe lowde and stille,   *aloud; silently*
To save that Cristen knyght
1385   That schulde yeve grace that geaunt,
That levyth on Termagaunt,   *believes in [a false god]*
That day schulde dey in fight.

Ther hare scheftis brake on sondir,
Everi stroke ferde as doundir;   *sounded like thunder*
1390   The pecis gan out springe.   *pieces*
Thei drowe swerdis bothe,
As men that weren wrothe,
And gan togadir dynge.   *strike blows together*
Everi man had wondur
1395   That Libeous nad go undur   *had not been killed*
At the first bigynnyng.
Sir Libeous smote Maugus tho
That his swerde fille him fro,   *his [i.e., Lybeaus's] sword*
Without eny lesyng.

1400   Maugus cowthe moche quede,   *knew much about evil*
And hit Libeous' stede on the hede,
And smote out the brayne.
Libeous nothing saide,
But stert up on a braide   *in a moment*
1405   Right ful sone againe.   *again*
An ax he hent ful sone
And hewe bi his nekke bone,
And smote to him with mayne,   *with strength*
That happid to his schilde.   *struck his shield*
1410   Hit flye fro him into the fielde   *so that it flew from him*
And fille right into the playne.

On fote bothe thei fought.
No man bitwene ham myght   *could [count the number of]*
The strokis bitwene ham two.

1415	Depe woundis thei raught,	*received*
	For thei were unsaught,	*furious in combat*
	And ever of ham othiris fo.	*each of them the other's foe*
	From the owre of the prime	*hour of prime (between 6:00 and 9:00 AM)*
	Til it was evesonge tyme	*evensong (i.e., vespers)*
1420	Of fighting were thei there.	
	Sir Libeous was athursti sore,	*extremely thirsty*
	And seid, "Maugus, thyne ore	*[may I have] your permission*
	To drinke thowe leve me go."	

	"Y schalle graunti thee	
1425	Whate bone so ever thou axi me,	*Whatever request*
	Suche grace may betide.	*Such grace [as] may be required [of me]*
	Grete schame it were for thee	
	A knyght for thurst to sle	
	And no more profite."	*accomplishment*
1430	Maugus graunte it welle	
	For to drink his fille	
	With more delite.	*pleasure*
	Whan Libeous lay on the wateris bank,	
	And throwe his helme he drank,	
1435	Maugus gan him smyte.	

	Into the ryvere he fille,	
	Armour and everi dele	*every bit*
	Ywette and evil ydight.	*Soaked and in bad condition*
	Up he stert also snelle	
1440	And swore bi Seint Michel:	
	"Nowe am Y two so light.	*twice as keen*
	Wyndist thow, fyndis fere,	*Did you think, companion of fiends*
	Uncristened that Y were?	*Unbaptized*
	To thee my trewthe Y plight.	*pledge; vow*
1445	Y schalle for thi baptise	*for your baptism [of me]*
	Wel quite thi service	*Well reward*
	Throwe the grace of God Almyght."	

	Thanne a newe fight bigan,	
	And everi to othir ran,	*each to the other ran*
1450	And gave ther dyntis stronge.	
	Many a gentil man	
	And ladies as white as swan	
	For him hare hondis wronge.	
	For Maugus in the filde	
1455	Clave atwo his schilde,	
	Throwe dyntis of armys longe.	*With the strokes of his long arms*
	Than Libeous ran away	

Ther Maugus' schilde lay,   *To where*
And up he gan hit fynge.   *seized*

1460   Than Libeous ran to him agayne
       And smote to him with mayne.
       Everi of ham othir gan asaile   *Each of them began to assail the other*
       Unto the day was done;   *Until it grew dark*
       After passid evensonge,   *past evensong*
1465   The knyghtis hilde bataile.
       Sir Libeous was werrour wight   *a strong warrior*
       And gave a stroke of myght
       Throwe splete, plate, and maile,   *metal reinforcements; chain mail*
       And throwe his schuldir bone
1470   That his right arme, anone,   *at once*
       Fille into the filde, sans faile.   *truly*

       The giaunt gan to se
       That he schulde yslayne be.
       He stode defens agayne.
1475   Sir Libeous so to him smote
       That at the secunde stroke
       He brake hys bak atwayne.
       The giaunt ther bilevyd.   *died*
       Libeous smote off his hevyd,   *off; head*
1480   Therof he was ful fayne.   *he was happy to do it*
       He bore his hede to towne,
       With a feire procescioune;
       The folke come him agayne.   *came to meet him*

1483a [A lady whyt as flowr],
       That men clepith Diamour,   *(see note)*
1485   Resceyvyd him fulle welle.
       The ladi thonkid him with honour
       That he was her socour   *rescuer*
       Agenst the giaunt felle.   *fierce giant*
       Til a chambur scho gan him lede   *To a chamber*
1490   And chaungid ther his wede.   *helped him change his clothes*
       In palle sho clothid him welle;   *fine cloth*
       Sho proferid him with worde   *offered*
       Ever to be hur lord   *her lord*
       Of cité and castelle.

1495   Sir Libeous graunt it in hast   *in haste*
       And love to hur cast,
       For sho was bright and schene.   *fair; beautiful*
       Alas, that sho nad be ychastid!   *had not been reformed (i.e., chaste)*
       For ever, at the latist,   *in the final analysis*

1500 Sho dud him trayne and tene.   *treason; wrong*
      Thre wokis and more   *weeks*
      Sho made him dwelle thore,   *there*
      And also maide Elyne,
      That he ne myght out breke   *break out*
1505 To helpe and awreke   *avenge*
      Of Synadowne the quene.

      For that feire ladi
      Cowthe more of sorsery   *Knew more about*
      Than othir wicchis fyve.   *witches*
1510 Sho made him melody,
      With al maner of mynstralsy
      That eny man cowthe discry.   *anyone could describe*
      Whan he sawe hur face,
      He thought that he wace   *was*
1515 In Paradis alyve.
      With fantasy and feiry   *fairy magic*
      Ever scho blerid his iee,   *blinded him*
      Therfore, evil mote scho thryve!   *may she have misfortune*

      Tille it bifille apon a day   *upon*
1520 He mette Elyne, that feire may,   *maiden*
      Bi the castelle towre.
      Til him gan scho say: *To him*
      "Knyght, fals is in thi lay   *your allegiance*
      Ayens Kyng Arthour!   *To*
1525 For love of a woman
      That moche of sorcery can,   *knows much sorcery*
      Thou dost thee dishonour!   *You dishonor yourself*
      My lady of Synadoune
      May longe ligge in prisoune,   *lie*
1530 That is ful grete dolour!"   *a great tragedy*

      Whan Libeous hurd hur speke,
      Him thought his hart wolde breke
      For that gentil dame.
      He toke with him his stede,
1535 His schilde and his othir wede,   *other equipment*
      And riden furthe in same.   *together*
      That ladiis steward hynde   *gracious steward*
      He made with him to wynde: *travel with him*
      Sir Jeffelot was his name.
1540 Thei rode furthe talkyng,
      And also fast syngyng,
      Laughe and made good game.

Sir Libeous and that may   *maiden*
Rode furthe on hare jornay
1545   On stedis bay and broune.
Til on the thrid day
Thei say a cité gay,
Men clepith Cinadowne,
With a castelle hie and wide,
1550   And palys proude in pride,   *palace splendid in structure*
And worke of feire facion.   *beautiful architecture*
Sir Libeous axkid that feire may   *asked*
Whos was that cité gay,
That stode ther in that towne.

1555   And scho him tolde anon:
"Sir," sho seid, "bi Seint John,
That is my ladyis fre.   *noble lady's [castle]*
And in one castelle
Woneth a giaunt felle,   *Dwells*
1560   Forsothe, witturly.
His name is clepid Lambert,
Of alle this lond is stewart,
Sothe, as Y telle thee,
And who so comyth to the gate
1565   For to axi herborowe therate,   *request [safe] harbor*
Justi with him wol he."   *Joust with him he will*

Quod Libeous: "Bi my lewté,   *On my honor*
That wolde Y blitheli se,   *blithely (willingly) see*
For ought that may betide!   *Whatever the outcome*
1570   And be he never so stout,   *formidable*
Y schal make him lowte!   *submit*
So schalle Y to him ride;
Forthi, maide Elyne,   *Therefore*
Thowe and the dworf bidene,   *together*
1575   In the towne ye me abide."   *wait for me*
Furthe than the maide rode.
The dwarf than nought abode;   *did not delay*
He rode hur side bi side.

Quod Libeous to Jeffelot tite: *without hesitation*
1580   "To me it were a spite   *an insult*
To lete for man on lyve   *To hinder any man alive*
To do Arthuris profite   *To increase Arthur's honor*
And wynne that lady white.   *And [fail to] deliver that beautiful lady*
Thedir wolle Y dryve.
1585   Sir Jeffelot, make thee yare   *ready*
With me for to fare,

Hastely and blithe!"   *hastily; at once*
Thei rode furthe algate   *straightaway*
Right into the castel gate   *the gate of the castle*
1590   With feire scheftis fyve,   *five superb lances [ready]*

And axid ther ostelle   *asked; hostel, accommodation*
Of that feire castelle
For two of Arthouris knyghtis.
The porter feire and welle
1595   Lete ham into the castelle,
And axid ham anone right: *asked*
"Who is your governour?"
And thei seid: "Kyng Arthour,
Man most of myght.
1600   He is kyng of curtesy,
chief of chyvalry,
Hys foo to fille in fight."   *defeat his foe in battle*

The porter, prestabelle,   *eager to serve*
To his lord the constabille
1605   This tale sone he tolde.
He seid, without fabulle:
"Thei bene of the Rounde Table,
Two knyghtis faire and bolde.
That one is armyd sure
1610   In ful riche armoure,
With thre lions of golde."
The lord was glad and blithe,
And seide also swithe,   *just as quickly*
With ham justi he wolde.   *He would joust with them*

1615   He bade ham make ham yare   *ready*
Into the fielde for to fare
Without the castelle gate.   *Outside*
The porter wolde nought spare,
So as the greyhound aftir the hare,
1620   Agen he toke the gate,
And seid anone right:
"One is come to thee, aventours knyght!   *adventurous knight*
For nothing ye ne lete: *neglect nothing*
Loke your schildis be strong
1625   And your scheftis longe,
Othir els your detheis gete.   *Or else receive your deaths*

"And ridith into the fielde;
My lord, with spere and schilde.
With you he wol play."

1630	Sir Libeous spake wordis bolde:	
	"This wordis bith wel ytolde	*These words are well spoken*
	And likyng to my pay!"	*satisfying to me*
	Into the fielde thei redyn,	*rode*
	And ther boldely abedyn,	*waited*
1635	And went thei nought away.	
	Lambert send aftir his stede,	
	His schilde and othir wede	*trappings*
	His tyre was ful gay.	*attire; very splendid*
	A schilde he bare, fyne,	
1640	Thre boris hedis ydentid therinne,	*inlaid*
	Blakke as bround bronde;	*a branch darkened by fire*
	The bordour was of ermyne.	
	He say never no suche a gyne	*splendid device*
	In londis where he went.	
1645	Two squyars rode bi his side;	
	Thre scheftis thei bare that tide	*at that time*
	To dele doughti dynt.	*strong strokes*
	He was wondir gay,	*splendid*
	And also large of pay,	*generous*
1650	In warre and in turnement.	
	Tho that stoute stewart,	*Then; princely*
	That hight Sir Lambert,	
	Was yarmyd at al right.	*at all points (completely)*
	He rode to the fieldeward,	
1655	Prowte as eny Lombard,	
	To abide the fightis.	*await the combat*
	He sie Libeous that tide,	*saw; then*
	And first to him gan ride	
	Whan he him sey with iee.	*eye*
1660	He than to him bare	
	A schefte that was square,	*squared*
	As man of moche myght.	
	Everi of ham smote othir in the schild;	
	The pecis fille into the fielde	*pieces*
1665	With hare strokis bidene.	*both their strokes*
	Everiche man to othir tolde,	
	Bothe yonge and olde:	
	"This yonge knyght is kene!"	*valiant*
	Lambert his cours out rode,	*rode his courser out of the field*
1670	As man that were wode,	*out of his mind*
	For ire and ful of tene,	*anger; rage*
	And seid: "Bringe me a schefte,	

And yef he can his crafte,   *if he knows his craft [of jousting]*
Sone hit schalle be ysene!"   *seen*

1675   Than toke thei scheftis rounde,
With hedis sharpe ygrounde,   *points*
And rode with grete renoune.   *power*
Thei prekid in that stounde   *they drove their horses hard*
To geven dethis wounde,   *in order to deliver a mortal wound*
1680   As egir as eny lyon.   *fierce*
Sir Libeous smote Lambert tho
That his schilde fille him fro
Into the filde adoune.
So harde he him hit
1685   That he myght nought sitte,
Of this was he yboune.   *prepared (i.e., he did not fall from his saddle)*

His schilde brake with power.
And Libeous smote Lambert
On his helme so bright,
1690   The pesyn, ventaile, and gorgare   *Collar; neckpiece*
Fly with the helme in fere.   *Flew with the helmet together*
And Lambert, upright,
That he sate rokkyng in his sadill
As a childe dothe in cradille,
1695   Without mayne and myght.   *Senseless and without strength*
Every man toke othir bi the lap,   *by his garment*
And fast gan with hondis clap,
Barons, burgeis, and knyght.   *citizens, burghers*

Sir Lambert fond to fight bette;   *tried; better*
1700   A newe helme ther was yfette
And scheftis unmete.   *extraordinarily large; (see note)*

Every to othir sette   *Each to the other set*
Strokis grym and grete.
Than the constable, Sir Lambert,
1705   Fille over his stede bakwarde,
Withouten more bigete.   *With no further gain*
Sir Lambart sware ful sone:
"Bi Him that schope sonne and mone,   *created*
He schalle my lady gete!"

1710   Ther Lambard was aschamyd.
Quod Libeous: "Be nought agrevyd."
And he answerid: "Nay!
For sith that Y was borne,
Y say never knyght biforne   *saw*

1715 So strong, bi this day.
Bi the thought that my hert is yn,
Thou art of Sir Gaweynis kyn,
That is so stoute and gay.
Thou art ful stoute in fight,
1720 And also stronge a knyght,
Ful sikir, bi my fay!"   *Most certainly, by my faith*

"Whate art thou," seid Libeous tho,   *then*
"That dothe so mochil wo   *create such suffering*
To the quene of Synadowne?
1725 Telle me er thou hens gone
Or Y thee telle, bi Seint John,
Y schal pare off thi crowne!"   *cut off the top of your head*
The steward answerid and seide:
"Sir, be thow nought evil apaide!   *displeased*
1730 For scho is my lady:
Sho is quene of this lond,
And Y hur steward, Y undirstond,
Forsothe, sicurly."   *Truly, indeed*

Sir Libeous answerid in hast: *at once*
1735 "Fight Y schalle for that lady chast
As Y hight Kyng Arthour!   *promised*
No man schal make me agast,   *frightened*
The while the life on me may last,
To wynne hur with honour!
1740 But Y ne wote wherefore ne whye,
Ne who hur dothe vilonie   *harm*
And bringith hur in dolour."
Lambart seid in that stounde:
"Welcome knyght of the Tabul Rounde,
1745 Bi God, oure Saviour!"

Anone, maide Elyne
Was ysend bi knyghtis kene   *sent for*
Bifore Sir Lambert.
Sho and the dwarfe bidene   *together*
1750 Tolde of the dedis kene
That thei had thedirward,   *on the way here*
And tolde howe Sir Libeous
Fought with many aventours
And him gevid nothinge.   *he surrendered (yielded)*
1755 And then were thei al blithe,   *content*
And thonkid fele sithe   *many times*
Jhesus, Hevyn kynge.

Anon with milde chere
Thei setten hem to soupere,
1760 With mochil gle and game.
Libeous and Lambert in fere   *together*
Of aventouris that thei in were
Talkid bothe in same.   *together*
Sir Libeous seid, withouten fable,
1765 To Sir Lambart the constable:
"Whate is the knyghtis name
That holdith in prison
The ladi of Synadon,
That is so gentil a dame?"

1770 Sir Lambart seid: "Bi Seint John,
Knyght, sur, is he none
That durste hur awey lede!
Two clerkis ben hur fone,   *foes*
Fals of blode and bone,
1775 That have ydo that dede.
Hit bene men of maistry,   *of special knowledge*
Clerkis of nigromansy,   *Clerks of black magic (sorcery)*
Sertis, right to rede.   *Certainly, to counsel truly*
Iran is, than, one brothir,
1780 And Mabon is that othir:
For ham we bene in drede.

"Iran and Mabon
Maden an hous of grete name,
A place queynte of gynne.   *ingeniously devised*
1785 Ther nys erle ne baron   *is not*
That had an hart as a lyon
That durst come therin.
Hit is made bi negromansy,
Ywrought it was with feyry,   *fairy (magic)*
1790 That wondir is to wynne.   *marvelously difficult; penetrate*
Therin lieth in prison
The ladi of Synadon,
Comyn of kyngis kynne.   *king's lineage*

Oft we hire hur crien,   *hear*
1795 But to se hur with ien,   *to see her with our eyes*
Therto have we no myght.
Thei dothe hur turmentry   *inflict pain on her*
And al maner vilony,
Bothe bi day and nyght.
1800 Thus Mabon and Iran
Have swore hare othe serteyne   *sworn their secure oath*

	To dethe thei wol hur dight,	*To inflict death upon her*
	But scho graunti ham tille	*Unless; grants to them*
	To do Mabonis wille,	
1805	And graunti him alle hur right,	*grant him all her rights*
	"Of alle this lond feire,	
	That my ladi of is eire,	*Of which my lady is heiress*
	To wynne alle with wille.	*get it all with force of will*
	And scho is meke and stille,	*meek; quiet*
1810	Forthei we bene in dispeire	*Therefore*
	Lest that thei bring hur in synne!"	*Lest they bring her in sin*
	Quod Libeous Disconious:	
	"Bi the love of swete Jhesus	
	That lady wolle Y wynne!	*rescue*
1815	Bothe Mabon and Iran	
	Y schalle hewe in the playne,	
	Hare hedis off bi the chynne!"	*off by the chin*
	Ther was no more tale.	
	In the castelle, grete ne smale,	*both those of rank and those below*
1820	But singith and makith ham blithe.	*merry*
	Barons and burgeis fale	*many*
	Come to that semely sale	*noble dwelling*
	For that to listen and lithe	*listen; be attentive*
	Howe that proude steward,	
1825	That men clepith Sir Lambert,	
	With Libeous his craft gan kithe.	*skill at arms made known*
	Thei fedde ham at sopere	
	And bade ham be blithe of chere,	
	Knyghtis bothe stoute and stithe.	*strong*
1830	Ther than gan thei dwelle	
	In that same castelle	
	Alle that longe night.	
	On morowe Libeous was prest	*prepared*
	In armour of the best;	
1835	Ful fresche he was to fight.	
	Sir Lambart lad him to the gate	*i.e., to the city gate*
	And to the castelle gate,	*i.e., the gate of the enchanted castle*
	That stode up ful right.	
	Further durste thei nought him bring,	
1840	Forsothe, withoute lesing,	
	Baron, burgeis, ne knyght,	
	But turnid ham agayne.	
	Sir Geffelot, Libeousis swayne,	*servant*
	With him fayne wolde ride.	*Would eagerly ride with him*

1845	Sir Libeous sware his othe, serteyne,	
	That he schulde Jeffelot slayne,	
	Yef he ther wolde abide.	*if he continued [with Lybeaus] further*
	Unto the castel ageyne he rode,	*[Jeffelot]*
	And with Sir Lambart ther he bode.	
1850	To Jhesus fast he cried	
	That he schulde send tithing glad	*glad tidings*
	Of him that longe had	
	Thedir ysought fulle wide.	

	Sir Libeous reyght his corcis	*arranged his corselet (breastplate)*
1855	And rode in to the palys	
	And at the halle alight.	
	Trumpis, pipis, and schalmys	*Trumpets, pipes, and shawms*
	He hurde bifore the highe deys	*high dais*
	And sawe ham with sight.	
1860	In myddis the halle flore	
	He sawe a fire starke and store,	*powerful (blazing) and large*
	Was light and brenden bryght,	*brilliant; burned bright*
	And furthe in he yede	
	And ladde with him his stede,	*steed*
1865	That helpith him in fight.	

	Libeous furthe gan pas,	
	Furthe into the plas	
	Ther the fire was in the halle.	
	Somme, of more and las,	*no one of greater or lesser rank*
1870	He ne sye in the plas,	
	But mynstrell clothid in palle,	*clothed in fine cloths*
	With setoll and with sawtry,	*citole; psaltry*
	And every maner mynstralci.	*kind of minstrelsy*
	Grete gle thei made alle;	
1875	Harpe, pipe, and rote,	*rote (like a harp)*
	Organs mery of note,	*merry*
	Was wrete in that walle.	*witnessed*

	Bi every mynstralle stode	
	A torche, feire and good;	
1880	Thei were ylightid and brende bright.	
	Sir Libeous in yode,	*i.e., proceeded further*
	To wite with egir mode,	*To discover eagerly*
	Who schulde with him fyght.	
	He yede abowte into the hall	
1885	To biholde the pelouris all,	*pillars*
	That were so feire in sight.	
	Of jasper and of fyne cristall	

Were thei ywrought alle,
That was so moche of myght.

1890 The doris was of bras,
The wyndowis were of glas,
Ywrought with ymagrye.
The halle ypeyntid was;
In the worlde a feirer nas *there was no fairer*
1895 That ever man sawe with ie. *eye*
He sette him on the des. *dais*
The mynstrals were in pece, *silent*
That weren so stourdy. *so loud [before]*
Torchis that weren so bright,
1900 Thei went out anone right —
The mynstrals weren away!

The dors and the wyndowis al
Beten in the halle,
As were dyntis of dondur. *claps of thunder*
1905 The stonys in the walle
On his hede gan falle;
Therof had he wondur!
The erthe bigan to quake;
The doris bigan to shake,
1910 As he sate therundur.
The halle rofe also, *roof*
Him thought it clave a-two
As it schulde asoundur! *split and collapse*

Sir Libeous therof had mervaile
1915 And seide, withouten faile:
"This is a wondur!
Y trowe the devill of helle *I believe [that]*
Be in this castelle
And hath here his resting! *his residence*
1920 Though the devil and his dame
Come with his brothir in same,
To dethe Y schalle him dynge. *kill him*
Y schalle never onis fle, *once (i.e., never ever)*
Er that Y se what he be,
1925 Aboute this biggyng." *building*

As he sate thus and saide, *sat*
Him thought he was betraide!
Stedis hurde he neye. *Steeds; neigh*
Than was he betir apaide *satisfied*
1930 And to himsilve saide:

"Yit Y hopy to play!"   *hope to*
As he lokid into the fielde,
He sawe with scheft and schilde
Men yarmyd twey   *Two armed men*
1935   In right good armour,
Was coverid with colour,
With golde garlondis gay.   *splendid gold garlands*

Thei come ride into the halle
And lowde bigan to calle:
1940   "Sir knyght of aventours,   *adventures*
Suche a cas ther is bifalle,
Yef thow be prowde in palle,   *If; splendid in rich clothing*
Fight ye must with us!
Y holde the man of kyn   *I consider the man to be my kinsman*
1945   Yef thow that lady wyn
That is so precious!"
Quod Libeous anone right:
"Redy Y am to fight,
Bi the love of Jhesus!"

1950   Sir Libeous, with good hert,
Into his sadulle he stert.
A spere on hond he hent.
Smertly he rode ham tille,
His fomen for to fille;   *foeman*
1955   Therto was his talent.   *That was his desire*
Whan thei togadur smote,
Everi on othir schildis hit   *Each man hit the other's shield*
With speris doughti of dynt.
Mabon his spere tobarst;
1960   Ther of was he sore agast   *extremely astonished*
And hilde him schamely schent.   *shamefully disgraced*

And with his sterk fauchon   *mighty sword*
Libeous bare Mabon doun
Undir his hors taile,
1965   That hors he bare to ground,
And Mabon fille that stound   *at that time, then*
Into the filde, sans faile.   *truly*
Nerehond he had be slayne,   *Nearly*
But than come Iraine,
1970   With helme, hauberk, and maile.
Ful fresche he was to fight.
Sir Libeous, anone right,
Thought him for to asaile.

Sir Libeous was of him yware,
1975 And his spere to him bare,
And left his brothir stille.
Suche dyntis thei gave thore   *then*
That hare hauberkis totore,   *their chain mail split open*
And that likid him ille!   *they did not like that*
1980 Hare speris brake on two;
Her swerdis drowe thei tho   *They drew their swords then*
With hertis grym and grille.   *grim; fierce*
Togadir gan thei fight,
Every of othir provid har myght   *tested their strength*
1985 Othir for to kille.

As thei togadir gan hewe,
Mabon, the more schrewe,   *greater rogue*
In the fielde aros.
He hurde, and wel knewe,
1990 That Iran gave strokis fewe;
Therof his hart aros.   *he swelled in anger*
To him he went ful right
To help to falle him in fight,   *To help [Iran] kill him [Lybeaus]*
Libeous of gentil los.   *of noble fame*
1995 But Libeous fought with hem bothe
As he were wode and wrothe,   *crazed; furious*
And kepid him in clos.   *kept himself protected*

Whan Iran sawe Mabon,
He smote a stroke of male felon   *evil treachery*
2000 To Sir Libeous with ire,
That evyn he clave doune,   *even struck down at*
With his swerde broune,   *bright sword*
Sir Libeousis stedeis swire.   *The neck of Lybeaus's steed*
Sir Libeous was wondir slighe,   *very skillful*
2005 And smote a-two his thighe

Ther helpid him none armour,   *(see note)*
His acton ne his charmour.   *protective jacket nor his sorcery*
He quitid wel his hire.   *[Lybeaus] acquitted himself well*

Libeous of hert was light   *keen*
2010 With Mabon for to fight,
In fielde, bothe in fere.   *both together*
Suche strokis gan thei dight,   *They delivered such strokes*
That the fuyre sprang out right   *fire*
Of schilde and helme clere.
2015 As thei togadir smette,
Hare strokis togadir mette,

As ye may lysten and lere.   *listen; learn*
Mabon smote to Libeous blythe   *quickly*
And brake Libeous swerde ful swithe   *at once*
2020   A-two quyte and clene.

Than was Libeous ful wo
For he had lorne so,   *lost*
Forsothe, his good swerde there,
And his stede was lame.   *disabled*
2025   He had wende to have come with schame   *expected*
To Kyng Arthour, his lorde.
To Iran fast he ranne
And hent his swerde thanne —   *seized then*
Of love ther was no worde!
2030   He ranne to Mabon right.
Ful fast than gan he fight,
As jestours tellith in borde.   *recite as entertainment (i.e., in romance)*

And ever faught Mabon,
As it were a lyon,
2035   Sir Libeous for to slo.   *In order to slay*
But Sir Libeous clave adoune   *thrust down*
His schilde with his fawchoune,   *falchion*
That he toke his brothir fro.   *i.e., Iran*
In right tale it is tolde,
2040   His right arme with the schilde
Awey he smote also.
Than seid Mabon him tille:
"Thy strokis bene fulle ille,
Gentille knyght, nowe ho!   *cease*

2045   "Y wol me yilde to thee,
With bodi and catelle fre,   *both my person and noble possessions*
And take alle thee tille.   *take all to yourself*
And that lady fre,   *gentle lady*
That is in my posté,   *in my power*
2050   Schalle be atte thi wille.   *will be at your will (i.e., in your power)*
For throwe thi swerdis dynt,
Myne honde is schent;   *ruined*
That wounde wolle me spille.   *destroy (kill) me*
Therfore, thowe savy my life   *spare my life*
2055   And ever, withouten strife,
Y schal be at thi wille."

"Nay," quod Libeous, "Bi my thrifte,   *By my good fortune*
Y wolle right nought of thi gifte,   *I do not want any part of*
For alle the worlde to wilde   *to wield (i.e., rule or possess)*

2060   Turne thee, yef thowe myght,
        For Y schalle, as I hight,   *promised*
        Hewe thi hed off bi the chynne!"
        Than Mabon and Sir Libeous
        Fast togadre hewe.   *traded blows*
2065   Thei left it for no synne.   *They did not cease for any cause*
        Sir Libeous was more of myght
        And clave his helme adoune right,
        And his hede off bi the chynne.   *his (Mabon's)*

        Than Mabon was yslayn,
2070   He ranne towarde Iran,
        With his swerde in fist
        For to se his brayne,   *expose his brains*
        I telle yowe, for certeyne.
        For to fight more him lust,   *he wanted to continue the fight*
2075   And whan he come thore,
        Awey he was ybore,   *he [Iran] had vanished*
        To whiche stede he ne wist.   *what place he did not know*
        He sought him, for the nonys,
        Fulle wide in that wonys.   *Throughout the dwelling*
2080   On trewthe ful wel he trust.   *trusted to fulfill his oath*

        And whan he myght not fynde Iran,
        He went agen, ful serteyne,
        And sought ful sore,
        And seide in dede and thought:
2085   "This wolle be dere ybought,
        That he is fro me yfare,   *has escaped me*
        For he wol with sorsery
        Do me grete turmentry,   *great harm*
        And that is my most care!"
2090   He sate and ful fast he thought
        Whate he best do mought.   *What he might best do*
        Of blys than was he bare!   *He was entirely devoid of happiness then*

        As he sate in the halle,
        Out of the stone walle
2095   A wyndowe feire unfolde.   *opened*
        Grete wondir, withalle,
        In his hert gan falle.   *arose*
        He sate and gan biholde   *sat; beheld*
        A worme ther out gan pas   *dragon to emerge*
2100   With a womanis face,
        Yonge and nothing olde.
        Hur bodi and hur whyngis

Shone in alle thingis,
As it were betyn golde.   *beaten gold*

2105   Hur taile was unmete;   *extremely large*
       Hur pennys were grym and grete,   *wings*
       As ye may lysten and lere.
       Sir Libeous swat for hete   *sweated from the heat*
       Ther he sate in his sete,
2110   As he had be in werre.   *in full combat*
       So sore he was agast,
       Him thought his hert tobarst   *would burst*
       As scho nyghid him nere,   *approached him*
       And ar Sir Libeous it wist,   *before; knew*
2115   The worme with mouthe him kist   *dragon*
       And hynge abowte his swire.   *embraced him around the neck*

       And aftir that kissing,
       Of the worme bothe taile and wyng
       Sone thei fille hur fro.   *Immediately fell from her*
2120   So feire in alle thing
       Woman, without lesyng,
       Sawe he never er tho.
       But scho was al nakid
       As the clerkis hur makid;
2125   Therfore Libeous was wo.   *distressed*
       Sho seid: "Gentille knyght,
       God yilde thee thi fight   *reward your fight*
       My fomen that thow wolt slo.   *In which you desired to slay my foes*

       "Thou hast ysley for sothe   *You have truly slain*
2130   Two clerkis that cowthe   *who knew [much sorcery]*
       And wrought bi the fende.   *performed [their magic] through the devil*
       Bi northe and bi sowthe,
       Bi maistry of hare mowthe.   *By the power of their words*
       Many men thei schende   *destroyed; (see note)*

2135   Ever in wo to wynde,   *To live ever in woe*
       Til Y had ykissid Gaweyn,
       That is ful doughti, serteyne,   *most excellent*
       Othir sum of his kynne.   *or someone of his kin; (see note)*

       And thowe savedist my lyve,   *Because you saved my life*
2140   Castels sixty and five   *sixty-five*
       Take Y wol thee tille,   *I wish to give them to you*
       And mysilve to wife,   *[Along] with myself to wed*
       Stilly, withouten strife   *Silently, without protest*
       Yif it be thi wille."

2145   Libeous was glad and blithe
        And lepe to hors also swithe
        And left that lady stille,
        And sore draddid Iran   *very much feared Iran*
        That he nad nought him slayn;
2150   With spere he thought him spille   *He sought to kill him with a spear*

        Sir Libeous, that knyght good,
        Into the sadil he yood   *went*
        To loke aftir Iran.   *seek*
        He lokid into a chambir,
2155   That was in an hie tour   *in a high tower; (see note)*

        And ther he sawe Iran.
        He drowe his swerde with myght
        And smote of his hed aright,
        For sothe, of Iran than.

2160   To the castelle than he rode   *i.e., Lambert's castle*
        Ther the folke him abode;   *awaited his return*
        To Ihesus gan thei cry.
        For Libeous to Lambert tolde,
        And othir knyghtis bolde,
2165   This tale ther ful pertly,   *publicly*
        How Mabon was slayn,
        And woundid was Iran,
        Throwe the myght of Marie;
        That the lady bright
2170   Til a dragon was dight   *Into the form of a dragon was transformed*
        Throwe myght of sorserye;

        And with a cosse of a knyght,   *kiss*
        Womman scho was aplight,   *She became a woman truly*
        A commely creature.
2175   But scho him stode byfore
        As nakid as scho was bore,
        And seid: "Nowe am Y sure
        My fomen thu hast slayn,
        Mabon and Iran.
2180   Therfore God joy thee send!"
        And whan Sir Libeous in that forward   *in that message*
        Had ytolde it to Sir Lambard
        Bothe worde and ende,

        A robe of purpure pris,   *valuable purple fabric*
2185   Yfurrid wel with grise,   *Edged well with gray fur*
        He sende hur to bigynnyng.

Suche riches and garlondis riche   *headpieces of gold*
He sende hur preveiliche;
A maide ham gan hur bringe.
2190   And whan scho was redy dight,   *ready and dressed*
Sho went with mayn and myght   *with her retinue*
Til hur owne wonnyng.   *dwelling*
Than alle the folke of Synadoune
With a feire processioune
2195   That ladi gan home brynge.

Whan scho come to towne,
Of golde a precious crowne
On hur hed was set.
Ther thei were glad and blithe
2200   And thonkid God fele sithe   *many times*
That hur balis were bete.   *misfortunes were overturned*
Than alle the knyghtis thrytté   *[her] thirty knights*
Send hur homage and fewté,   *homage; fealty*
As hit was lawe in lond.
2205   And whan thei had this ydone,
Thei toke hare leve and went sone,   *took their leave; departed soon*
Alle men bowid to hur honde.

Seven daies thei made hare sojour   *days they; their sojourn*
With Sur Lambert in the tour
2210   And alle the folke in same.   *together*
Than went thei with honour
Unto Kynge Arthour
With moche gle and game.
Thei thonkid God of his myght,
2215   Kynge Arthour and his knyght,
That scho had no schame.   *[the Lady of Synadoun] had no disgrace*
Arthour, he gave blyve   *eagerly*
Libeous that may to wyve,   *maiden [the Lady of Synadoun]; marry*
That was so gentil a dame.

2220   The myrthe of that bridale
May no man tel in tale,
Ne sey in no gest.   *Nor describe in any romance*
In that semely halle
Were lordis gret and smalle   *i.e., of all ranks, high and low*
2225   And ladies ful honest.   *most noble ladies*
Ther was wel sertayne
Servise fulle good wone,   *Food; in great abundance*
Bothe most and lest.   *nobility and commoners*
Forsothe, the mynstrals alle

2230	That were in the halle	
	Had giftis at that fest.	
	Sir Libeous' modir so fre	*mother so noble*
	Yede to that maungeré.	*Went to that feast*
	Hur rode was rede so rys.	*Her complexion; as red as rose*
2235	Sho knewe Libeous wel bi sight	
	And wist welle, anone right,	
	That he was of moche pris.	
	Sho went to Sir Gaweyne	
	And seid, withouten delaye:	
2240	"This is our childe so fre!"	
	That was he glad and blithe	
	And kissid hur fele sithe,	*many times*
	And seid: "That likith me!"	*I am very pleased*
	Sir Gaweyne, knyght of renoune,	*renown*
2245	Seid to the Lady of Synadoune:	
	"Madam, trewliche,	
	He that wanne thee with pride	*won you*
	I wanne him bi a forestis side	*sired*
	And gate him of a giantis lady."	*begot*
2250	That ladi was blithe	
	And thonkid him many a sithe	*many a time*
	And kissid him, sicurly.	*truly*
	Than Libeous to him ranne	
	And ever kissid that manne,	*man*
2255	Forsothe, trewly.	
	He fille on kneis that stound	*at once*
	And sate knelyng on the ground,	
	And seid: "For God alle weldond,	*all-wielding (i.e., all-ruling)*
	That made this worlde round,	
2260	Feire fadir, wel be ye found!	
	Ye blis me with your hond!"	
	The hyndy knyght, Gaweyne,	*gracious*
	Blessid his sonne with mayne,	*heartily*
	And made him up to stond.	
2265	And comaundid knyghtis and swayn	*knights; squires*
	To calle Libeous "Gyngelayn,"	
	That was lord of that lond.	
	Forty daies they dwellid there	
	And hare fest thei hilde yfere	*together*
2270	With Arthour the kyng,	
	As in romaunce it is tolde.	
	Arthour with knyghtis bolde	

Home he gan ham bryng.
Ten yere thei levid in same   *years; together*
2275   With moche gle and game,
He and that swete thinge.   *i.e., the Lady of Synadoun*
Jhesu Crist our Saviour
And His modir, that swete flour,
To blys He us alle bryng. Amen.

2280   *Qui scripcit carmen sit benedictis. Amen.*[1]

Hic explicit Libeus Disconyus.   *Here ends Libeus Disconyus*

He that lovyth welle to fare
Ever to spend and never spare quod More   *declares More [the scribe]*
But he have the more good   *increasing material wealth*
2285   His here wol grow throw his hood[2]

Hic pennam fixi penitet me si male scripsi.[3]

---

[1] *Blessed may he be who wrote/copied/recited [this] song/poem. Amen*

[2] *Hair will grow through his hood (i.e., a threadbare hood indicates poverty)*

[3] *Here I set my pen down. I [not the pen] am blameworthy if I have written poorly.*

EXPLANATORY NOTES

Line references are consistent for both texts in the early part of the poem. Thereafter we have listed Lambeth (L) first followed by the corresponding line numbers in Naples (N) in parentheses; when lines are omitted in L, N is the first text referenced. Short stanzas or missing lines are noted for both manuscripts. Perhaps these omissions are deliberate or the lines could have been missing from the scribe's copy-texts.

ABBREVIATIONS: **A**: Ashmole 61 (Oxford, Bodleian Library, MS 6922) (see Shuffelton); *AND*: *Arthurian Name Dictionary*; **C**: London, British Library, MS Cotton Caligula A.ii (see Mills); **L**: London, Lambeth Palace, MS 306; *LBD*: *Li Biaus Descouneüs*; *LD*: *Lybeaus Desconus*; **LI**: London, Lincoln's Inn, MS 150 (formerly known as Lincoln's Inn, MS Hale 150) (see Cooper); *MED*: *Middle English Dictionary*; **N**: Naples, Biblioteca Nazionale, MS XIII.B.29; *NAE*: Lacy, *New Arthurian Encyclopedia*; *ODOS*: Farmer, *Oxford Dictionary of Saints*; **P**: London, British Library, MS Additional 27879 (Percy Folio); *SGGK*: *Sir Gawain and the Green Knight*; Shuffelton: *Codex Ashmole 61*.

Incipit   L: *A tretys of one Gyngelayne othir wyse namyd by Kyng Arthure Lybeus Dysconeus that was bastard son to Sir Gaweyne*. This extended incipit in L is unique among the extant manuscripts. N: *Libious Disconious*.

1–6   The invocation to Christ and his mother is conventional and appears to include the audience in its storytelling. Renaut de Bâgé's poem begins with an encomium to the poet's lady: "Cele qui m'a en sa baillie / cui ja d'amors sans trecerie / m'a doné sens de cançon faire — por li veul un roumant estraire / d'un molt biel conte d'aventure" (For my sovereign lady I have written and sung of a love that knows no falsehood, according to the direction she gave. Now I wish to compose a romance for her from a beautiful tale of adventure) (*Le Bel Inconnu*, lines 1–5). The substitution of the Virgin Mary in the English version underscores similarities between religious discourse and the quasi-religious discourse of courtly love, marking perhaps a shift in emphasis toward piety. The Virgin is the recipient of a number of pleas in the poem, most notably when the maiden Violet is abducted and about to be assaulted by two giants.

4   L: *That lysteneth of a conquerour*. N: *That listenith of a conquerour*. The cues of oral poetry are retained, even though this is a late version of the poem; the oral story-telling tradition and minstrelsy are particularly strong in both L and N. Musical instruments, the dwarf's ability to entertain as well as to advise, and several musical allusions draw attention to the debt that metrical poetry and music owe to each other. See Zaerr, "Music and Magic." Purdie notes that the rhymes

"conqueror/warrior" appear also in the opening of *Otuel and Roland* (*Anglicising Romance*, p. 125n111); see *Otuel and Roland*, lines 3, 11.

7   L: *His name was Sir Gyngelayne*. N: *His name was hote Gyngeleyn*. L's manner of naming the protagonist "Sir Gyngelayne" has the effect of legitimating the natural son of Gawain by dubbing him a knight, whereas N does not. The moniker "Lybeaus Desconus" (spelled in various ways in Lambeth and Naples) is later bequeathed upon the hero by Arthur for practical purposes (see L, N, line 80), an act marked by a marginal note in L. In Renaut's poem, the hero's name is not revealed until the end.

7–30   The story of the hero's *enfances* in Renaut's text enters the narrative after the defeat of the enchanters (Mills, *LD*, p. 42). In *LBD*, however, the events of the "enfances" differ from the English versions. Following the *fier baiser*, the disembodied voice of la Pucele as Mains Blancs (the Maiden of the White Hands) informs Guinglain that his father was Gawain and that his mother is Blancemal le Fee (lines 3235–37). The mother of the Middle English Lybeaus, however, is not a "fay" who arms her son to send him to the Round Table. There are several romances where the hero's mother, estranged from the hero's father, either because she has been abandoned or because of the father's death, leaves the court and makes a life in rural seclusion, often in a forest, with her son whom she isolates and protects from the world. In *Sir Perceval of Galles*, for example, Acheflour retires from court upon the death of her husband and lives secluded in a forest with her young son Perceval. Whereas Lybeaus's acquisition of a chivalric identity begins with his discovery of a dead knight in full armor, Perceval's chivalric identity begins when he meets fully alive Arthurian knights. Further, the illegitimacy of Gyngeleyn is lessened by the fact that his father is Sir Gawain, one of Arthur's most honored knights. Gawain ranks among "the most complex Arthurian characters"; he often exemplifies courtesy and chivalric ideals, but his frequent womanizing also receives attention (Shuffelton, p. 474n8). The stigma of illegitimacy imposed upon Lybeaus at the beginning of the poem is somewhat mitigated at the end by full recognition of the Arthurian court and his marriage to the regal Lady of Synadoun. N and A continue and conclude the hero's *enfances* with the return of Gyngeleyn's mother to Arthur's court in the final scene, a family reconciliation not present in the other manuscripts. Sir Degaré, like Lybeaus, is an illegitimate son, but he manages to reconcile his parents and promote their marriage, whereas in *LD*, Sir Gawain and Lybeaus's mother do not marry.

9   L: *Under a forest syde*. N: *Bi a forestis side*. The location of Lybeaus's conception at the edge of a forest also places him at the outer limits of legitimacy. As Shuffelton notes, "bastardy was often imagined as manifesting itself in moral or physical defect" (p. 475n15); moreover, in the realm of the law, an illegitimate child could not legally inherit property from either parent (Brand, "Family and Inheritance," p. 73). This medieval context thus provides motive for Lybeaus's strong drive for public recognition by the Arthurian court and confirms the underlying narrative sense that he is to some extent legitimized by his paternal bloodline and his father's reputation. According to Thomas Wright, "The story

of rising from an obscure beginning is a very common one in medieval literature, and belongs to a principle of medieval sentiment, that noble blood was never lost . . . and that if a knight, for instance, met with a woman, or however low the circumstances under which the child received its first nurture, the blood it had received from the father would inevitably urge it onward till it reached its natural station" (quoted in Hales and Furnivall, *Bishop Percy's Folio*, 2:405).

11   L: *With Arthur at the Roun Table.* N: *With Arthur at the Round Table.* The Round Table, added to the Arthurian cycle by Wace in the twelfth century in his *Roman de Brut* ("Fist Artur la Runde Table" [Arthur had the Round Table made], line 9751), has become a symbol of Arthurian governance. The Winchester Round Table shows the names of twenty-four knights, one of whom is Lybeaus Desconus, written "S(ir) lybyus dyscony(us)." See Badham and Biddle, "Inscriptions in the Painting," pp. 255 and 280.

19   L: *For he was full savage.* N: *For that he was so savage.* Narratives of *l'enfant sauvage* (the wild child) abound in the Middle Ages. In Middle English romance, the wild child trope may include characters such as Gowther, whose kinship with Merlin (as half-brother) renders him a good candidate for taming; that he is conceived by a demon disguised as his mother's husband (an episode akin to Arthur's as well as Merlin's conception) contributes to his lack of civility. His wild behavior is particularly noteworthy when he is described as having suckled nine wet nurses to death (*Sir Gowther*, lines 119–20). Lybeaus exemplifies his inner wild child in that he inhabits the forest and, like young Perceval, he flagrantly disregards the rules of chivalric behavior.

26   L: *His moder clepte him Bewfiz.* N: *His modir callid him Beaufits.* The name means literally "Beautiful Son" (Beau Fitz) and is a term of endearment bequeathed upon the boy by his mother, whose name is unstated, although in *LBD*, Guinglain's mother is Blancemal le Fee. It is tempting to see a pun as well on "Bewvisage." See N, line 72, where Lybeaus is praised for being "so feire of vis" and similarly in L (same line number): "so fayre a vice." Naming is an important feature of medieval romance, a genre often concerned with questions of identity and chivalric education. His mother's term of endearment is later supplanted by Arthur's dubbing of the young man as Lybeaus Desconus, although both names allude to the young hero's good looks and, by implication, his noble blood through kinship with Gawain and Arthur. Lybeaus's testing through adventure confirms the outward sign of noble blood, that is, his masculine beauty, and explains his natural prowess.

28   L: *And this childe was so nyse.* N: *And he him silve was nyse.* Lybeaus is called a child here not only because of his apparent youth (as indicated by Arthur in L, line 103: "But me thinketh thou arte to yonge" or N, line 106: "But ever me thinkith thee ful yong") but because his identity is partially defined by his biological kinship with Gawain and by his mother. "Child" also means a young man who aspires to be a knight or a young knight at the early stages of his career. To say that Lybeaus is a "child" because he has not been fully enfolded into chivalric masculinity and Arthur's court is pertinent to the use of the term here, since Lybeaus's identity is fully aligned at this point in the narrative with a mother wholly responsible for

her son's nurture. Like other orphaned, abandoned, fostered, or quasi-legitimate male protagonists of medieval romance (e.g., Tristan, Perceval, Lancelot, and Arthur), Lybeaus cannot be fully masculinized until he has been properly trained in the precepts and practices of chivalry. Only A and P assign a specific age to Lybeaus: "Ten yere olde I ame" (A, line 52) and "14 yeere old I am" (P, fol. 157r, line 52 [Cooper]). The typical age at which a young man could be knighted was twenty-one. This rite of passage varied among literary knights: at twenty Chaucer's Squire is still a squire, while Bevis of Hampton becomes *Sir Bevis* at fifteen, as does Sir Gowther.

37   L: *He toke off that knyghtis wede.* N: *The childe drowe off the knyghtis wede.* In a system predicated upon honor and prowess, armor stripping is a dishonorable and frowned-upon practice. The scene recalls a similar incident in the tales of Perceval in which the young rustic, with the help of Gawain, appropriates the armor of a dead knight. He, like Lybeaus, is unfamiliar with courtly etiquette. Lybeaus's ignorance and naiveté in this scene illustrate the "savagery" and "outrage" mentioned in lines 19 and 20.

41   L: *Glastynbury.* N: *Glastonbury.* A traditional placename associated with Arthurian literature. Its use in the Middle English romance situates Arthur and his court in that part of Britain known as Logres. In Wirnt von Grafenberg's *Wigalois*, Arthur's court is located in Brittany, whereas in *LBD*, Arthur's court is in Caerleon in Wales.

45   L: *This childe knelyd downe on his kne.* Despite his lack of chivalric training, C and L's Lybeaus seems to know what to do in front of a king, a gesture that tacitly indicates the boy's innate nobility, an apparently inherited character trait that allows the disadvantaged Lybeaus to claim his proper heritage in this early scene. N, A, and P (the stanza is missing completely in Ll) omit Lybeaus's gesture of kneeling, perhaps in order to underscore his rustic ways. In N, he simply greets (*grete*, line 45) the king and his *knyghtis alle* (line 44).

48   L: missing expression. N: *Y pray yow, par amour.* Literally, for the sake of love, this is a conventional courtly expression added to requests. The expression is used only in N and P.

49   L: *I am a child unkowthe.* N: *Y am a childe unknowe.* The boldness of this pronouncement in a court obsessed with gestures of civility and courtesy indicates lack of training in these skills. The translation of L's *unkowthe* as *uncouth* is certainly plausible, but N's *unknowe* suggests that it could also mean "unknown," or that the scribe understood it as a word relating to the overall themes of the poem; the notion that to be unknown is also to be outside the realm of chivalry renders both interpretations possible.

52   L: *Lorde, I pray thee nowthe.* N: *Lord, Y pray you nowthe.* This line differs considerably from the other redactions that indicate Lybeaus's age. (See note for line 28.)

61   L: *Sayde Gyngelayn, "Be Seint Jame!"* N: *The childe seid, "Bi Seint Jame."* L alone among the manuscripts cites the name "Gyngelayn" here. The naming of saints is significant throughout the narrative. This reference is probably to James the

Great, the first apostle of Christ to die and to be martyred for Christianity. The shrine with which he is most often associated is Santiago de Compostela in Spain. His cult was so thoroughly linked to pilgrimage that his emblems, the scallop shell and wide-brimmed hat, frequently became the garb of medieval pilgrims (see *ODOS*, p. 135).

66   L: *Clepped me Bewfice*. N: *Callid me Beaufice*. This second occurrence of Lybeaus's informal moniker underscores its importance to the narrative. In the *Promptorium Parvulorum*, the nickname means "more beautiful son;" the entry reads "*Byfyce. Filius, vel pulcher filius* (1:28). Shuffelton's suggestion that Rate, the presumed author/scribe of A, "may be evoking another famous romance hero, Bevis (or Beuis) of Hampton, who is not otherwise connected to this story" (p. 475n26), lends another dimension of meaning to the designation. Good looks appear to foreshadow a hero's success.

69   L: *Be God and Seint Denyce*. N: *Bi God and Seint Denyce*. Although the naming of saints is a common feature of the English version of the poem, in passages focused on the renaming of the protagonist, the utterance of saints' names calls attention to their value as mediators between human and divine realms. This saint, for whom the abbey of St. Denis was named, was popular in France and also in England, with forty-one churches named in his honor (see *ODOS*, p. 135).

80   L: *Lybeus Disconeus*. N: *Lybeus Dysconius*. This short line, consisting only of the two words that compose the protagonist's name, calls attention to itself metrically as well as visually. In L, the name *Lybeus Disconious* in a later hand appears in the margin; interestingly, the spelling *Disconious* resembles the Naples spelling *Dysconious*.

88–93   L: *"Now Kyng Arthur hathe made me knyght."* Alone among the manuscripts, L attributes a verbal response to Lybeaus that suggests an innate graciousness and proclaims his new status to the court.

89   L: *I thanke him with all my myght*. N: *And with a swerde bright of myght*. Nancy Cooper ("*Libeaus Desconus*," p. 400) believes that "bright" is erroneously repeated here from the previous line. A reads "suerd of might" (line 89), C: "swerde of might" (line 77), and P rearranges the lines thus: "K[ing] Arthur anon right / with a sword ffaire and bright / trulye þ[at] same day / dubbed that child a knight / And gave him armes bright" (fols. 157r–v, lines 85–89 in Cooper).

92–93   L: *to say . . . in feere*. N: *with a swerde bright of myght* (line 89). *say* ("assail"). See *MED saien* (v)d: "to test one's strength on, do battle with; an aphetic form of *asseien*; to try, test, challenge" *in feere* (in the company of men). Having been knighted, Lybeaus is eager to prove himself in combat. In N, he is taught by Gawain.

93   L: Short stanza. Following Arthur's investiture of Lybeaus, Gawain trains him in knightly combat and provides him with a shield only in N, A, P, and C. The passage is missing in both L and LI. Gawain's mentorship is important to the shaping of Lybeaus's identity as a knight and a tacit if unacknowledged recognition of their father-son relationship and Lybeaus's innate nobility. The shield,

of course, marks a knight's identity in the field. N: *Aftur, him taught Gaweyn . . . He hongid on him a schilde* (lines 91–94). Also missing in L and LI, the details of the shield appear in C, N, A, P. The griffon, a hybrid fabled animal with traits of a lion and eagle, appeared in medieval bestiaries, encyclopedias, and travel literature, and was adopted as a common feature in heraldry. It is somewhat ironic that the Fair Unknown should be given such a well-known identifying heraldic device. At N, line 264, however, the shield has only one griffon as its device. N: *a schilde / With grefons overgilde, / Ipeyntid of lengthe ful gay* (lines 94–96).

95   L: *Of Arthure a bone he bade.* N: *Anone a bone he bade* (line 98). The novice knight's request for the king's granting his petition is reminiscent of a similar scene in Chrétien de Troyes's *Perceval*, though such a request is an important trope of romances and of Arthurian literature more generally. Notice how N's "Anone" creates a Lybeaus more impetuous than L's.

103   L: *But me thinketh thou arte to yonge.* N: *But ever me thinkith thee ful yong* (line 106). Arthur's assessment here emphasizes the youth and inexperience of Lybeaus and perhaps refers back to the king's initial reluctance to dub him without proof of his abilities or lineage. If Lybeaus is as young as ten or fourteen as some manuscripts suggest (see note for lines 28 and 52), then Arthur's hesitancy is well justified, although medieval boys were expected to engage in adult activities earlier than modern boys. Aristocratic males, for example, were generally imagined to be ready for marriage at age fourteen (for girls, age twelve). Military training also began early. William Marshall served as a squire for eight years, during which time he trained for combat; he was thirteen when he entered the service of William, lord of Tancarville (Painter, *William Marshal*, pp. 16–17).

108   L: *Wesshed and went to mete.* N: *Thei weschid and went to mete* (line 111). The motif is found in *Emaré*, *Sir Orfeo*, *Le Bone Florence of Rome*, and *Robyn Hode and the Potter*. This custom is reiterated in several different ways in courtesy books that advocated teaching children, particularly boys, from a young age, e.g., *The Young Children's Book* from Ashmole 61, *Dame Courtesy* from Ashmole 61 (previously published as *The Babees Book*, ed. Furnivall; see Shuffleton, *Codex Ashmole*, p. 447), etc. See also the texts in Furnivall's edition of *The Babees Book*, including *Aristotle's A B C*, *Urbanitatis*, *Stans Puer Ad Mensam*, etc., as well as the texts in Johnston, *Medieval Conduct Literature*.

115   L: *Ther con a mayde in ryde.* N: *Ther come a maid in ride* (line 118). As often happens in Arthurian narratives, an adventure ensues just as the court sits down to dine (perhaps the best time to catch everyone at home). There is a strong resemblance to Lunete in Chrétien's *Yvain* here.

116   L: *And a dwerfe by hir syde.* N: *A dwarfe rode bi hur side* (line 119). The dwarf is a stock character of medieval romance, but this particular dwarf has a name and description of his own. Unlike most medieval dwarves he is more virtuously construed (see notes for lines 130–40 below).

118   L: *The may hight Ellene.* N: *The maid was yhote Elyne* (line 121). In *LBD*, the messenger is named *Helie*. Other variations include *Elene* (C), *Elyn* (A), and *Hellen* (P). The line is missing in LI.

124–26   L: *She was clothed in tarse, / Rownd and nothinge scarse, / I-pured with blawndenere.*
          N: *The maiden was clothid in tarsis, / Round and no thing skars, / With pelour blandere*
          (lines 127–29). References here to *tarse* and *blawndenere* suggest an exotic opulence
          to Elene's dress. *Tarse* refers to a costly fabric associated with Tharsia, whereas
          blawndenere refers to rich fur, possibly ermine. The dwarf in *Sir Degaré* has a
          surcoat "iforred with blaundeuer apert" (line 794). Other manuscript variants
          include *blandere* (N, line 129), *blaunner*, (C, line 117), *blaundyner* (A, line 129), and
          Blaundemere (P, fol. 157v). The line is missing in LI. Editors have found *blauwndener*
          (L) or *blandere* (N) difficult. The Auchinleck editors of *Sir Degaré* transcribe the
          word as "blaunchener" (line 794), but the manuscript reads "blaundener."

129   L: *Milke white was hir destere.* N: *Mylke white was hur desture* (line 132). According
          to the *MED*, the term refers to "a riding horse of noble breed, a knight's mount."
          Later in the poem, the horse is called a palfrey, a steed more closely identified
          with women and ordinary riding rather than a steed used for battle, although the
          terms appear to be used interchangeably in *LD*. The luxurious saddle decorations
          as well as the milk white color of the horse indicate the high status of both.

130   L: *The dwerf was clothed in ynde.* N: *The dwarf was clothid in ynd* (line 133). *Ynd(e)*
          could be the color of the cloth (indigo) or a kind of cloth associated with India,
          extravagant and exotic, distinguishing the dwarf as a special envoy from a signifi-
          cantly noble court. The manuscripts do not agree on the color or the fabric of the
          dwarf's clothing; P clothes him "with scarlett ffine" (fol. 157v). N's "hynd" is
          probably an error for "ynd." Mills (*LD*, p. 208–09n121–32) notes the similarity
          between this description of Theodeley (N's Deodelyne) and the dwarf in the
          Auchinleck *Sir Degaré*, lines 781–94.

132   L: *Stoute he was and pertte.* N: *For he was stout and pert* (line 135). The term *pertte*
          means "attractive" or "comely," according to the *MED*. The dwarf here
          resembles the lady of *Sir Launfal* as described in lines 292 and 294, "Sche was as
          whyt as lylye yn May . . . He seygh nevere none so pert." *Stoute* here does not
          represent portliness but rather strength or courage.

135   L: *His surcote was so ryche bete.* N: *His sircote was overte* (line 138). Mills (*LD*, p.
          209n126) corrects L with a reading from C, here corroborated by N. The
          reference is to the *surcot ouvert*. Mills directs readers to Joan Evans, *Dress in
          Mediaeval France*, frontispiece, pp. 17, 31, and fig. 67 (p. 209n126). A reference to
          sorcot overt also appears in *Sir Degaré*, line 793. This is another instance where N
          agrees with C and not with L, A, or P (the line is missing in LI); C reads "Hys
          surcote was ouert"; P: "His cercott was of greene"; and A: "His sircote was yalow
          as floure."

136   L: *His berde was yelewe as wax.* N: *His berde was as yelow as wax* (line 139). Dwarves
          play an important part in medieval romance, and not all conform to negative
          stereotypes of this stock character. Many function similarly to Shakespeare's
          "licensed" fools as messengers, philosophers, or counselors to the king. Some-
          times they are wicked and treacherous as is the dwarf in the Tristan narratives;
          at other times they are loyal as in Malory's "Tale of Sir Gareth." Physiognomy,
          the medieval science of physical form and shape thought to correspond to one's

intrinsic worth, appears not to apply to these characters. The dwarf in *LBD* and *Wigalois* enters Arthur's court riding on the back of his lady's saddle. Perhaps it is only by coincidence that the dwarf's "yellow beard" matches the color of his lady's hair. However, as Mills notes (see the quotation Mills cites on p. 208n121–32), the dwarf in *Sir Degaré* has hair as "crisp an yhalew as wax" (line 786).

137   L: *To his girdyll hange his fax.* N: *To his gurdul [henge] the plax* (line 140). C also reads "To hys gerdell henge the plex" (line 128), once again agreeing with N and opposed to L, A, and P. (See Mills, *LD*, p. 209n128.) According to the *MED*, *plax* refers to braided hair or beard, whereas *fax* refers to the hair of the head.

142   L: *Theodeley was his name.* N: *Deodelyne was his name* (line 145). See C *Teandelayn*; A *Wyndeleyn*, P *Teddelyne*. The line is missing in LI. These are the Middle English versions of Tidogolain, the dwarf in *LBD*, who serves Helie, the lady-in-waiting to Blonde Esmeree, the French text's equivalent to the Lady of Synadoun. Vernon J. Harward, Jr., *The Dwarfs of Arthurian Romance*, places this character within a category he defines as "romance dwarfs," whom he describes as often having characteristics such as "beauty or handsomeness of countenance, excellent proportion of body and limbs, and, twice, [as described in this poem, having] fair hair" (p. 29). Theodeley/Deodelyne is clearly what Harward calls a "petit chevalier" (p. 29). The messenger's name Elyne (the spelling in N) is incorporated into N's spelling of the dwarf's name, Deod*elyne* (italics added). Both dwarf and Elyne function as metonymic surrogates for the Lady of Synadoun, whose messengers they are. Together their attitudes and comments challenge, test, and later confirm the prowess and knightliness of Lybeaus.

146–47   L: *Sotill, sawtrye in same, / Harpe, fethill, and crowthe.* N: *Sotil, sawtre in same, / Of harpe, fethil, and crowthe* (lines 149–50). These are the stringed instruments — citole, psaltery, harp, fiddle, and crowthe — that Theodeley/Deodelyne apparently masters, indicating that he is indeed a "petit chevalier" educated in courtly accomplishments pleasing to aristocratic ladies. Music and minstrelsy appear also in the Golden Isle and the enchanted castle of Synadoun. (See Zaerr's discussion in "Music and Magic.") The debt that medieval poetry pays to music is addressed in Strohm and Blackburn, *Music as Concept and Practice*, especially in the section on minstrels and their education (pp. 98–103) as well as the section on instrumental music (see below note 216), "Soft Instruments," pp. 147–56.

148–50   L: *He was a gentill boourdour / Amonge ladyes in boure, / A mery man of mouthe.* N here (lines 145–53) appears to have a defective stanza, missing L's triplet. Mills (*LD*, p. 289) notes that L 148–50 are lacking in N, but that they are present in all other versions of the poem (except LI, where this entire section of the poem is missing). These lines, however, carry an almost sexual implication concerning the relationship of the dwarf to women in their bowers, and they appear in neither *Sir Degaré* (see note to line 136 above) nor *LBD*. In other words, the omission in N may be intentional, a way of evading an unnecessary sexual implication.

160   L: *Mi lady of Synadowne.* N: *My lady of Synadowne.* The imprisoned heroine of *LBD*, la Blonde Esmeree, the queen of north Wales, is presented by Helie as the "daughter of King Guingras" (line 177). See the note for L, line 1772. Synadoun

refers to the ancient Roman station of Segontium, called later by the Welsh Cair Segeint, Caer Seint, or Caer Aber Seint, at the base of Mount Snowdon in Wales. It became known as Snauedon and later simply Snowdon (see Loomis, "From Segontium to Sinadon," pp. 526–28). Synadoun was also associated with magic and a history relevant to the curse placed upon the queen. According to the *AND*, a curse inhibited construction on Vortigern's fortress at Snowdon, which could only be removed by the blood of a fatherless child. His emissaries brought before him Ambrosius (in Nennius) or Merlin (in Geoffrey of Monmouth), who stayed his execution by showing a hidden lake beneath the foundation, where two dragons fought, one white, the other red; the victory of the white dragon, Merlin said, "foretold Vortigern's eventual defeat" (*AND*, p. 449). In the Welsh *Lludd and Llefelys*, the dragons had been buried there by Lludd. In the *Historia Meradoc*, Snowdon is the capital of Wales, whereas in *LBD*, it is at the base of the Snowdon mountains laid waste by two sorcerers, Mabon and Evrain, until disenchanted by Guinglain, the son of Gawain (p. 449).

162   L: *That was of grete valure.* N: *That was of grete honour.* This description appears to refer to the lady and not the prison, since virtue typically resides in human subjects rather than in inanimate objects. The term valor or honor applied to a woman is significant, however, since, according to the *MED*, the term embodies chivalric virtues of "nobility of character," "spiritual worth," "courtliness," "refinement," "bravery," "courage," "physical strength," "stability," and "endurance."

164   L: *That is of wer wyse and wight.* N: *In warra that were wyse and wight.* N's reading "warra" conflicts with L and A, which have "wer" and "were" respectively. C deviates completely, omitting the concept of war, and substituting the line "With herte good and light" (line 155). The line is missing in LI, but P carries forth the idea of war in a much altered line, "For to win her in fight" (line 170 [Cooper]; fol. 157r). Given that the manuscripts disagree, N's "warra" is a possible variant of *ware* or *wara*. The phrase "in warra" is probably a variant of "on warra," meaning watchful or alert (*MED*). The line thus describes an alert or keen knight who is both wise and courageous.

165   L: *To wynne hir with honoure.* N: *To wyn hur with honour.* In *LBD*, Helie forewarns the Arthurian court that the knight who frees her lady must first accomplish the "Fier Baissier," the Fearsome Kiss (line 192). Here, in the ME narrative, Lybeaus has no prior knowledge of this expectation and so is taken completely by surprise when the dragon kisses him later.

166   L: *Uppe startte that yonge knyght.* N: *Than stert up a yong knyght.* In *LBD*, Arthurian knights hesitate to volunteer for the task, whereas here Lybeaus simply asks first.

178   L: *The mayde began to chide.* N: *Than gan Elyne to chide.* Shuffelton calls Elene a "*demoisele mesdisante*, a sharp-tongued maid who never hesitates to voice severe criticism, particularly when the hero engages in something foolhardy" (p. 476 n181). One might consider her to be the prick of Lybeaus's conscience since she reminds him of his promise to Arthur at crucial points in the narrative.

183   L: *lose.* N: *loce.* The term refers to "reputation" or "being known." The Naples scribe frequently uses *c* and *s* interchangeably.

197–200   L: *He shall do bataylles thre . . . At Poynte Perilowse, / Besyde the Chapell of Awntrous.*
           N: *Bataile five othir thre . . . At Poynt Perillous, / Biside the Chapel of Aventours.*
           Lybeaus has many more fights than predicted by the dwarf (William Selebraunch
           and his three nephews, two giants, Sir Jeffroun, Sir Otis de Lile, Maugys, and Sir
           Lambert; before he actually sees the Lady of Synadoun, he must fight Iran and
           Mabon). Nor does Lybeaus begin his adventures at Poynt Perillous by the Chapel
           of Adventours. In *LBD*, Tidogolain does not speak or prophesy in this scene.
           According to Mills, Poynte Perilowse "roughly corresponds to *le Guè Perilleus* of
           the same episode in BD (323), but the Old French romance makes no mention
           of the *cause* with which the *Poynte* is presumably identified in L 301" (p. 213).
           Perhaps its mention here creates a bridge to the French romance and a reminder
           that Lybeaus is Gawain's son. According to the *AND*, this is "a treacherous ford
           in the land of Galloway that no knight dared to cross. Gawain reached it during
           his travels and tried to jump his horse across it, but his horse jumped badly and
           dumped him into the river" (p. 401). Lybeaus will win against his opponent(s)
           here but will experience a river dunking later in the poem. Moreover, "chapel"
           is as likely to refer to a haunted place or fairy mound (as in *SGGK*) as to an
           orthodox parish church. The *MED*, in fact, cites this line, (chapele, n5c, "a
           haunted place, a fairy mound"). According to Shuffelton, "*Antrus* is a corrupt
           form of the name found in other manuscripts, *Awntrous*, and the Chapell of
           Antrus may be translated as 'the Chapel of Adventures'" (p. 476n202–03).

203–16   The punctuation that Mills provides in his edition to L (lines 207–10) exaggerates
           the boast to the point of dissembling, as Lybeaus seems to claim experience in
           mortal combat that he does not yet have. A slight alteration in punctuation, how-
           ever, makes more sense in context and avoids vilifying the hero. He has *some*
           training in weapons (see note to lines 90–93 above). The remainder of the
           passage expresses Lybeaus's firm conviction that to flee the potentially fatal
           battle is reprehensible.

216–25   L: short stanza. This stanza is missing in L and C, but present in all other
           manuscripts (N, A, P, and LI). It includes two rather stunning lines quoted in
           The Squire of Low Degree: "Therfore the dwarfe was full wo, / And sayd: 'Arthur,
           thou arte to blame. / To bydde this chylde go sucke his dame / Better hym
           semeth, so mote I thryve'" (lines 620–23). The Naples lines spoken by the dwarf
           are strikingly similar: "Go home and sowke thi dame / And wynne ther thi
           degré" (lines 224–25). With this particularly insulting remark, the dwarf cuts
           Lybeaus down to size and manifests the threat to the young hero indicated as
           well through his association with music. See note 146–47 above.

223–28   L: *The mayden for ire and hete / Wolde neyther drynke ne ete. . . . N: The maide for noye
           and hete / Wolde nought drinke ne ete . . .* (lines 232–37). In *LBD*, Helie and
           Tidogolain leave once Arthur has given his decree, before the meal, so that
           Lybeaus has to catch up with them later. Here the two messengers remain at the
           table and do not eat, but all three begin the quest together.

227   L: *Tyll the table was raysed.* N: *Til the tabul was unleide* (line 236). Shuffelton
           remarks that "in medieval halls, the large dining tables were movable boards,
           taken up and stored after meals to make space for other activities" (p. 476n239).

231 L: *Foure of the best knyghtis*. N: *Four of the best knyghtis* (line 240). L adds a fifth knight in the arming of Lybeaus, Lawncelett, who gives him a spear (line 258). In L, the first four knights are Gawain, Perceval, Ywain, and Agravain. N's four differ in identity and order, and where L lists Gawayne, Persyvale, Iwayne, and Agfayne (Agravain), N lists Percevale, Gawayn, Ewain, and "Griffayn," and excludes Lancelot (see the note for L240 [N250]). Shuffelton believes that the N, A reading of Gryffayn or Geffreyn is a corruption of Agravain (p. 476n257), and although this is plausible, the name may also be a corruption of Griflet (also known as Girflet or Jaufre). The names connected to Gawain, that is, Perceval and Ywain, may have evoked the name Griflet. For an account of the connections among Jaufre/Griflet and Chrétien de Troyes's *Yvain* and *Perceval*, see Hunt, "Texte and Prétexte." Griflet in Malory's *Morte d'Arthur* is one of the knights killed by Lancelot in his rescue of Guinevere. For a history of Sir Griflet in French and English Arthurian tales, see Reno, *Arthurian Figures*, pp. 133–34.

232 ff. L: short stanza. N: *Of the best armour that myght be found* (line 242).

235 L: *That in the flome was baptiste*. N: *That in the flem Jourdan was baptist* (line 245). As the passage makes clear, this is a reference to the archetypal baptism of Jesus in the Jordan River. The trope is recalled later in the poem when Maugis/Maugus dunks Lybeaus in a river during a battle (see L, lines 1413 ff. and N, lines 1436 ff.).

240 L: *To armen him the knyghtis were fayne*. N: *To army him the knyghtis were fayn* (line 250). In *LBD*, the Fair Unknown appears in Arthur's court fully armed. Arthur does not knight the young warrior (he accepts him into his service as a knight of the Round Table), nor do his companions give him arms and weapons. The knights "fayne" named in the following lines are interesting, particularly since Gawain is first on the list and his brother Agravain is also included. In the middle are Perceval and Yvain, two knights arguably made most famous by Chrétien de Troyes; Lancelot is named shortly hereafter as the knight who provides lance and sword. Purdie links this scene in LD to the arming scene in *Otuel and Roland* (*Anglicising Romance*, p. 125 and n111). N, lines 271–72 (C, lines 235–36; L, lines 261–62) thus corresponds to *Otuel and Roland* 312, 315. However, where C, line 232 (L, line 258) recalls *Otuel and Roland* 303 (Purdie, *Anglicising Romance*, p. 125n111), N does not. Lancelot does not number among the arming knights in N, A, and P as he does in C and L (the episode in LI is illegible).

242 L: *Syr Persyvale*. N: *Sir Percevale* (line 251). In *Sir Perceval of Galles*, Perceval resembles Lybeaus in that he appears in Arthur's court without chivalric upbringing and demands to be knighted; he also subsequently confirms his knightly worth. Ironically Perceval and Gawayn, the knights Elyne would have preferred as champions of her lady, are the first knights to prepare Lybeaus for his quest.

244 L: *The fourthe highte Agfayne*. N: *The fourth was Sir Griffayn* (line 254). See note 254 below where a griffon becomes part of the heraldry not found in L.

246 L: *They kestyn on him of sylke*. N: *Thei cast on him of sylke* (line 256). The arming scene depicted in L beginning at this line and in N at line 256 is an important set piece of chivalric romance and takes on the symbolic meanings of sacred ritual

and the dressing of a knight or a priest. See Ramón Lull, chapter 6 "The Sig-
nificance of a Knight's Arms," *The Book of the Ordre of Chyvalry*, pp. 76–89, a
popular text that circulated in England in "numerous manuscripts of French
versions" (p. xvi), e.g., St. John's College, Oxford, Codex 102 (late fourteenth
century) and BL MS Additional 22768 (first half of the fifteenth century) and
translated with some elaboration into English prose in 1456 by Gilbert of the
Haye (the Abbotsford manuscript). For Haye's version of chapter 6, see pp.
xli–xlii. The most memorable literary example in Middle English perhaps is the
arming of Gawain in *SGGK*, though Chaucer's arming of Sir Thopas may be a
close second, with its mirror of mockery [*CT* (VII[(B²)] 857–87]. The attention
paid to the description of the arming contrasts interestingly with both the
undressing of the enchanted lady and her subsequent redressing as Lybeaus's
bride.

254   L: *A shelde with one cheferon.* N: *A schilde with on griffoun* (line 264). Only L varies
from the heraldic griffon at this point (but see note for line 93 above). C has
gryffoun (line 231); A: *gryffyn* (line 267); P: *griffon* (fol. 158v); and LI *griffown* (fol.
4r). Guinglain's shield in *LBD* has a "lion of ermine" emblazoned on it (line 74).
The shield hung around Lybeaus's neck by Gawain is significant, especially in
relation to its emblem. Noteworthy in this regard, as Hahn observes, may be "the
fifteenth-century depiction of a coat of arms composed of a green field
emblazoned with three gold griffins registered to 'SIR GAWAYNE *the good knyght*'
(Harleian MS 2169; this is reproduced in *The Ancestor: A Quarterly Review of County
and Family History, Heraldry and Antiquities* 3 [1902], p. 192" (*Sir Gawain*, p. 390).

257   L: *Sir Percyvale sett on his crowne.* N: *Sir Persevale set on his croun / A griffon he
brought with him* (lines 267–68). Gawain has just set a helmet on Lybeaus's head,
and Perceval seems to add a crest in the figure of a griffon, which is also the
heraldic animal depicted on his shield. This reference to a helmet crest is unique
to N. Helmet crests, although first devised in the twelfth century, became
fashionable in the fifteenth (Bradbury, *Routledge Companion to Medieval Warfare*,
p. 266). Chaucer appears to ridicule such pretensions in the Tale of Sir Thopas,
CT (VII[(B²)] 906–08): "Upon his creest he bar a tour, / And therrinne stiked a
lilie flour— / God shilde his cors fro shonde!"

260   L: *And a fell fauchone.* N: *And a fel fouchone* (line 270). For a good note on
falchions see Ewart Oakeshott's *European Weapons and Armour* and *The Sword in
the Age of Chivalry*. See also Oakeshott, *Archaeology of Weapons*, p. 235, and *Arms
and Armour of the Crusading Era 1050–1350*, by David Nicolle. The *MED* defines
a falchion as "A large, broad sword with a curved blade, a falchion; also, a short
stabbing-sword or dagger." The Middle English Breton lay *Sir Gowther* features
a falchion as a weapon that represents in part Gowther's identity and prowess.
As David Salter puts it in a chapter on the poem, this is a weapon that only
Gowther "is strong enough to wield" (*Holy and Noble Beasts*, p. 72).

264–66   L: *The knyght to hors gan sprynge / And rode to Arthure the kynge / And sayde, "My lorde
hende."* N: *The yong knyght to hors gan spring, / And rode to Arthour the kyng, / And
seid: "My lord so hynde"* (lines 274–76). N here agrees with L (and C, lines
241–42). According to Purdie (*Anglicising Romance*, p. 125n111), these lines link

LD to *Otuel and Roland*, lines 324–25. Lybeaus departs on the quest here with Elene and the dwarf, whereas in *LBD* he leaves the Arthurian court only with his squire Robert, as Helie and Tidogolain have already left (see note for lines 223–28 above). Throughout *LBD*, Squire Robert assists Li Biaus, but Squire Robert is not a character in *LD*.

270–71   L: *Arthur his honde up haffe / And his blessyng him gaffe.* N: *Arthour his hond up hafe, / And his blessyng he him yafe* (lines 280–81). The blessing by the king authorizes the mission. The upraised hand of a monarch with Arthur's authority is significant in itself, but to have a blessing (here more a sanctioning of the mission than a religious blessing) from him indicates his confidence in Lybeaus's ability to carry out his mission.

281–82   L: *Faste he gan to chide. / And saide, "Lorell, caytyfe."* N: *Ever sho gan to chide, / And seid: "Thou wrecche, thou caitife"* (lines 291–92). L seems in error here, since Elene is the one who needs to be convinced that Lybeaus is in fact a worthy knight, and since the dwarf has already made his opinion clear, his chiding seems superfluous. Like N, C also attributes the chiding to Elene: "sche be-gan to chyde" (line 258) as does LI, "schee gonne chide" (fol. 4), although in A and P, both Elene and the dwarf combine efforts ("gan thei chyd" [A, line 294] and "they gan to chide" [P, fol. 158v]). Helie also chides at this point in *LBD*.

288   L: *He hat Syr William Delaraunche.* N: *William Celabronche* (line 298). William's role as the first major opponent of Lybeaus is unique to the Middle English version of the poem. In *LBD*, Li Biaus's first opponent is Blioblïeris, guardian at the Perilous Ford (see Theodeley's/Deodelyne's "prophecy" earlier) (see note to lines 197–200). Blioblïeris seems to be a crusader; he wears "a silk tunic from the Holy land" over his hauberk (lines 357–58). Li Biaus defeats him and sends him to Arthur's court. However, his three companions, "Elin the fair, lord of Graie, / the strong knight of Saie, / and William of Salebrant" (lines 527–29) encounter him prior to his departure and seek to avenge his defeat. The English romance substitutes the name William Delaraunche/Celebronche for Blioblïeris, and his three companions become three unnamed kinsmen, probably because of the demands of rhyme scheme. "Celebronche" rhymes in N with "stonche" and "honche" and "lonche"; see also below, lines 376–77, where "Celebronche" again rhymes with "lonche." Later "William" rhymes with "schame" and "St. Jame" (lines 431, 433). "Blioblïeris," placed in the same rhyming position, would not rhyme so easily in English. As the main opponent, William is given a more expansive role in the ME version. Lybeaus's decision to fight against a knight who has just been described as "a werreour oute of wytt" (L, line 290) suggests Lybeaus's impetuosity and lack of experience in battle, if not in matters of mature deliberation. That he is victorious and does not kill his opponent in this version as he does in *LBD* places greater emphasis on William's importance as a witness to Lybeaus's growing prowess; he is expected to tell his story of defeat when he returns to Arthur's court. Also noteworthy is that *LD* appears in the Percy Folio along with *The Squire of Low Degree* in which there is a reference to Salebraunce, though in the *Squire* the name refers to a chapel where five battles are to be fought rather than to a person: "Than for to do these batayles fyve / At the

chapell of Salebraunce" (lines 624–25). See Kooper, *Sentimental and Humorous Romances*, pp. 127–79.

306–07   L: *He bare a shelde of grene / With three lyons of gold shene*. N: *He bare a schilde of grene / With three lions of golde schene* (lines 316–17). Heraldry is part of an elaborate sign system, a means by which knights could be identified even when their faces were covered by a visor and helmet. Colors, animal totems, design features, and other details signify the status, if not the identity, of the knight.

309   L: *Of sute lynnell and trappes*. N: *To suche lengels and trappis* (line 319). The sense here seems to be that the device of the lion on William's shield is replicated on the harness and trappings of his horse, a typical medieval practice.

314   L: *And sayde, "Welcome bewfere."* N: *And seid, "Welcome, Beaupere."* (line 324). William's familiar greeting seems to suggest that he knew Lybeaus was coming or perhaps that the young knight's distinctive physical features lend him a generic identity, thus prompting a remark akin to "hey, good lookin'."

368 ff.   L: short stanza. N: *A quarter fille to ground*; / *Sir Libeous in that stound* / *In hart he was agast* (lines 379–81). William has sliced away a quarter of Lybeaus's shield. C has a "kantell," which the *MED* (cantel) defines as "A chunk, piece, slice."

382   L: *For the love of Mary*. N: *For the love of Seint Marie* (line 395). William's call to the Virgin, the emblem of mercy, suggests his desperation. The act recalls Gawain's plea for aid from the icon of Mary painted inside his shield immediately after which Bercilak's castle appears in *SGGK* (lines 753–62).

395   L: *Thou shalt to Artor wende*. N: *Thou schalt to Arthour wynde* (line 408). Shuffelton suggests that "Arthur acts as both a lordly receiver of tribute and as a recording authority or audience who validates the accomplishments of the hero" (p. 477n411). He cites a discussion in Maddox's *Arthurian Romances of Chrétien de Troyes*, pp. 14–25.

400   L: *Lybeus Disconeus*. N: *Libeous Disconious* (line 413). The iteration of the hero's name in a line of its own calls attention to its significance. The name is repeated at several points in the poem and again at the end, thus trumping the number of times Gyngelayn is used (in L, four times including the incipit). Here the stress pattern guiding the pronunciation of the name appears to be Lýbeŭs Díscŏnéus. Contrast with line 423 following.

423   L: *Lybeus Disconeus he highte*. N: *Libious Disconious he hight* (line 436). The pronouncement of a name that literally signifies nothing recalls the scene in Homer's *Odyssey* in which Odysseus says his name is "nobody" when asked by the Cyclops who has just stolen his sheep and done injury to him. Medieval writers are not likely to have known Homer's epic poems directly but rather through Virgil's *Aeneid* and its retelling of the Trojan War. The *Lybeaus* poet frequently uses amphibrach (unstressed, stressed, unstressed syllables).

428   L: *And eke a well fayre berne*. N: *And eke a wel faire schene* (line 441).   The description here is of Lybeaus's squire, who is otherwise not a prominent player in the English version. In *LBD*, however, he has a name (Robert) and an identity

as a squire. That he is also a fair youth is in keeping with the emphasis on Lybeaus's level of maturity and good looks. The squire becomes something of a reflection of his knight. The equivalent line in N describes the lady "schene" who accompanies the knight.

430–31   L: *That he hathe made me swere / By his fauchone bryght.* N: *That he hath made me swore / Uppon his bronde bright* (lines 443–44). Chivalric society is dependent upon honor by word as well as deed, hence the importance of oaths. There is also an implicit threat in the falchion/brond.

451   L: *His hambrek we will to-rasshe.* N: *We schul his hauberk of bras* (line 464). The manuscripts disagree on what exactly the three knights will do with Lybeaus's hauberk. They will "to-rasshe" it, which Mills renders "tear to pieces" (L, line 451). P and A have them unlacing his hauberk ("unlace" in both). C does not have this line, and in LI the passage is missing. N's reading "of bras" makes sense, however. William's nephews do not accuse Lybeaus of having a hauberk made of an inferior metal (brass); rather the verb "bracen" can mean to seize or grasp, to impale, or to wrap or fasten together. The sense here suggests that the brothers threaten to "of bras," that is, unravel or break Lybeaus's chain mail to pieces.

452 ff. L: short stanza. N: also missing. Appears only in C as follows:

> Now lete we Wylyam be,
> Þat wente yn hys jorne
> Toward Artour þe Kyng.
> Of þese knyȝtes þre
> Harkeneþ, lordynges fre,
> A ferly fayr fyȝtynge.
> Þey armede hem full well
> Yn yren and yn stel,
> With-out ony dwellyng
> And leptede on stedes sterne
> And after gon y-erne
> To sle þat knyȝt so yenge.
> (lines 430–41)

454   L: *Syr Lybeus that yonge knyght.* N: *Ne Libeous, the gentil knyght* (line 467). While L emphasizes age, N emphasizes nobility.

458   L: *Gamen and grete solas.* N: *Game and grete solas* (line 471). It is unnecessary to understand the line as indicating, as Mills does, "a night of love-making" (*LD*, p. 58), a reading recently repeated by Shuffelton (p. 477n474) and Cory Rushton, "Absent Fathers, Unexpected Sons," p. 145. The innocence of the couple's mirth is evoked by the final line of the stanza, indicating that the dwarf served them "Of alle that worthi was" (L, line 464; N, line 477). For the argument countering the reading by Mills, see Weldon, "'Naked as she was bore,'" pp. 70–71.

470   L: *Rydynge from Carboun.* N: *Come ridyng fro Karlioun* (line 483). As suggested by N and the other versions, this is probably Caerleon, a small town in southeast Wales on the River Usk. According to the *NAE*, Caerleon is a castle important to Arthurian legend "as the place where Geoffrey of Monmouth has Arthur hold

a plenary court, after organizing the conquests made in his first Gallic campaign. Geoffrey may have chosen it simply because it was near his native Monmouth and he had seen the ruins, which in the twelfth century were still conspicuous" (*NAE*, p. 65).

488   L: *That he to-brake Gowers thiegh.* In C and L, the eldest brother is Gower; in A, he is Banerer; in P, Baner; and in N, Gawer (LI has a missing folio here). Also, in C, L, A, and P, Lybeaus breaks the eldest brother's thigh or leg, but in N, Lybeaus breaks his spine: *And brake his rigge bone* (line 500). In general, N presents Lybeaus as more aggressive and violent in his early formative adventures.

499–501   L: *Than loughe this mayden bright / And seide that this yonge knyght / Is chose for champyon.* N: *Than louge that maide bright / And seid: "This yong knyght / Was wel ychose champioun"* (lines 511–13). That Elene has finally been convinced of Lybeaus's capabilities as a knight is indicated in the sense of relief conveyed in her "loughe." That women often provide the encouragement for a knight's achievement can also take the form more traditionally associated with courtly love; the knight becomes a better combatant in arms when he fights for his beloved, at least in theory. Chrétien's *Lancelot* provides a study in how much power a lady (i.e., Guenevere) could have over her champion.

518   L: short stanza. N: *Sir knyght, bi Seint John* (line 527). Most probably this refers to John the Apostle, a privileged witness to special events in the Gospels, such as Christ's agony in the Garden. John was known for his ardent temper, and his invocation here would be appropriate in the context of Lybeaus's deadly prowess in his battle with the three nephews of William. See *ODOS*, p. 262. The oath by Saint John at this point in the text appears only in the N, A, P tradition. See also note to line 731 below.

581–82   L: *Thei dight a loge of leves, / With swerdys bryght and browne.* N: *Thei made a logge of levys / With swerdis bright and broun* (lines 593–94). The detail of making a lodge out of leaves and swords is not in *LBD*, but using their swords Bevis and Terri build a lodge of leaves for the pregnant Josian in *Bevis of Hampton* (see lines 3621–23).

586   L: *And evyr the dwerf can wake.* N: *And ever the dwarfe gan wake* (line 598). N streamlines the narrative here by omitting three lines in the C, L, A, LI, and P accounts, which attribute the dwarf's inability to sleep for fear of theft: L: *That nothinge shulde betake / Here hors aweye with gyle. / For dred he ganne quake* (lines 587–89).

597   L: *Be God and be Saint Gyle.* N: *By God and by Seint Gile* (line 606). Giles is the patron saint of cripples, lepers, and nursing mothers (see *ODOS*, p. 211). Saint Giles's shrine was on the pilgrim's route to Compostela. He founded a monastery at Saint-Gilles in Provence (*ODOS*, p. 211).

598–99   L: *Lybeous was stoute and fayre / And lepte upon his desteyre.* N: *Sir Libious was stout and gay, / And lepe on his palfray* (line 607–08). In *LBD*, combat with the giants takes place between Blioblïeris and his companions Elin of Graie, the lord of Saie, and William Salebrant. Also, after their defeat, the lord of Saie with the wounded Elin

(William has been killed) returns Clarie, the victim of the giants, to her family. In the ME version, Lybeaus takes Violet to her father himself. In Wace's *Roman de Brut*, a giant abducts Eleine, the niece of Arthur's kinsman, Hoel, and he carries her to Mont St. Michel, intending to rape her; she dies in the attempt. Arthur, Bedevere, and Kay interrupt the giant as he is roasting a wild boar on a spit, and Arthur kills him. (See Wace, *Wace's Roman de Brut*, ed. Weiss, lines 11287–560). The story is retold in the *Alliterative Morte Arthure*, where the giant not only slays a maiden but feasts on children. He has men and beasts roasting on spits when Arthur approaches him, and is more elaborately described in animal terms: "He grenned as a grayhound with grysly tuskes" (line 1075). See the description later of Maugis, who is also cast as a stereotypical subhuman giant. Although this episode is originally found in Geoffrey of Monmouth's *History of the Kings of Britain*, subsequent versions elaborated his representation of the giant, who is *not* portrayed in explicitly animal terms despite his animal behavior. Further, Geoffrey of Monmouth's scene of Arthur to the rescue on Mont St. Michel recalls the biblical story of David and Goliath, where the child David defeats the gargantuan threat to the Hebrew nation. One might say that these implications are suggested in every scene of giant slaying in medieval romance. Other exempla include *Bevis of Hampton*, *Guy of Warwick*, *Sir Launfal*, *Sir Degaré*, *Sir Eglamour of Artois*, and *SGGK*; Spenser's Orgoglio is the giant whose defeat moves Redcrosse into eventual recognition as a figure for St. George.

603   L: *Two gyauntes he sawe there.* N: *Two jeyauntis he founde at the last* (line 611). See Jeffrey Jerome Cohen's discussion of this scene in *Of Giants*, pp. 73–76.

604–05   L: *That one was rede and lothelych, / That other black as eny pyche.* N: *That one was blak as picche, / That othir rede and lotheliche* (lines 613–14). There has been considerable debate about whether the color of knights and the giants they fight refers to skin color or the color of armor. (A special issue of the *Journal of Medieval and Early Modern Studies* 31 [2001] contains a number of essays that address matters of race and ethnicity pertinent to a reading of otherness.)

607–08   L: *The black helde in his arme / A mayde i-clypped in his barme.* N: *The blake gan holde in barme / A feire maide bi the arme* (lines 616–17). There is an allusion here to Arthur's battle with the rapist giant of Mont St. Michel (see note to lines 598–99 above). In Wace's *Brut* (and in Geoffrey of Monmouth's *History*), the maiden dies during the giant's assault, and so does not suffer the indignity of rape. In *LBD*, the rape is interrupted, and the maiden does not die (see lines 707–16, p. 45), as is the case in *LD*.

609   L: *So bryght as blossom on brere.* N: *Bright so rose in brere* (line 618). This detail alludes to the flower (rose) on a branch in springtime, and evokes conventional female beauty. Although brief, it gestures to the rhetorical *effictio*, an elaborate description of (noble) feminine pulchritude consisting of stereotypical details arranged from head to toe (see Geoffrey of Vinsauf's *Poetria Nova*). Here the line metonymically suggests the conventional beauty of Violet. Later a similar phrase describes Lybeaus's mother in N: "Hur rode was rede so rys" (line 2234).

615   L: *For some man shuld it wit.* N: *For sum man schulde it wete* (line 621). This appears
        to be a legal term equivalent to "witness." In English law, witnessing a crime in
        the making required the witness to call attention to the deed by raising the hue
        and cry. The maiden's prayer to "Mary mylde" appears to be gender specific and
        notable in that way. As patron saint of childbirth, the Virgin Mary seems an odd
        choice, but, given the sexual nature of the threat and the Virgin's traditional
        function as mediatrix, perhaps all the more understandable.

626   L: *Hit is no childes game.* N: *It is no childis game* (line 635). According to the author
        of *Ratis Raving,* a child's game could include gathering flowers, building houses
        with sticks, making sailing ships with any available materials, making and dressing
        dolls or "poppets," and playing at sword fighting (among others). Many children's
        games were enacted in imitation of adult activities, including "war games" played
        by boys. (See Nicholas Orme, *Medieval Children,* especially chapter 5.) Since
        Lybeaus is still a "child" in terms of his chivalric experience, if not his specific age,
        depending on which version of the narrative one is reading, the reference here is
        significant. In L, C, LI, and P this line forms part of Lybeaus's speech. In N and
        A, however, the fearful observation that two of these grim foes pose a threat
        belongs to the narrator, not the hero. The N, A Lybeaus, in other words, appears
        more courageous and determined and less timid. Also noteworthy is the proverbial
        nature of the expression. According to Whiting C221 (p. 83), this line and
        variations on it appear in several ME narratives, including *Otuel and Roland,*
        Gregorius, Octavian, Tottenham, and old Januarie's lines in Chaucer's Merchant's
        Tale, *CT* (IV[(E)] 1530–31): "I warne yow wel, / it is no childes pley / To take a
        wyf," and *Le Morte Darthur.* The use of a related proverb in line 1683 (L) to
        describe how one of Lybeaus's opponents rocks in his saddle after their combat
        emphasizes the connection between chivalric readiness and maturity.

643–44 L: *And besought swete Jhesus / Helpe Lybeus Disconeus.* N: *And bisoughte Jhesus, / That*
        he wolde helpe Libeus Disconyous (lines 649–50). That Elene prays to Jesus for aid in
        helping Lybeaus underscores the specificity of the request for divine intervention.
        Here Mary is not asked to play her traditional role of mediatrix but rather her Son
        is called upon to intervene. When envisioned in his role as the sword-wielding
        apocalyptic Christ, this seems an appropriate choice for a knight.

646–47 L: *The rede gyaunte smote thore / To Sir Lybeous withe the bore.* N: *The rede geaunt*
        smote thore / To Libeous, with the wilde bore (lines 652–53). Mills (*LD,* 218n616–18)
        links this idea of the giant striking with a roasted boar on a spit to *Wace,* where
        a giant is roasting a *char de porc;* he sees the passage as perhaps inspiring this
        event in *LD.*

648   L: *As wolfe oute of wede.* N: *As wolfe that wolde of wede* (line 654). The poet deploys
        similes rather infrequently, and the repetition of this particular phrase at line
        986 in L calls attention to that fact. It may also be calling attention to a trope of
        the wild beast as a thematic concern of the poem, as well as a reality of medieval
        life in England. According to a relevant entry in *The Dictionary of Medieval Terms*
        and Phrases, "there were enough wolves in England during the reign of King
        John (1199–1216) for a bounty of 5s to be offered for their catching and killing.
        There are many AS placenames which indicate the presence of wolves, e.g.

Woolley in Yorkshire [<wolves' + OE leah=wood] and Woolmer in Hampshire, [<wolves' + OE mere=lake]. In 1209 two colts were killed and eaten by wolves in Hampshire. There are also sufficient records of wolves being caught in the king's forests to make it unsurprising that during the 1130s there were full-time royal wolf hunters, with a pack of two dozen hounds and also greyhounds. A wolf-catcher in Worcestershire in the early 13c was paid 3s a year. No records survive to show how many, if any, he caught, or whether indeed there were any wolves left in that part of England. Certainly, wolves were killing deer in the Forest of Dean in 1290s [*sic*]. Wolves appear to have survived in England until the 17c, and longer in Scotland" (ed. Corèdon and Williams, p. 300).

657 ff. L: short stanza. N: *The bore was ful hote than*; / *On Sir Libeous the grece ran* (lines 670–71). The detail of the hot grease causing a wound or pain as well as the extended description of the red giant reaching a height of fifteen feet appears in the N, A, and P tradition only (it does not occur in LI). Mills (*LD*, p. 218n657) compares this scene to one in the *First Continuation of Perceval* (*Continuations*, ed. W. Roach), where a knight strikes Sir Kay with a bird that has been roasting over the fire (see lines 9373–75).

657 L: *To quyte the gyaunte his mede*. N: *To yelde the geaunt his mede* (line 663). The exchange of blows is construed as payback and retribution, literal acts reversed by the notion of redemption. Coming on the heels of a plea for rescue, this line appears to be ironic.

662 L: *A tronchon oute he laught*. N: *A tronchon up he caught* (line 680). The giant demonstrates his strength by pulling a fully grown tree out of the ground. As he lifts it to deliver a blow, Lybeaus recognizes an opportunity to prune the limb by which the giant just uprooted the tree.

673 L: *In Frensshe as it is ifounde*. N: *In Frensche tale as it is found* (line 691). Although a convention of romance is to acknowledge a French source, whether or not it is the actual source, this is probably an allusion rather than an explicit reference to *LBD*. Shuffelton, who presumes Chestre to be the author of *LD*, comments: "Though this phrase suggests that Chestre is working directly from a French source, several factors limit the certainty of this interpretation. Several other manuscripts preserve entirely different readings of this line, and it is a common formula used by many other Middle English romances" (p. 477n699).

674–75 L: *He that he gave the fyrste wounde,* / *He servyd hym so aplyght*. N: *Tille that othir he went that stound* / *And servid him aplight* (lines 692–93). The idea of a "first wound" appears only in L. Mills (*LD*, p. 219n643–44) notes that N (C, A, P, LI) makes more sense here than L, which contradicts the earlier slaying of the black giant by suggesting that he had only been wounded by "the fyrste wound" (line 674). Mills argues for the superiority of L, however, by noting the repetition of the tag line in N, lines 690 and 693, "in þat stound" and "that stound," which suggests a scribal error of repetition. He also observes that "Chestre . . . [was] unconcerned to accommodate statements made in one part of his work with those found at another." The possibility of a scribal error with tags, however, does not invalidate the more sensible reading of N (C, A, P, LI).

676–77   L: *And then toke the hedis two / And bare the mayden thoo.* N: *Tho he toke hedis tway / And bare ham to that may* (lines 694–95). Lybeaus displays the severed trophy heads to a grateful maiden before sending them to Arthur's court. Cohen's comment is worth noting here: "Following the structure received from the David and Goliath story, the display of the conquered giant's head is often in its simplest terms part of the rite de passage from boyhood to manhood, from mistakes and potential ambiguity into the certainties of stable masculinity" (*Of Giants*, p. 73).

690   L: *His name is Syr Anctour.* This line in which Violet names her father is missing in N. Mills's note on Anctour is useful: "The name of this character recalls the Antore who in AM 9751 meets his death at the hands of giants, but in his function he more closely resembles the aged father of Enide (E 375 *in passim*). The corresponding figure in BD [*LBD*, i.e., *Li Biaus Descouneüs*] is not characterized at all (see 892), but in Platin's *Giglan* he is described as *ancien*, and it seems possible that the name in LD [*LD*, i.e., *Lybeaus Desconus*] may have arisen from a contracted form of the adjective *anci(e)nor* (? *ancīor* l. ivv) in the OF source. But whatever the provenance of the name it was sufficiently unfamiliar to be replaced by that of Arthur in two of the less reliable texts of LD. . . . This king is also associated with the scene in the version given of it in the *Didot Perceval*, since the giant there waits for the girl's father to set out for Arthur's court, before abducting her" (p. 219n660). According to the entry in the *AND*, Antor (with variations of spelling including Antore, Antour, Anton, and Entor) is "Arthur's foster-father, and the father of Kay, in the Prose and Vulgate *Merlins*, the Didot-*Perceval*, and Tennyson. Robert de Boron seems to have originated the character . . . [where] Antor raised Arthur after Merlin presented him with the child. . . . His character appears in the Post-Vulgate and Malory as Ector" (p. 28). J. D. Bruce suggests that the origin of the name lies in a possible corruption of Arthur, "given the literary tradition of naming children after their foster fathers" (*AND*, p. 28). As Shuffelton notes, "A character with a similar name (Antor, Antour) appears in several Arthurian romances as Arthur's foster father and the father of Kay the Seneschal. See *The Erle of Tolous* (Shuffelton item 19), line 853 and note. Perhaps the name is meant to evoke loose associations of benevolent paternity" (p. 477n716). The name of Violet's father in L is Anctour (line 690) or Antore (C, line 3660), Anter (A, line 716), Antory (LI, line 372), or Arthore (P, line 723 fol. 161v. [Cooper line 72]). The omission in N appears to be an error because later reference is made to Lybeaus donning armor, "That the erle of Auntouris was" (N, line 804). Only C preserves a stanza in which the earl offers Lybeaus his daughter in marriage, which Lybeaus refuses. Mills (*LD*, p. 220n688–99) argues for the authenticity of this stanza on the basis of content and rhyme scheme. However, in *LBD*, the maid's name is Clarie, and she is taken back to her unnamed father's castle by the surviving nephews of Blioblïeris (the events are different). The passage authenticated by Mills, in other words, may not be authentic at all. It does not appear in the original and exists only in C. Mills (p. 221n688–99) locates the origin of the offer of Violet to Lybeaus in the episode of the gerfalcon in *Erec et Enide*, in which Erec expresses his wish to marry the host's daughter, Enide.

691   L: *They clepen me Violet*. N: *Mi name is Violette* (line 709). In a scene that recalls the beginning of the poem, the maiden is asked to identify herself. Unlike Lybeaus she is able to name her father (except in N), and she describes him as "of riche fame" (L, line 686) The name of the lady is unusual, and the only other reference appears to be Violet the Bold, "one of many ladies at King Arthur's court to fail a chastity test involving a magic goblet" (*AND*, p. 488). Gerbert de Montreuil, who wrote the continuation of Chrétien de Troyes's *Perceval*, has a romance called *Roman de la Violette* (c. 1220), where the heroine has a birthmark resembling a violet. Jean Froissart wrote *La plaidoirie de la rose et de la violette*, an allegorical debate between two courtly ladies, one of whom is named Violette.

698   L: *Oute of the busshes con sprynge*. N: *Out of a busche gan sprynge* (line 716). The description of Violet's abduction recalls the abduction of Guenevere by Meleagant, though here it is construed as an ambush done without much premeditation. Mills notes that "Chestre's account seems to have been influenced by the later scene at the Île d'Or, in which he tells how another black giant (Maugrys) besieges a city to gain possession of a lady (lines 1243–51): this modification makes it seem strange that Vyolette should wander about, so freely and unsuspectingly, on her own" (*LD*, p. 220n661–66). The idea that a giant lurks in the bushes conventionally associates him with rural, uncivilized, even nonhuman behaviors and values. See the description of Maugis/Maugus below.

713–14   L: *To Kynge Arthour in present, / With mekyll glee and game*. N: *To Kinge Arthour, in present, / With moche gle and game* (lines 731–32). The severed heads are sent to the court as proof of Lybeaus's prowess and growing reputation. The "glee and game" here indicate something of a victory celebration.

717 ff.   L: short stanza. N: also missing. The passage is supplied here by C:

> The Erl Antore also blyue
> Profrede hys doftyr hym to wyue:
> Vyolette that may;
> And kasteles ten and fiue
> And all after hys lyue
> Hys lond to haue for ay.
> Than seyde Lybeaus Desconos,
> "Be the loue of swete Jhesus,
> Naught wyue yet Y ne may;
> J haue for to wende
> Wyth thy mayde so hende.
> And therfore, haue good day!"
> (lines 688–99)

719   L: *Yave him full riche mede*. N: *Gave Sir Libeous to mede* (line 737). The earl rewards Lybeaus with armor and a horse tested "in turnament and in fyght" (L, line 723). These items are notable for their material value, but also stand as an indication of a formal recognition of Lybeaus's status as a knight. See note to line 690 above.

727 ff.   L: The adventure of the knight with the gerfalcon begins here. Compare N, 745 ff. In *LBD*, the adventure with Otis precedes the gerfalcon story. Renaut's source for his version of the story is the sparrowhawk episode in Chrétien de Troyes's

Erec et Enide. In *LBD*, Helie, Robert the Squire, and the dwarf spy a castle, Becleus, and on their journey, they come upon a maiden (Margerie) whose lover-knight has been killed. She explains to them the conditions set by the lord of the castle, Giflet (French Giflés), son of Do: any maiden who dares take the beautiful sparrowhawk that sits on a golden perch must have a knight willing to claim her to be the most beautiful maiden of all. He will then be challenged by the lord of the castle. The party proceeds to where the sparrowhawk sits, and Li Biaus asks Margerie to take it. The lord of the castle appears with his beloved, Rose Espanie; he defends her position as the most beautiful of women, despite the fact that she is "ugly and wrinkled" (*LBD*, line 1727). Li Biaus defeats him. In *LD*, the hero's motive for the challenge lies neither in revenge for past personal insult, as in *Erec and Enide*, nor to avenge the wrong committed against a maiden, as in *LBD*, but in Lybeaus's personal sense of adventure, a motive criticized by the dwarf. Margerie and Robert disappear in *LD*, and decapitation becomes the loser's reward. Mills (*LD*, pp. 220–21n.L 750–53) contends that decapitation, which makes the episode more forbidding, has been transferred from Renaut's later episode with Malgiers.

731   L: *Suche sawe he never none*. N: *Suche sawe he never none* (line 749). Although opulent and marvelous castles are common in romance, Lybeaus's lack of chivalric experience and his early life in the woods away from Arthur's court help to explain his awestruck response, "Be Seynt John!" (L, line 733; N, line 751).

744   L: *He hathe done crye and grede*. N: *He had do crye and grede* (line 762). The phrase suggests an official and public announcement, here of a challenge to combat.

746   L: *A gerfawkon, white as swanne*. N: *A jerefawken as white as swane* (line 764). Possibly the white gerfalcon of Iceland (*MED*), a large hawk used for hunting and much prized. This hunting bird is a substantial reward for what amounts to a beauty contest between Lybeaus's lady and the lady of his opponent, Jeffron. Like people, birds of prey were often classified in a hierarchical system. According to Richard Almond, "The basic division in the manual is between *hawks of the tower* and *hawks of the fist*, which conveniently corresponds largely to the falcons (*Falconidae*) and the hawks (*Accipitridnae*). The short-winged hawks were more popular with the French whereas the long-winged hawks, generically falcons, were more favoured in England. The latter birds include the peregrine, merlin and hobby, all of which were, and still are, used by falconers to fly at live quarry. *Roy Modus*'s division differs somewhat from the basic classification. He places the peregrine falcon, lanner, saker and hobby as hawks of the tower, whereas the goshawk, sparrow hawk, gyrfalcon and merlin are classed as hawks of the fist" (*Medieval Hunting*, p. 42). This episode of the gerfalcon, while in *LBD*, is likely to have derived from Chrétien de Troyes's *Erec et Enide*.

754 ff. L: short stanza. N: *Ther stont on every cornelle* (line 773). Mills translates C's "karnell" — "Ther stant yn ech a karnell" (line 737)—as battlement. The word means corner or angle, or the front of a building (*MED*).

757   L: *By God and Saint Michelle*. N: *Bi God and bi Seint Mighelle* (line 776). This
         probably refers to Michael, the avenging archangel and principal combatant
         against the dragon/devil of Apocalypse. Perhaps not surprisingly, given the
         Arthurian themes of this narrative, his most famous shrine is Mont Saint Michel,
         celebrated as a place of divine judgment in *The Alliterative Morte Arthur*, where,
         according to the *ODOS*, "a Benedictine abbey was founded in the 10th century"
         (p. 349).

761   L: *A lemman two so bright*. N: *A lemman two so bright* (line 780). This beauty contest
         motif is also present in *Sir Launfal* when Tryamour and her ladies are compared
         to Guenevere (Gwenore) who has insulted Launfal and made a false accusation,
         thereby necessitating a trial. Because Launfal has broken his pledge of discretion
         and silence to Tryamour, he is no longer able to call upon her for aid. The
         outcome of the trial will depend on whether his claim of a lady more beautiful
         than Guenevere is true.

768   L: *Jeffron le Freudous*. N: *Geffron le Frediens* (line 787). All manuscripts have
         trouble with this name; C: Gyffroun le Fludous (line 772) or Flowdous (line 751);
         L: Jeffron le Freudous (line 768) or Freudys (line 789); LI: Jeffron le Frondous
         (fol. 8v); A: Gefferon lefrondeus or lefrendeus (fol. 46r); P: Giffron la ffrandous
         (fol. 162r), and Cooper, line 802, has Giffron La ffraudeus. In *LBD*, the knight's
         name is Giflés, li fius Do (line 1805). Mills notes that "Gyffroun is in himself one
         of the most polite and reasonable of all the hero's antagonists" (*LD*, p.
         221n785–89). While Jeffron is clearly more chivalrous than the other
         antagonists, "polite" and "reasonable" are perhaps exaggerations.

785   L: *That Er Aunctours was*. N: *That the erle of Auntouris was* (line 804). This refers
         to the earl Antore mentioned earlier in L, C, and A as the father of Violet but
         omitted in N. The bestowing of the earl's armor upon Lybeaus, however, is
         mentioned at N, lines 736–38, so N's omission of the earlier passage is likely an
         error. See note to line 690.

794   L: *Come prickande with pryde*. N: *Come prikyng as prins in pride* (line 813). The
         resonance of this with Spenser's Redcrosse Knight, who goes pricking across the
         plain at the beginning of Book 1 of the *Faerie Queene*, is worth noting, though
         there is no evidence that Spenser knew *LD*. To "prick" means to spur a horse to
         move at a quicker pace, but also connotes "distress," "grief," "goading," or
         "urging to action" as used in the devotional work, *The Prick of Conscience*.

805   L: *Ther is no woman so white*. N: *That woman is none so white* (line 824). The color
         gestures to the conventional *effictio*, the formal rhetorical description of ideal
         beauty, where "white" signals the delicacy of a woman's skin rather than its color.
         Thus the line means "that no woman is as beautiful."

817   L: *In Cordile cité with sight*. N: short stanza. The site is probably Cardiff as is the
         case with Cardyle in L, line 830. Variant spellings are: Cardelof, Cardull, Karlof,
         Cardeuyle, Kardeuyle, Kardill, Karlill, Cardigan. Shuffelton speculates that the
         city is "[p]ossibly Carlisle, in northern England," but, as Mills argues, the Welsh
         city of Cardiff is more likely (Shuffelton, p. 478n844; *LD*, p. 222n800).

837   L: *And hit the mayde Elyne*. N: *And seide to maide Elyne* (line 853). Lybeaus's election
          of Elene to the role of substitute maiden differs from source and cognate tales.
          Chrétien's *Erec* selects his host's daughter, Enide, whom he later marries, as his
          fair maiden to champion in the contest. *LBD* has the wronged Margerie claim
          the sparrowhawk for him so that he can avenge her. Lybeaus, however, has
          neither love nor justice as a motive here; his is a subterfuge that allows him to
          meet his opponent in combat and utilize chivalry to promote himself and his
          reputation.

850   L: *Thow doste a savage dede*. N: *Nowe is this a wondir dede* (line 866). The wise dwarf
          in L reminds the still-churlish Lybeaus that this is not what chivalry is supposed
          to be, whereas in N he reminds Lybeaus that he is not evincing appropriate
          adult (chivalric) male behavior. Using ladies as tournament prizes undermines
          the central tenets of chivalry, that is, to honor ladies and fight on their behalf,
          and to champion their causes, especially if they involve unlawful captivity. This
          is the damsel-in-distress motif so prevalent in Arthurian romance. This stanza
          is not in C. N and A draw attention to inexperience and youth, L, to churlishness
          and madness (*madd hede*, line 853).

854   L: *As lorde that will be lorne*. N: *As man that wolde be ylore* (line 870). Despite the
          apparent similarity between L's "lorne" and N's "ylore," the two words are
          different. L's "lorne" means "lost," as the dwarf chastizes Lybeaus for acting
          mad, as someone who is either "lost" mentally or a suicide (running toward
          certain death). N, however, alters the charge of madness to childishness; the
          dwarf accuses Lybeaus of juvenile behavior, acting as a schoolboy who has yet to
          learn something of value.

857   L: *And in Bedlem was borne*. N: *That we ne come him bifore* (line 873). L's reference
          to Bethlehem and the birth of the Christ Child points to an archetypal event that
          underscores the religious ideals of chivalry, that is, humility and obedience to
          one's Lord, even when He appears in the body of an infant. This will stand in
          stark contrast to the necromancers depicted later. Lybeaus's response here
          indicates his misunderstanding of these chivalric ideals (much akin to Perceval's
          early misunderstanding of the purpose of the Grail quest) and his sensitivity to
          the imputation of his prowess.

861   L: *The mayde Ellyne, also tighth*. N: *That maide feire and fre* (line 877). Mills (*LD*, p.
          222n844–91) notes similarities between this description of Elene and Dame
          Tryamour in *Sir Launfal*. The description of Elene's attire, ornamentally
          beautified with precious metals, jewels, and furs, indicates the wealth supporting
          Elene, perhaps provided by her lady, the queen of north Wales, also known as
          the Lady of Synadoun. The rest of Elene's attire reflects the "best" of the
          "empire" she represents, that is, North Wales. L adds to her apparel "a robe of
          samyte" (line 862), a costly fabric that enhances her appearance even further.

885–87   L: *He bare ... gold the bordure*. N: *He bare ... golde was the border, ryngid with floris*
          (lines 901–03). Although the details differ, both texts offer a depiction of
          Jeffron's heraldic device; heraldry and its emblems were an important means by
          which identity could be ascertained when a knight was unknown and his face was

covered by a visor. The description of the shield, like the description of the ladies' attire, typically signals allegiance to a court and kinship group. Its obvious display of material wealth suggests the high standing of the knight in his relation to the court. See notes to lines 93 and 254 above.

898–99   L: *A lady proude in pryde, / Iclothed in purpyll palle.* N: *A lady ful of pride, / Yclothid in purpul palle* (lines 914–15). The description of Jeffron's lady differs somewhat from the description of Elene. Jeffron's lady wears purple, while Elene wears white. In her edition of *LBD*, Karen Fresco adds that "purple was a rare and costly fabric, probably made out of silk imported from Tyre and Alexandria. It came in several colors and seems to have been worn by royalty. In *LBD* only Blonde Esmeree, a princess, wears *popre*" (p. 393n3279). In *LD* there is also an elaborate description of the lady's rosy complexion and her blond hair, "as gold wyre shynynge bryght." Blond hair is considered desirable in ladies of medieval romance in general, but in the French version hair color is particularly important as indicated by the name of *LBD*'s Lady of Synadoun, that is, la Blonde Esmeree. For a classical medieval description of idealized female beauty, see Geoffrey of Vinsauf's *Poetria Nova*, pp. 36–37.

912   L: *Hir browes also blacke as sylke threde.* N: *Hur browys as silken threde* (line 928). Well-shaped, clearly separated, and darkly colored eyebrows were considered a sign of beauty, as were gray eyes, milky white complexion, and an elongated "swyre," that is, neck. A woman's eyebrows, if not separated but rather as one continuous growth across the forehead, were considered a sign of sexual promiscuity. There is an interesting contrast to be made with the later description of the eyebrows of the Saracen giant Maugis.

930–31   L: *Ellyne the messangere / Ne were but a lawnder.* N: *Elyne the mesynger / Nas but a lavender* (lines 946–47). When it becomes apparent that Elene cannot win this beauty contest, an unflattering comparison to a laundrywoman ensues. In *Erec et Enide*, the sparrowhawk contest over the most beautiful woman resides less in the relative merits of each woman and more in the power of love to influence the judgment of lovers. Renaut takes this idea to an extreme in that Giflet's damsel is truly ugly, so that there is no real contest between her and Margerie; instead, Renaut's narrator marvels at how "love could so disturb his judgment . . . for Love makes the ugliest woman seem a beauty"(lines 1731,1734). In *LD*, by contrast, the contest is real, and onlookers declare that Elene, though fair, is much less beautiful than Jeffron's maiden. Unlike Jeffron (or Erec or Giflet), however, Lybeaus is not in love; only pride motivates him here. This is the first of two or three episodes that project weakness or bad judgment by the hero (see note to line 837 above). The mistaken motives are also marked by Lybeaus's severely violent defeat of Jeffron, who has his "rigge tobrake" (N, line 1006; L, line 990, "Geffrounes backe to-brake"), the same excessive result of violence inflicted upon one of William's nephews earlier, so that he has to be carried to town on his shield. Shuffelton notes that "In comparison to other versions of this motif, the outcome here is surprising. Usually the hero's lady is judged more beautiful, prompting a combat to settle the dispute. Though Elyne has been described as *bryght, schene*, and *sembly* (lines 120–32), perhaps her beauty is downplayed here so that Lybeaus's attempt to win the falcon seems all the more rash" (p. 478n953).

944   L: *Magré thyne hede, hore* (so, too, C, line 915). N: compare line 960. In agreement with L, C has "*Maugre thyne heed hore*" (line 915) and LI, "*Mawgre thy berd hore*" (Cooper line 513; fol. 8v), whereas in agreement with N, P has "*Maugre thy head indeed*" (Cooper line 978; fol. 163r) and A, *Thoff thou be wroth therforn* (line 971); LI, C, and L imply that Geffron is an older or an old man, which does not make sense here.

951–52   L: *Her shaftis brosten asondre, / Her dyntis ferden as thonder.* N: *Here schaftis brake in sondir, / Hare dyntis fyrde as dondir* (lines 967–68). The sound and fury signifies the intensity of this confrontation between the brash young upstart and his experienced opponent.

960   L: *This yonge frely freke.* N: *So this yonge freke* (line 976). The description here likely is more positive than it appears to be to modern readers since "frely freke," according to the *MED*, denotes the fair, noble, freeborn knight rather than the more negatively construed modern word for one who resides outside the norm in terms of appearance or behavior, that is, "freak."

967–68   L: *As Alysaunder or Kyng Arthur, / Lawncelot or Syr Percevalle.* N: *As Alexaundre or Kyng Arthour, / Launselake or Persevale* (lines 983–84). The comparison to these particular figures, all of whom had similar childhood experiences and a distinctive fearlessness in combat, underscores one of the central themes of romance, that is, that even those fairly unknown can acquire a legitimate place in the annals of literary history, if not history itself. The *enfances* of *LD* is often compared to the *enfances* of Sir Perceval of Galles; both are examples of the fair unknown motif and both men come to Arthur's court knowing little of chivalry. That all these historic icons are products of a traumatic or atypical childhood appears to be a prerequisite of transformation in narratives of heroic triumph.

986   L: *As wolfe that wolde at wede.* N: *As a man that wolde of wede* (line 1002). The shift from wolf to man signals recognition of a proverbial expression and alters the more typical and negative aphorism of a wolf in sheep's clothing. (See note for line 648.)

1000   L: *Was borne home on his shelde.* N: *Geffron in his schilde / Was ybore out of the filde* (lines 1015–16). Carrying bodies off the field using a shield as a stretcher is an ancient practice, maybe one reason shields were designed to be as large as possible. See also note for line 488.

1003   L: *By a knyght that hight Cadas.* N: *Bi a knyght that hight Clewdas* (line 1019). This may refer to Cadoc the king who "fought in a Castle of Maidens tournament, where he was defeated by Gawain's son Guinglain" in Renaut's version (*AND*, p. 93, s.v. "Cadoc"). In A, this character is named Lucas; other variants are Gludas (C), Caudas (LI), and Chaudas (P).

1011–13   L: *He hathe sent me . . . he fyrst byganne.* N: *He hath sende me . . . Sithe he furst bigan* (lines 1027–29). Arthur's recognition of Lybeaus's deeds vis-à-vis the "trophies" he sends back to the court points to the central tenet of feudal relations, that is, the king's duty to reward his knights and the knight's duty to fight on behalf of the king. Lybeaus has fought, at this point, William, his three nephews, two giants, and Jeffron: seven opponents in four battles.

1019   L: *Kardill towne*. N: *Karlille toune* (line 1035). This refers to Carlisle, the chief residence of King Arthur, or perhaps Cardiff. See note for line 817.

1034–35   L: *For youre frely sale*: / *Hit blowis motis jolelye*. N: *Fer yere ferly falle!* / *Sir Otis hit blewe, de la Ile* (lines 1050–51). The dwarf, presumably speaking to Elene, recognizes the sound of the horn as coming from the vicinity of Synadoun, thus signaling the company's progress. This marks the beginning of the episode with Sir Otis de Lile (or de la Ile), once a loyal servant of the Lady of Synadoun, who has since abandoned her to her fate. As Mills notes, this name is equivalent to Orguillous de la Lande, the huntsman knight of Renaut's *LBD*, line 1486, whose name translates to "Proud Knight of the Glade." In *LBD*, the story of the hunter (*li venere*) and the brachet takes place before the adventure of the sparrowhawk. Clarie, the maiden rescued from giants by Li Biaus, catches up with him and his party. They spy a stag followed by hunting dogs with a small brachet trailing behind. Clarie picks up the brachet, saying that she will take the dog to her lady, when the hunter rides up and demands the return of his brachet. In this version, Li Biaus attempts to persuade Clarie to return the brachet, but she refuses, and at this point the hunter conspires to take the dog back by force. One might compare this situation to Malory's Torre and Pellinore, a section in which knights go out to claim hounds or deer that belong to someone else, resulting in deaths and destruction that call into question the tenets of chivalry. In *LD*, the hero seems more at fault for having given Elene the brachet himself and therefore he is completely responsible for refusing to return it to Otis, once more placing himself in the wrong. In *LBD*, Orguillous de la Lande attacks Li Biaus alone, whereas in *LD*, Sir Otis later waylays Lybeaus with a host of knights; this proves to be his most difficult combat yet, one in which he is seriously wounded. Mills (p. 226n1009) points out that the name in *LD* may derive from Duke Otus, who in *Guy of Warwick* is Guy's entrenched enemy.

1040   L: *West into Wyralle*. N: *West into Wirale* (line 1056). This refers to what was known as the Wilderness of Wirral, a forested area northwest of Liverpool, next to Wales. Gawain finds himself in the "wyldrenesse of Wyrale" (line 701) in *SGGK*.

1042   L: *They sawe a rache com renynge*. N: *Ther come a rache rennyng* (line 1058). Unlike the greyhound bred to hunt by sight, this breed of dog hunts by scent.

1047   L: *He was of all coloures*. N: *For he was of alle colours gay* (line 1063). Although N indicates the variegated colors of the canine, "of alle colours gay," missing from this short stanza are the lines that complete the description, "That man may se of floures / Bytwene Mydsomer and Maye" (L, lines 1048–49).

       As Mills (*LD*, p. 227n1021–23) suggests, the description of the brachet may reflect the multicolored Peticrewe in *Sir Tristrem*: "He was rede, grene and blewe" (line 2404), although in that narrative the animal is not a hunting dog but a lap dog presented to Duke Gilan of Wales by one of the goddesses of Avalon. The bell around its neck was thought to bring happiness to the owner of the dog, hence Isolde, in her efforts to be as unhappy as Tristan, rips it off. Lybeaus's chasing of the diminutive canine recalls a similar episode in Chaucer's *Book of the Duchess*, only there the attention-getting whelp leads the dreamer to a grieving knight (lines 386–449). References to this particular breed of dog appear also in other notable ME romances (see Lupack, *Lancelot of the Laik and Sir Tristrem*, pp. 224–25, lines 2399–2420).

1048   L: *That man may se of floures*. This line is missing in N, but the sense survives there without it, namely that the many colors are those nature brings forth between Midsummer and May (see below).

1049   L: *Bytwene Mydsomer and Maye*. N: *Bitwene Mydsomer and May* (line 1064). Mid-summer, usually in June, marked a time of festive celebration of the longest day of the year.

1083   L: *Quod Sir Otis de Lile*. N: *Quod Sir Otis de la Ile* (line 1098). Mills identifies this name as equivalent to l'Orguillous de la Lande, the huntsman knight of *LBD*, line 1486 (Mills, *LD*, p. 236; Fresco, p. 88). The name may also refer to the treacherous Duke Otoun in *The Stanziac Guy of Warwick*. In A, this character is named Otys de la Byle. See note to line 1034 above.

1088   L: *Chorle*. N: *Chourle* (line 1103). The use of *churl* here suggests Lybeaus's own lack of training in the finer points of courtesy. He resorts to name-calling to which Otis responds with verbal indignation and an identification of just who his parents were, that is, "My fader an erle was . . . the countesse of Carlehille, / Forsothe, was my dame" (lines 1092–93). Shuffelton notes that "Rate's spelling of the insult, *carle*, and the place name, *Carlehyll* has created a little joke here, perhaps inspired by another Middle English romance, *Sir Gawain and the Carle of Carlisle*" (p. 478n1120).

1108   L: *Rode home to his toure*. N: *Rode home in that schoure* (line 1123). N's phrase is a variation of "a god schoure," that is, quickly.

1117–18   L: *Though he were the grymmer grome / Than Launcelet de Lake*. N: *Though he were also stronge / As Launcelet de Lake* (lines 1132–33). The comparison here is interesting, since Lancelot is known as much for his fierce loyalty and devotion to Guenevere as he is for his fierceness in battle. So too the term refers to Lybeaus's immaturity. The *MED* defines *grome* as ranging in meaning from "infant" to "boy" to "young man" as well as social ranking: "A man of low station or birth; also, a worthless person."

1146   L: *arblast*. N: *areblast* (line 1161). This is a synonym for a crossbow as well as a term for the missile discharged from the weapon.

1153   L: *This is the devyll Satan*. N: *Here comyth the devil Satan* (line 1168). Another example of misidentification and name-calling; this name is often used in romance to describe giants, heretics, and pagan others.

1161   L: *For twelve knyghtis, all prest*. N: *Twelve knyghtis prest* (line 1176). There is a distinct imbalance between opposing sides here.

1179–80   L: *Lybeous slowe of hem three, / The fourthe begon to flee.* N: *And four awey gan fle* (line 1194). N omits a line here and changes the text so that *four* flee rather than the *fourth*.

1183   L: *And his sonnes foure.* N: *And his sonnys fowre* (line 1197). Mills notes that "the huntsman's sons are not mentioned in any of the cognates," and he cites a similar passage in *Bevis of Hampton*: "Two ffosters he smote adowne / Wyth the dynte of hys tronchon / vi he slewe at dyntys thre / And odur vi away can flee" (*LD*, p. 229n1153–58). Shuffelton observes that "The appearance of Sir Otys's sons is not otherwise mentioned, and seems an afterthought on the part of Chestre" (p. 478n1210).

1186   L: *He one agaynes fyve.* N: *He alone ayenst fyve* (line 1200). The imbalance between oppositions heightens the degree of aggression and makes the next line — *Faughte as he were wode* — necessity rather than the hyperbole typical of chivalric romance. As the scene suggests, getting into a state of battle frenzy enables Lybeaus to overcome the inequity. He is even able to kill three horses, one stroke each. In this instance, Lybeaus does not balk at being outnumbered, as he did when faced with two giants.

1194   N: Short stanza. See L, lines 1180 ff.

1202   L: *Bothe mayle and plate.* N: *Throwe helme and basnet plate* (line 1216). That Lybeaus is able to cut through chain mail or helmet as well as steel-plated armor suggests his extraordinary strength. Just as Havelok the Dane demonstrates his manpower in feats of strength that later enable him to reclaim his patrimony and avenge the death of his sisters, so too Lybeaus demonstrates his martial prowess. Havelok, unlike the others, goes through a number of contests literally designed to test his strength as a man, not as a knight. He is also described as taller than other men.

1217   L: *Under a chesteyne tree.* N: *Undir a chesteyne tre* (line 1231). As Mills aptly observes "the submission of one character to another under a (chestnut) tree occurs in a number of romances. Sometimes the dominating character possesses supernatural powers, as in *Sir Gowther*. . . where a fiend begets a child on a lady; sometimes both characters are human, as in *Le Bone Florence*" (*LD*, p. 230n1189–94). Other romances in which this motif may be found include *The Erle of Tolous*, *Bevis of Hampton*, and *Sir Orfeo*.

1247   N: short stanza. See L, lines 1233 ff.

1263   L: *Kynge Arthur had gode game.* N: *Kyng Arthour had good game* (line 1274). Arthur's delight in storytelling prior to sitting down to a meal is extended to his reception of prisoners. The submission and recounting of the narrative and the knight responsible for the defeat contributes to Lybeaus's burgeoning reputation, a necessity for a knight who needs to prove himself. Lybeaus's growing list of credentials convinces the king that he has chosen wisely. This is the first instance where Arthur and the court recognize Lybeaus as an accomplished knight of the Round Table.

1269–71   L: *Nowe rest we here a while / Of Sir Otys de Lyle / And tell we forthe oure talis*. N: *Rest we nowe a while / Of Sir Otys de la Ile / And telle we of othir talis* (lines 1280–82). As is typically found in tail-rhyme romance, these lines mark a transition from one episode to the next.

1273–74   L: *And sey awntours the while / And Irlande and in Walys*. N: *In Cornewaile and in Walis* (line 1285). Requisite adventures for the aspiring knight are suggested here. Although crossing the Irish Sea is not a formidable challenge to the resourceful knight, the link between these two Celtic kingdoms is a feature of Arthurian literature, particularly the Tristan thread. Both N and A place Lybeaus's adventures in Cornwall and Wales, whereas P has him in England and Wales. L and C place him in Ireland and Wales. A journey to Ireland would take Lybeaus out of his way, and there is no such itinerary in any of the sources. Mills, following Schofield, sees the reference to Ireland as a misunderstanding of a source passage, suggesting that C and L represent the author's line (*LD*, p. 231n1222–24). N, A, and P, however, place Lybeaus within the conventional settings for Arthurian adventures and offer a more reasonable and typical area of sojourn rather than an extended period of quest such an Irish journey would require. See also the note for line 1479 below, where N also reduces the amount of time Lybeaus spends with Dame Amoure / Diamour. These are examples of N (and often A, P) revising or correcting the excesses of the other manuscripts' details (see Mills, "Mediaeval Reviser").

1276   L: *Whan fenell hangeth al grene*. N: *Whan levys and buskis ben grene* (line 1287). L's specific reference to fennel refers to a perennial plant described in one of the quotations in the *MED* as having a "double manner of kynde, wilde and tame" (p. 487). Although less specific, N, too, marks a shift in the narrative with a shift in seasons, when leaves and bushes were green; see Malory's opening of "The Knight of the Cart" and "Slander and Strife" in *Le Morte Darthur*.

1280   L: *And notis of the nyghtyngale*. N: *Of the nyghtingale* (line 1291). Nightingales have long been associated with pivotal moments in romance narrative. In Marie de France's *Laüstic*, the songbird provides an excuse for the lovers to communicate at night. When the jealous husband discovers the ruse, he kills the bird and throws its body at his wife, staining her white chemise with blood. In Chaucer's *Troilus and Criseyde* (Book 2, line 918), the nightingale sings outside Criseyde's window as she dreams of the white eagle who steals away her heart. There the mirage is ominous in that it recalls the allusion to the myth of Philomela and Procne at the outset of the fated day (Book 2, lines 64–70).

1290   L: *Men clepeth this Il de Ore*. N: *Men clepith hit Il d'Ore* (line 1301). Literally the Isle of Gold or Golden Isle, this place appears in *LBD* as the island replete with a castle belonging to the Maiden of the White Hands (la Pucele as Blances Mains); in *LD*, the castle belongs to Dame Amoure/Diamour, whose name evokes the seductive love she will later proffer Lybeaus.

1291   L: *Here be fightis more*. N: *Ther hathe ybe fighting more* (line 1302). P (line 1337) reads: "*There hath beene slaine knights more*" (fol. 165v, line 1337 in Cooper).

1296   L: *A gyaunt that heght Maugys*. N: *A giaunt that hat Maugus* (line 1307). The
        corresponding figure in *LBD* is Malgiers li Gris, a knight who guards the
        fantastic castle, l'Isle d'Or, the Golden Isle (line 1930) and who is the suitor of
        the enchantress la Pucele as Blances Mains, the Maiden of the White Hands (line
        1941). La Pucele has promised to marry him if he can defend the causeway that
        leads to the castle:

> The maiden had decreed that any knight who could defend her island for
> seven years, against any knight who passed that way, could marry her. Malgier
> set his sights on accomplishing the goal, although he was so loathsome that the
> Maiden would have found some way to get out of the marriage anyway. After
> five years, he had killed 140 knights and seemed undefeatable, but he was
> finally killed by Gawain's son Guinglain. (*AND*, p. 340)

Malgiers has defeated all would-be suitors and placed their helmeted heads on
stakes before the causeway. Although he is an evil knight ("fel, cuvers et mals /
mais trop ert plains de mautalans" [cruel, base, and wicked, / a faithless
scoundrel]) (lines 2035–36), he is not, like Maugis, a *Saracen* giant. Mills assumes
that the author has confused Malgiers li Gris with "the typical Saracen giant of
heroic romances" (*LD*, p. 232n1243–48). This may not be a matter of confusion.
Maugus does resemble stock Saracen giants, who are racially distinct. Maugus
is called a "devil so blak" (N, line 1374), as is the Saracen giant in *Octovian
Imperator*, which, like *Sir Launfal*, has been attributed to Thomas Chestre. The
giant in *Octovian Imperator* does not wear black armor, but he has "blake yghen"
(line 935), is similarly associated with animal traits, and has an inhuman height:
"He was of lengthe twenty feet" (line 925). Giants in medieval romance are also
associated with "unbridled lust," functioning as emblems of lower or bestial
human aspects (Saunders, *Rape and Ravishment*, p. 209). This reinvention of
Maugus, then, may have to do with the parallel shift in the characterization of
the lady of Il d'Or. In *LD*, she is a malevolent enchantress who sidetracks
Lybeaus from his true quest to rescue the Lady of Synadoun, while in *LBD* la
Pucelle is a benevolent sorceress who helps him. It is generically and
aesthetically appropriate, therefore, for an evil enchantress to have a Saracen
giant associated with lust to challenge Lybeaus. The combination of evil
enchantress and stock evil giant, then, brings two conventional villains to bear
on Lybeaus, whereas Li Biaus fights a combatant who turns out to be another
suitor and thus a competitor for la Pucele's affections. The name "Maugys/
Maugus" has eluded modern scholarship, though the *chanson de geste* hero
Maugis bears some kinship to the Maugus of *LD*. Maugis belongs to the
Charlemagne stories of France, and his family exploits are contained in what is
known as the "Renaud de Montauban cycle" of tales. Maugis or Maugris was a
foundling raised by the fairy Oriane; he became a great enchanter, learned in
both white magic and the black arts. Later, he becomes the lover of the
enchantress/fairy Oriane. At one point, Maugis dons Saracen arms. Maugus in
LD similarly has Saracen arms and battles in the service of an (evil) enchantress.
The Middle English author may have imported and adjusted his material in
order to develop his version of the *LBD*, especially his adjustment of the alliance
between the "Saracen hero" Maugus and the malevolent Diamour.

1305   L: *He is thirty fote on leynthe.* N: *He is furti fote longe* (line 1316). As Mills notes,
       "the description of Maugys's size . . . makes his fighting on horseback
       unexpected." He remarks, moreover, that Chestre "was not wholly consistent in
       remodelling Malgiers on the lines of a Saracen giant" (*LD*, p. 233n1291–93).
       Perhaps this giant is more akin to Ascopard in *Bevis of Hampton*, who begins as
       a supporter of Bevis and Josian but becomes a traitor later in the narrative. Also,
       Amoraunt, the giant in *Guy of Warwick*, may be alluded to in this
       recharacterization. Only N has Maugus's height as forty feet, clearly
       exaggerating his gigantic size in order to develop the stock Saracen villain. A's
       Magus (the name is perhaps a play on the Latin word for magician, *magus*) is
       "thryty fote longe" (line 1331): P reduces his height to "20 ffoote of length" (line
       1351, fol. 165v). The line is missing in LI.

1317 ff.   L: missing stanza. N: *And so is he grymly, / As Y telle thee, wittirly. / He is also grete
       / As is an ox or a kowe . . . Or as grete as any nete* (lines 1328–33). Mills (*LD*, p.
       232nL1316) notes that this stanza, which expands the giant's description,
       appears only in A and N. It follows the typical elaboration of comparisons to
       animal traits common to stock giants in medieval romance. See note 1305 above.
       A, however, introduces an ass and a cow as beasts scarcely able to draw Maugis's
       cart of equipment. N, by way of contrast, introduces animals as comparisons to
       the giant; Maugis is as large as an ox, a cow, or any "nete" (ox). The Naples text,
       then, emphasizes animal characteristics, and we might say that the poet
       "transforms" Maugis by moving him in the direction of the bestial, which is
       perhaps intended to link him more firmly to the Circean Dame
       Amoure/Diamour.

1331   L: *That men calleth Ile Dolour.* N: *That men clepith Il d'Ore* (line 1354). L seems to
       veer away from the original name of the island to suggest perhaps its dark side,
       a cause of human pain and sorrow, but N repeats the name of the Golden Isle
       in anticipation of Lybeaus's encounter with the sorceress, Dame Amoure or
       Diamour, who dwells there. In *LBD*, the Isle d'Or is an enchanted island with a
       fabulous castle where la Pucele lives.

1337   L: *Thre mawmentis therin wes.* N: *Four mawmetts therin was* (line 1360). ME
       romance often represents Saracens as idol worshipers. Mawmetts are pagan idols.
       The word comes from Old French *Mahomet*, a corruption of Mohammed, whose
       name thus became synonymous with "idol." A and N characteristically enhance the
       stock, villainous nature of Maugis, here increasing the mawmetts on his shield
       from three to four; so too, C, line 1275.

1343   L: *Tell me whate arte thowe.* N: *Telle me whate art thowe* (line 1369). In *Ywain and
       Gawain,* Colgrevance tells a story in which a peasant asks him, "What ertow,
       belamy" (line 278), and later King Arthur asks Ywain the same question, "What
       man ertow?" (line 1341). Such questions in medieval romance foreground the
       theme of chivalric identity, and therefore Lybeaus identifies himself here as an
       Arthurian knight. His full identity, his true name and parentage, is later
       revealed in stages by Sir Lambard, the Lady of Synadoun, and (in N, A only)
       Lybeaus's mother.

1353–54   L: *Syr Lybeus and Maugis / On stedis proude in prise.* N: *Maugus on fote yode, / And Libeous rode to him with his stede* (lines 1376–77). L and C present Maugis on horseback, which, as Mills (*LD*, p. 233n1291–93) notes, is unlikely given his size. A, N, P place Maugis on foot, thus eliminating the inconsistency. See also Mills, "Mediaeval Reviser," pp. 13–14.

1363   L: *That levyd on Turmagaunte.* N: *That levyth on Termagaunt* (line 1386). Termagaunt is the name of another pagan god sometimes said in ME romances to be worshiped by Saracens.

1375   L: *That his shelde fell him froo.* N: *That his swerde fille him fro* (line 1398). A, N agree that Lybeaus loses his sword here, whereas L, C, P have him lose his shield at this point in his fight with Maugis, which later proves inconsistent. Since Lybeaus reaches for an ax as a weapon in the next stanza, it seems reasonable that he has lost his sword. N omits the detail of the ax's location found in A, C, L, and P (the stanza is missing in LI); e.g., "That henge by his arsowne" (L, line 1384).

1378   L: *And smote Lybeous stede on the hede.* N: *And hit Libeous' stede on the hede* (line 1401). Horses die as frequently as the knights they carry in this romance. Lybeaus will retaliate against Maugis's horse by driving his ax "Through Maugis stede swyre"(L, line 1386). The killing of a knight's horse may be read as a symbolic act, indicting that in chivalry equine lives are also at risk.

1383   L: *And an ax hent ybowne.* N: *An ax he hent ful sone* (line 1406). Note that here N once more presents a more coherent text; where L, C, and P have Lybeaus smite off the head of Maugis's horse (which he is too large to ride), N has him aim at Maugis's neck, missing, and striking the giant's shield instead so that it flies away, thus remaining consistent to the idea that Maugis fights on foot and not on horseback. Maugis is depicted in A as losing only a piece of his shield. Later, however, Lybeaus runs to recover that shield: N's version presents the more credible adventure.

1395–96   L: *From the oure of pryme / Tyll hit were evensonge tyme.* N: *From the owre of the prime / Til it was evesonge tyme* (lines 1418–19). It was customary for fighting to cease at evensong or vespers.

1399   L: *"Maugis, thine ore."* N: *"Maugus, thyne ore"* (line 1422). Combat would seemingly have few rules, but there are still common courtesies to be expected. Here Lybeaus requests a moment to refresh himself with a drink of water, after which Maugis "smertly hym smytte" (L, line 1412). Maugis's unchivalric action endorses the medieval stereotype of the Saracen giant.

1422   L: *I shall for this baptyse.* N: *Y schalle for thi baptise* (line 1445). The irony of this retort suggests the symbolic meaning of Lybeaus's refreshment. Like Spenser's Redcrosse Knight, his strength has been renewed by water from the well (or stream). Mills's remark expands the allusion to a scene in *Guy of Warwick* in which the eponymous hero battles the giant Amoraunt: "Guy agrees [to allow Amoraunt to drink from the river] and Amoraunt quenches his thirst, but later denies Guy permission to do the same unless he discloses his identity to him. But even when he has done this, Amoraunt refuses to let him go, and he has to make a dash for the river. While he is drinking he is knocked into it by the giant, but he quickly recovers, curses the giant for his treachery, and says that although 'baptized' by Amoraunt, he does not owe his name to him" (*LD*, p. 234n1333–62). The reference to "baptism" is found in the Anglo-Norman *Gui* and in the ME texts of *Guy* found in manuscripts Caius 107 (8514–17) and CUL MS ff.ii.38 (8265–68) (Mills, *LD*, p. 234n1333–62). The allusion to baptism is not in the *Stanzaic Guy of Warwick*, however.

1445   L: *jepowne*. The jupon (gipon) may refer to the tunic worn under the breastplate, but more likely here it designates his surcoat bearing his coat of arms worn outside chain mail and breastplate. See *OED*, jupon, n. 1.

1449–50   L: *The gyaunte this ganne see / That he shulde slayne bee*. N: *The giaunt gan to se / That he schulde yslayne be* (lines 1472–73). Mills (*LD*, p. 235n1384–94) observes a close correspondence between this scene and the scene in *Octovian Imperator* where Florent kills the giant Guymerraunt (in the *Northern Octavian* the giant's name is Arageous or Aragonour).

1462   L: *la Dame Amoure*. N: *Diamour* (line 1484). La Pucele in *LBD*, this lady's symbolic name literally means Love in L, but in N perhaps it is more akin to Duessa in *The Faerie Queene*. A, C, and P retain the image of "whiteness" found in *LBD*: A, line 1498, "That lady was whyte as flower;" C, line 1399, "A lady whyt as flowr," added to N here to retain the sense, and P, line 1507, "A Ladye white as the Lyllye flower." L and LI mention only that she is "bright" (L, line 1461; LI, line 694). It seems likely, therefore, that N would have retained the image of whiteness captured in A and P. As Maria Bendinelli Predelli (*Bel Gherardino*, p. 235) suggests, whiteness conventionally marks noblewomen as fitting objects of knightly love, and the phrase "white as flower" or "white as lily flower" is merely a chivalric stereotype. However, it may be a direct echo of *LBD* or a similar version, where "whiteness" is a significant attribute of la Pucele, figured not only in her name but in her description (see lines 2238, 2403–10): her whiteness, too, is compared to a lily flower — "Mains ot blances con flors de lis" (line 2241) — which conveys a dimension of sanctity to her role, since the lily is traditionally associated with the Virgin Mary. Unlike la Pucele, however, Dame Amoure/Diamour is cast as a malevolent enchantress. Blancemal's name and the attribute of whiteness serve to mark her ambiguity, much like la Fata Bianca in *Bel Gherardino* or Li Biaus's mother in *LBD*. In both *LD* and *Bel Gherardino*, the figure of the sorceress retains the "whiteness" of la Pucele, even while their narrative roles have changed. Sanctity, however, is rendered ambiguous in the Old French name, Blancemal, a combination of *blance* (white) and *mal* (evil), and perhaps this is why Lybeaus's mother is not named in *LD*. Like Circe, Dame Amoure/Diamour tempts Lybeaus away from his quest to liberate the Lady of Synadoun and to disregard Elene: "he forgate mayde Elyne" (L, line 1481). In Chrétien de Troyes's *Yvain*, the eponymous knight forgets to return to his wife, Laudine, in a year as promised.

1473   L: *Lybeous graunted hir in haste*. N: *Sir Libeous graunt it in hast* (line 1495). Dame Amoure/Diamour offers Lybeaus what appears to be her hand in marriage together with all of her cities and castles, that is, her inheritable lands and properties as well as the cities owing her allegiance (and taxes). Lybeaus accepts this proposition. Only N inserts the pronoun "it" in Lybeaus's acceptance, a pronoun that logically connects his agreement to Diamour's offer. The other manuscript variants include C, line 1411, "Lybeauus grauntede yn haste"; A, line 1510, "Lybeus grantyd hyr in haste"; and P, fol. 166v, "Sir Lybius frened her in hast," where *frened* probably signifies "frended," that is, he became friends with her (Cooper's text, line 1519 reads *frened*). The variants without the pronoun perhaps imply his consent to her proposition of marriage, but when combined with "her" might also suggest that his consent was primarily to her person, her beauty. N makes it clear that his consent is to her proposition first, and then afterwards he "love to hur cast" (line 1496). The distinction of the pronoun is significant, given the text's focus on marital consent throughout; this illegitimate marriage based upon magical coercion contrasts markedly with Lybeaus's later legitimate marriage, which is based upon free consent. See Weldon, "'Naked as she was bore.'"

1475–76   L: *For she was bright and shene. / Alas, she hadde be chaaste.* N: *For sho was bright and schene. / Alas, that sho nad be ychastid* (lines 1497–98). Shuffelton notes that these two lines are missing in A and suggests that the omission may be deliberate: "Though the lines may have been missing in Rate's exemplar, it is also possible that he omitted them due to their suggestion of a sexual liaison [as in L and N]. But line 1513 [A]— 'sche dyde hym traye and tene'—nevertheless hints at Denamowre's seduction of Lybeaus" (p. 479n1511), as does his protracted stay with her and her offer of marriage. In L and N, the narrator immediately characterizes the enchantress as an improper match for Lybeaus.

1479   L: *For twelve monthes and more.* N: *Thre wokis and more* (line 1501). In *LBD*, the hero spends only one night with the sorceress, whereas Lybeaus spends a year or more with her in C, L, P but only three weeks in A, N. The length of his stay is illegible in LI, line 712, although the reference to "monyth and more" clearly indicates more than several weeks. The reduced amount of time of Lybeaus's enchanted stay with Diamour in A, N to some extent lessens his culpability as well as the power of the enchantress over him.

1487   L: *Than other suche fyve.* N: *Than othir wicchis fyve* (line 1509). N, together with C and LI, introduces the term *wicchis*, further intensifying the impression that the sorcery practiced by Dame Amoure/Diamour is aligned with the occult. Further, her enchantment is associated with minstrel music ("She made hym suche melodye / Of all maner mynstralsye" (L, lines 1488–89). As Linda Marie Zaerr, "Music and Magic," points out, a conjunction of magic and music appears in the enchanted hall of Iran and Mabon, where Lybeaus hears and sees minstrels: "Trumpys, hornys, sarvysse, / Right byfor that highe deys, / He herde and saughe with sight" (L, lines 1836–38). As he proceeds further, he sees minstrels in the niches of the walls and again hears their music: "Suche maner mynstralsye / Was never within wall" (L, lines 1855–56). That the necromancy of Mabon and Iran involves magic and music, similar to the musical sorcery of Diamour, is suggestive. Also important to note is that the analogues frequently depict Lybeaus's mother as a woman of fairy or possibly an enchantress. In *LBD*, for example, the protagonist's mother is Blancemal le Fee. In the ME romance,

Lybeaus's mother is not depicted as either a fairy or a sorceress, although in N she is referred to as "a giantis lady" (line 2249).

1498   L: *He mete Elyne that may.* N: *He mette Elyne, that feire may* (line 1520). That Elene hangs around until she can catch Lybeaus alone to correct his errancy underscores her loyalty to the cause of her lady as well as her confidence in Lybeaus's now-proven abilities to accomplish the mission.

1520   L: *Jurflete was his name.* N: *Sir Jeffelot was his name* (line 1539). Also known in other variants as Gyrflete, Jerflete, Jeffelot, or Gesloke. A squire made into a steward marks a distinctive move up the social ladder. In A, this character is called Syr Gesloke. R. W. Ackerman suggests a link with Girflet, son of Do of Carduel, who became a knight of the Round Table and was "slain by Lancelot in the abduction of Guinevere" (*Index of the Arthurian Names in Middle English*, p. 112). See also note to line 240 above. In *LBD*, squire Robert accompanies the hero from the Arthurian court together with Helie and the dwarf. Furthermore, Gyflet, son of Do, in *LBD*, is the name of the knight of the gerfalcon. See note to lines 727 ff.

1533–35   L: *Cor and fenne full faste, / That men hade ere oute caste, / They gadered ynne iwysse.* The custom of carrying waste products outside the boundaries of the city is reversed in these lines. That the use of the word "cor" may suggest the presence of one or many corpses is in accord with the uncanny effects of the occult forces conjured up by Mabon and Iran. In C this passage reads: "For gore and fen and full want / That there was out ykast / To-gydere they gadered ywys" (lines 1471–73); N omits the passage entirely, as does A, while in LI it appears as follows: "Bothe gor and fen faste, / That hadde out beo caste, / Th . . . gedred yn iwis" (lines 763–65); and in P: "They gathered dirt & mire ffull ffast; / Which beffore was out cast, / They gathered in Iwis" (lines 1579–81; fol. 167r). That the city is called "Gaste" or "Desolate" or "Waste" City as an analogous name for Synadoun underscores an implicit connection to the dead and to practices of necromancy, though the term appears to be used ambiguously. Roger Sherman Loomis notes in "From Segontium to Sinadon: The Legends of a *Cité Gaste*" that the city was built on or near the site of Segontium, the ancient Roman fortress located in north Wales. Also relevant to the haunting elements of this part of the poem may be the site's association with the defeat and death of the British king Vortigern prophesied by Merlin when he interpreted the symbolic meaning of opposing red and white dragons discovered underneath the tower that Vortigern was attempting to build. The prophecy revealed the demise of the red dragon and the ascendancy of the white, a sign of victory for the Saxons.

1539–40   L: *They taken in the goore / That ar was oute yboore.* This line and stanza are missing in N. The custom in this enchanted castle appears to be atypical for medieval waste management but perhaps typical for the strangeness of this section of the poem. As Derek G. Neal points out, "Lybeaus arrives with the go-between Elaine and her steward at a town where 'filth and ordure' are 'collected back in' rather than 'thrown out.' In this strange place lurks humiliation rather than death: Lybeaus risks being spattered with filth if he loses the challenge of Sir Lambard, hence (according to Elaine) to be known as a coward" (*Masculine Self*, pp. 220–21).

1549 L: *That hight Syr Lanwarde*. N: *His name is clepid Lambert* (line 1561). Also Lambard, Lambarte, Lamberd, Lambardys, and Lancharde, this character is the constable or steward of the Lady of Synadoun's castle; he is in a position that bequeaths him responsibility for overseeing everything that goes on both inside and outside. Here he assumes the role of porter, the most relevant example of which is found in *SGGK*. The name also recalls a character in the Anglo-Norman *Gui*, who, as Mills explains, "is a vassal of Otes (Otus *Guy*) and who equals him in villainy. . . . In *LD*, Lambard is essentially a 'good' character, but his habit of fighting with all visitors to the castle, including those who had come to rescue his lady, could easily have raised doubts about his real nature and caused the author of the OF *Lybeaus* [*sic*] to bestow upon him a name with associations of treachery" (*LD*, p. 236n1487). Shuffelton notes that no version is entirely coherent in its portrayal of Lambert (p. 479n1574). Stephen Knight suggests that the name evokes the Lombards, the great bankers of the later Middle Ages, and their powerful importance to aristocratic landholders ("Social Function," pp. 107–08). See Richard Kaeuper, *Bankers to the Crown*, on England, Lombardy, and mercantilism. In Thomas Chestre's *Sir Launfal*, Lombardy, the setting of Sir Launfal's tournament with the gargantuan Sir Valentine, provides an amusing satire on such mercantile/chivalric inequalitites.

1549 L omits the detail of the castle-dweller as giant. N: *a giaunt felle* (line 1559). This line is also missing in C, P, LI but present in A, line 1572, "a gyaunt felle." Found only in N and A, the phrase seems to suggest (erroneously) that Lambert is a giant, like Maugis. Also in N, A the lines describing the habits of the citizens of Synadoun to throw garbage on the loser (L, lines 1560–68) are omitted (see note to lines 1539–40 above). Mills (*LD*, p. 236nL1530–68) suggests that the comparison to a giant represents an attempt to make Lambert more negative and that the poet/reviser dropped this effort later, reverting to the more positive characterization of Lambard in *LBD*. See also Shuffleton, p. 479n1574. N's use of "giant," however, differs. The point here is that Lambert is a man of extraordinary size or strength (*MED*) rather than the folktale villain or stereotypical giant; in other words, N makes him a formidable opponent.

1554 L: *And ere he do thi nede*. N: omitted. Why Lambert should humilate Arthurian knights or why there is an assumption that all challengers are Arthurian knights is not clear. See Textual Note to N, line 1554.

1581 L: *And axed ther ostell*. N: *And axid ther ostelle* (line 1591). Medieval hospitality required monasteries and castles to admit travelers, especially at night or in inclement weather. This custom appears in romances; Gawain tells the porter of Bercilak's castle that he comes "herber to craue" (*SGGK*, line 812).

1587 L: *Who was here governours*. N: *Who is your governour* (line 1597). This expression recalls *SGGK*, when Bercilak, in his guise as the Green Knight, enters Arthur's hall, he asks, "Wher is. . . / Þe gouernour of þis gyng" (lines 224–25). See also note 1581 above.

1593 L: *The porter prophitable*. N: *The porter, prestabelle* (line 1603). The chain of command is made clear: the porter reports to the constable before letting the knights in. This contrasts sharply with the actions of the porter in *SGGK* wherein Gawain is admitted immediately once he is recognized as one of the most famous knights of Arthur's court. According to the *MED* "prestabelle" may mean "eager to serve" but may also be related to the sixteenth-century French word, *prestable*, meaning "remarkable," in which case it would be close in meaning to L's "prophitable."

1597   L: *"Syre, of the Rowne Table."* N: *"Thei bene of the Rounde Table"* (line 1607). The identification of Arthur's knights differentiates them from all others in terms of renown and respectability.

1609   L: *As a greyhounde dothe to an hare.* N: *So as the greyhound aftir the hare* (line 1619). In another rare simile the poet creates a hunting image against which the porter is compared ironically — this is what he is *not*. The greyhound was noted for its speed, and the point here is that porter races to inform Lambard as speedily as a greyhound pursues a hare.

1629–30   L: *His shelde was asure fyne, / Thre beer hedis therinne.* N: *A schilde he bare, fyne, / Thre boris hedis ydentid therinne* (lines 1639–40). L's azure shield differs from N's merely fine one. Blue is one of the most frequently used colors (or tinctures) in heraldry. Others commonly used are red, black, and green, while more uncommonly used tinctures are purple, sky-blue, and mulberry. The ermine on the shield refers to a pattern, not fur; see Friar, *Dictionary of Heraldry*, p. 343 and p. 159. The two versions also differ in the animal heraldry, where L has bears' heads and N, boars' heads. Both emblems suggest formidable strength. The two shields seem to bring together the details of the shield belonging to Sir Degaré's father, a fairy knight, who bears a shield "of asur / And thre bor-hevedes therin / Wel ipainted with gold fin" (lines 997–99).

1641 ff.   These lines confirm Lambert's powerful build, which N and A express as giant-like (see note to line 1549 above). L, A, and P compare him in this stanza to a leopard (L: "lebard" [line 1645]; A: "lyberd" [line 1662]; P: "Libbard" [fol. 167v]; missing in Ll), whereas only N makes Lambert a Lombard (line 1655). In Chestre's *Sir Launfal*, Sir Valentine, another Lombard, is "fyftene feet" tall (line 512), but there is no suggestion that he, any more than Lambert, is a Saracen giant or stereotypical villainous or rustic giant. It is worth noting here that Lambert has none of the inhuman and animal characteristics associated with Maugis or the two giants who abduct Violet.

1655   N: *Prowte as eny Lombard.* Lombardy is more famous for its bankers than "prowte" knights. Compare the satiric battle between Launfal and the giant of Lombardy in the ME *Sir Launfal*. See note 1549.

1683–84   L: *Sate and rocked . . . in his cradill.* N: *That he sate . . . in cradille* (lines 1693–94). Lybeaus has given his opponent a taste of his own medicine in this scene of role reversal. Whiting lists this line in *Proverbs, Sentences, and Proverbial Phrases*, p. 83.

1701 ff.   N and A arrange this stanza differently from L. The details of the fighting part of the stanza are abbreviated, and Lybeaus, rather than offer more violence (see

L, line 1702, "Wilt thou more?"), immediately responds generously to Lambert's shame at having been unsaddled: "Be nought agrevyd" (N, line 1711).

1701	N: short stanza. See L, lines 1689–1700.

1708   L: *Thowe arte of Sir Gawynes kynne.* N: *Thou art of Sir Gaweynis kyn* (line 1717). Unlike what happens in *LBD*, the Lady of Synadoun's constable, Lambard, recognizes Lybeaus as a kinsman of Gawain, the most formidable British knight in Arthur's court and, in a deft maneuver of self-preservation, pledges his loyalty to the stronger knight. Further, in *LBD*, la Pucele reveals his identity, whereas in *LD* Lambard partially reveals it; the Lady of Synadoun, after her disenchantment, also recognizes Lybeaus's identity in terms of kinship with Gawain, but it is Lybeaus's mother who finally and fully completes his identity when she attends her son's marriage feast at Arthur's court and reveals that Lybeaus is not only a kinsman to Gawain but his son (N, A only).

1709   N: *He schalle my lady gete* (line 1709). See also A: *He schall my lady gete* (line 1709). Lambard's prophecy that Lybeaus is the champion who shall rescue the Lady of Synadoun is missing in L and occurs only in A and N.

1736   L: *God and Seint Leonarde.* N: *Jhesus, Hevyn kynge* (line 1757). Although N invokes Christ, L refers to Saint Leonard, one of the most popular saints of western Europe. Leonard was patron saint of hospitals, prisons, pregnant women, and captives. The evocation of his name seems appropriate considering the Lady of Synadoun's imprisonment.

1756   L: *Clyrkys of nigermansye.* N: *Clerkis of nigromansy* (line 1777). Necromancy, according to the *MED*, refers to sorcery or black magic. Corinne Saunders, in *Magic and the Supernatural*, notes that necromancy may refer to demonic practices and the conjuring of the dead, but observes that "it is very rare for romances to describe explicitly demonic magic practised by humans" and that romance writers "employ 'nigromancy' not to depict rituals wholly different in kind from natural magic . . . but rather to suggest more dangerous rituals that enter further into the conscious practice of magic" (p. 154). Helen Cooper, in *The English Romance in Time*, writes, "Middle English 'nigromancy' is magic on the edge of acceptability, not magic conducted through the agency of the dead" (p. 161). In *LD*, necromancy is only mentioned twice, in the lines above and later in L, lines 1767–68: "Hit is by nygrymauncye / Iwrought with fayreye." In N the comparable lines are "Hit is made bi negromansy, / Ywrought it was with feyry" (lines 1788–89). The text implies perhaps that the ghostly magicians who perform in the enchanted hall and vanish suddenly are necromantic spirits, but as the text offers no explicit reference to the dead, they seem more illusory than necromantic. The magic of the clerks appears elsewhere in the poem as *chambur* (L, line 1975; N: *charmour*, line 2007), *chauntement* (L, line 2103; N, missing line), *chawnterye* (L, line 2132), and *sorcerye* (L, line 2055; N: *sorsery*, line 2087; N: *sorserye*, line 2171).

1758   L: *Irayne ys that o brother.* N: *Iran is, than, one brothir* (line 1779). Variants include Yrayn, Jrowne, and Evrain in *LBD*.

1759   L: *And Mabon is that other.* N: *And Mabon is that othir* (line 1780). Variants include
            Maboun and Mabouunys. A likely derivation of "an enchanter and hero from
            Welsh legend derived from the Celtic god Maponos. He was the son of Mellt and
            Modron (herself taken from the goddess Matrona). He is named as a servant of
            Uther Pendragon in an early Welsh poem. In *Culhwch and Olwen*, Culhwch needs
            his assistance in the hunt for the boar Twrch Trwyth" (*AND*, p. 333). In *LBD*,
            Mabon and his brother, Evrain, enter the city of Snowdon disguised as
            jongleurs; they cast spells so that the populace believed they were insane, and
            they laid waste to the city, which became known afterwards as the Desolate City.
            Mabon attempted to coerce la Blonde Esmeree into marriage by transforming
            her into a snake, a form she would endure while she refused him or until
            rescued by "the greatest knight . . . from the court of Arthur" (see *LBD*, lines
            3319–62, especially 3353–59).

1772   L: *That is of knyghtis kynne.* N: *Comyn of kyngis kynne* (line 1793). C, L, P make the
            Lady of Synadoun "of knightis kin." A is silent on her kinship. Ll, fol. 10v, refers
            to her as "so gent a dame." Only N raises her status to a king's daughter, thereby
            elevating Lybeaus's station as her (future) husband.

1790   L: *Luste they done hir synne.* N: *Lest that thei bring hur in synne* (line 1811). The
            sense here seems to be that Iran and Mabon are trying to force the Lady of
            Synadoun to give Mabon all her inheritance, that is, to marry him. Lambard and
            the townspeople fear that they may "force" her into sin, that is, if Mabon rapes
            her and then claims her as his wife. The enchantment of the Lady of Synadoun,
            in other words, has coerced marriage and propertied wealth as its motive.

1833   L: *Syr Lybeaus, knyght curtays.* N: *Sir Libeous reyght his corcis* (line 1854). L reads here
            "knyght curtays," so too, C, A, Ll, and P. N's reading is unique; Lybeaus arranges
            his "corcis," that is, corset, a piece of body armor or corselet, in preparation to
            enter the enchanted hall. The action suggests the young knight's trepidation.

1850   L: *Butt mynstralis cladde in palle.* N: *But mynstrell clothid in palle* (line 1871). The
            negative association between fairy magic and music links the enchanted castle
            to the enchantment of the Golden Isle and Dame Amoure/Diamour. For a useful
            discussion of minstrels and minstrelsy of the time, see Howard Mayer Brown and
            Keith Polk, "Instrumental Music." See also the note to line 1487 and Zaerr,
            "Music and Magic."

1854   N: *Sir Libeous reyght his corcis.* This line appears only in Naples, which the *MED*
            locates under "righten" v. 1c, "to aim (a weapon), point; direct (one's course), in
            which case the line would mean "Sir Libeous directed his course." All other
            manuscript versions of *Lybeaus* have some form of "curtays" in a line similar to
            A's "Syr Lybeus, knyght curtays" (line 1830). However, "righten" v. 2a and 2b
            may also involve armor, as in "set one's gear in order" or "to make weapons
            ready"; the *MED* gives the example, "right her armour" (*Merlin*, line 150).
            Similarly, in the *Prose Merlin*, Leodogan acquires armor: "And [thei] hym
            unbounden, and right his armoure, and sethen made hym to lepe on a steede
            that was stronge and swyfht" (*Arthur at Tamelide*, lines 222–24). The difficulty of
            the Naples line is compounded by the ambiguity of the word *corcis*. If the word

refers to "course," as implied in the *MED* reading, then the Naples line is an anomaly, as *MED* gives no other example of "righten" connected with course or direction; all other *MED* examples under 1c collocate "righten" with weapons aimed or pointing, not with setting out on a "course" or "direction." It may be that the noun *corcis* is a scribal distortion of *cors, corset,* or *corselet*. Hewitt describes fourteenth-century inventories that support this reading: the inventory of Louis Hutin (1316) mentions a "cors d'acier," that of Humphry Bohun (1322) includes a "corset de fer," and that of the Earl of March (1330) a "corsetz de feer" (*Ancient Armour and Weapons*, 2:136). *Corcis* as *cors, corset,* or *corselet* thus preserves the usual *MED* senses of *righten* 1.a.b. and c. and 2.a. and b. Lybeaus does not direct his course or point his horse in the right direction, then; rather, he arranges his armor properly before riding into combat.

1872   L: *The halle ypeynted was*. N: *The halle ypeyntid was* (line 1893). The splendor of the locale enhances its enchantment. The hall is reminiscent of other enchanted places, most significantly in ME narrative, such as in the otherworldly palace of the fairy king in *Sir Orfeo*: "Amidde the lond a castel he sighe, / Riche and real and wonder heighe, / Al the utmast wal / Was clere and schine as cristal" (lines 355–58). Orfeo thinks "it is / The proude court of Paradis" (lines 375–76). Also resonant is the enchanted hall encountered by Sir Degaré, a palace filled with beautiful women, mirth, music, and a sumptuous feast.

1888   L: *The erthe began to quake*. N: *The erthe bigan to quake* (line 1908). The natural world marks the impending battle as in the earlier scene of thunder and lightning. It is also possible that the earthquake, thunder, and lightning are illusory, wrought by magic.

1892 ff.   L: missing stanza. N: *Sir Libeous therof had mervaile . . . Er that Y se what he be, / Aboute this biggyng"* (lines 1914–25). This stanza is unique to N. See Sir Gawain's musings about the "dele" and "fende" that might fittingly inhabit the green chapel, "a chapel of meschaunce" (*SGGK*, lines 2185–98).

1975   L: *His chawntementis ne his chambur*. N: *His acton ne his charmour* (glossed as sorcery, line 2007). There clearly appears to be a scribal error in L since "chamber" makes little sense, even if one stretches the imagination to define the word as "body." Hence, we have glossed the word as "charms" (sorcery).

2006–08   N: short stanza. See L, lines 1974–75.

2021–22   L: *The venym will me spille; / I venymed hem bothe*. The mention of venom occurs in C, L, and P (the lines are missing in LI); no venom is mentioned in N or A. The poisoned sword is another means by which Mabon and Iran engage in a nonchivalric mode of combat. Shuffelton notes that "Like N, Rate's copy-text had these lines instead of three lines in the Cotton manuscript and in L explaining that Mabon has poisoned the swords. As a result of this foul play, Lybeaus's refusal to spare Mabon's life seems more explicable in those manuscripts" (p. 480n2009–11).

2037   L: *Tho Mabon was slayne*. N: *Than Mabon was yslayn* (line 2069). Lybeaus cleaves the skull of Mabon; in Renaut's version smoke comes from the skull's mouth:

"Donné li a si grant colee / que mort l'abat guile baee. / Del cors li saut une fumiere / qui molt estoit hideusse et fiere / qui li issoit par mi la boce" (lines 3059–63). (The Fair Unknown dealt him such a great blow / that he knocked him down dead, his mouth agape. / From his body there arose / a horrid and fearful plume of smoke, / which spewed out of his mouth.) Meanwhile Iran appears to disappear.

2060 ff.   Both L and N are missing this stanza. Only P includes it as follows:

> Then he was ware of [a] valley;
> Thitherward he tooke the way
>   As a sterne Knight and stout.
> As he rode by a riuer side
> He was ware of him that tyde
>   Vpon the river brimm:
> He rode to him ffull hott,
> & of his head he smote,
>   Ffast by the Chinn;
> & when he had him slaine,
> Ffast hee tooke the way againe
>   For to haue that lady gent.
> (Cooper, lines 2104–15; see also fols. 120r–v)

2067   L: *A worme ther ganne oute pas.* N: *A worme ther out gan pas* (line 2099). *Worm* is a word typically equated with *serpent* or *dragon*. The woman/beast here is clearly a dragon since she is a worm with wings and a tail. Medieval portrayals of the Fall often depict the serpent as a woman; for example, the serpent in the sculpture above the left portal, west façade, Notre Dame Cathedral, Paris, looks like the archetypal Eve. See page 83 for an image of Eve and the Dragon-Serpent in *Speculum humanæ salvationis*, and for more on this point, see Weldon, "'Naked as she was bore,'" pp. 73–77.

2069   L: *"Yonge Y am and nothinge olde."* N: *Yonge and nothing olde* (line 2101). In L, the Lady of Synadoun addresses Lybeaus directly as a dragon-woman, whereas in N, the dragon-woman does not address him, and this line represents indirect narratorial comment. No form of this line appears in the French *LBD*.

2083   L: *The worme with mouth him kyste.* N: *The worme with mouthe him kist* (line 2115). This is the *fier baiser* episode at the heart of the Fair Unknown narrative and the effective cause of the disenchantment of the Lady of Synadoun. Other "fearsome kisses" take place in *Ponzela Gaia, Carduino,* and *Lanzelet,* as well as in *LBD,* but in no other episode is the dragon/serpent endowed with a "womanes face." Similar to the loathly lady narrative, the kiss disenchants the dragon-lady, transforming her into her previous form, a beautiful woman. This is also the moment in which Lybeaus's identity is manifestly revealed, for only the kiss by a blood relative of Gawain can affect the disenchantment.

2085–87   L: *And aftyr this kyssynge / Off the worme tayle and wynge / Swyftly fell hir froo.* N: *And aftir that kissing, / Of the worme bothe taile and wyng / Sone thei fille hur fro* (lines 2117–19). In *LBD,* as Ferlampin-Acher notes, the transformation of disenchantment is never seen (*La Fée et la Guivre,* p. lixn128); so too, in *Lanzelet* and the other

European analogues where the transformation also occurs "off stage" or is never directly described. Only in *LD* does the disenchantment take visible form.

2091 ff.   L: *But she was moder naked, / As God had hir maked:* . . . *As naked as she was bore.* N: *But scho was al nakid / As the clerkis hur makid*; . . . *As nakid as scho was bore* (lines 2123–24; L, line 2137, N, line 2176). The disenchantment involves the disappearance of the serpent-Eve-dragon disguise ("Off the worme tayle and wynge / Swyftly fell hir froo" [L, lines 2086–87]), suggesting that the transformation returns the lady to a state of innocence equivalent to a prelapsarian Eve, the mother of all humankind. Not only is she innocent but without shame. N's original reference to clerks recalls the enchantment caused by Iran and Mabon, and perhaps implies their malicious disrobing of her prior to covering her with the magic dragon disguise. Later, however, when Lybeaus recounts the story to Lambard, he describes her, "As nakid as scho was bore" (N, line 2176). Another parallel to this striking image is the story of Saint Margaret, patron saint of childbirth, who is swallowed by a dragon but erupts from its belly reborn. See Weldon, "'Naked as she was bore,'" p. 81.

2120 ff.   L: missing stanza. N: *To loke aftir Iran* (lines 2153 ff.). This passage dealing with the search for and killing of Iran occurs after the disenchantment only in the N, A tradition. For Mills, it is a revised passage that corrects the unsolved mystery of Iran's disappearance and provides closure. N omits the repetitive lines from A at this point: "And ther sone he wane. / He went into the towre / And in that ilke chambour" (A, lines 2113–15). Of the two, N is more sensible than A, and from line 2153, the passage is original with N.

> Syr Lybeus, the knyght gode,
> Into the castell yode
>   To seke after Irain.
> He lokyd into the chambour
> Ther he was in towre,
>   And ther sone he hym wane.
> He went into the towre
> And in that ilke chambour
>   He saw Irain that man.
> He drew hys suerd with myght
> And smote of hys hede with ryght,
>   For soth, of Irain than.
> (Shuffleton, A, lines 2108–19)

2134   N: Short stanza. See L, lines 2097 ff.

2137   L: *As naked as she was bore.* N: *As naked as scho was bore* (line 2176). See note for line 2091 above.

2138   N: Short stanza. See L, lines 2109 ff.

2160 ff.   N: Short stanza. See L, lines 2121 ff.

2178   L: *Arthur gave also blyve.* N: *Arthour, he gave blyve* (line 2217). Arthur's blessing and consent to the marriage sanctions it and renders Lybeaus's mission complete. He has literally won the lady's hand in marriage. In *LBD*, this is a bittersweet reward, since in that poem Lybeaus's true love is the Maiden with the White Hands whom he had left abruptly to complete his mission.

2192 ff.   L: missing stanza. N: 2232 ff. The arrival of Lybeaus's mother is unique to A and N, and solves what Mills perceives as an inconsistency in the other manuscript versions, where Gawain's sudden recognition of his son is left unexplained ("Mediaeval Reviser," pp. 17–18). The appearance of Guinglain's mother not only solves what Mills perceives as an inconsistency, Gawain's sudden recognition of his son, which is left unexplained in C and L but added to A and N; it also provides reconciliation of the separated and "lost" parents. The family reunion motif appears in *Sir Degaré*, *Octovian Imperator* and the *Northern Octavian*, *Emaré*, and *Sir Isumbras*. Illegitimate but chivalric sons occur in the story of Lancelot and Galahad, *Le Livre de Caradoc*, and *Ysaÿe le triste*.

Gawain's address to the Lady of Synadoun (N: 2244 ff.) is unique to N, A, P, and LI. Only in N, however, does Gawain refer to Lybeaus's mother as a "giantis lady" (line 2249) — see note to line 1487 above. A refers to her as a "gentyll lady" (line 2209); so, too, LI, "gentil lady" (Cooper, line 1077; fol. 12v). Although her description as a giant's lady might seem incongruous, there is a sense in which N's reading restores the idea that Lybeaus's mother is kin to a race of nonhuman beings. *LD* belongs to a group of folkloristic narratives in which the hero's *enfances* is obscure; he is raised outside of civilization and his parents or one of his parents and/or guardians is divine or animal (Walter, *Bel Inconnu*, pp. 49–72). In *LBD*, Guinglain's mother is Blancemal le Fee (line 3237), for example; in, *Wigalois*, she is Florie, daughter of a fairy king. If, as a giant's lady, Lybeaus mother is meant to be a giant's daughter, then she recalls folklore tradition in which a giant's daughter helps the hero or marries the hero, as in the British folktale "Nix Nought Nothing." In the Celtic story *How Culhwch Won Olwen*, Culhwch weds Olwen, the beautiful and nonmonstrous daughter of the giant Ysbaddaden. In folklore and myth, giants, like fairies, live outside human communities, so the N association of Lybeaus's mother with giants maintains the obscure and uncivilized (nonhuman) parentage of the hero lost in the other versions of *LD*. It is also possible that the "giant" status of Lybeaus's mother indicates her "otherness" — that she resides outside the court and is marginalized by her unwed, single-parent status.

2199   L: *Sevyn yere they levid same*. N: *Ten yere thei levid in same* (line 2274). The marriage in N lasts longer than L's, although neither text (nor any other version) mentions children, which are often the conventional index of a successful medieval marriage.

2204   L: *Grawnte us gode endynge. Amen*. N: *To blys He us alle bring. Amen* (line 2279). Despite the naming of Lybeaus in the incipit of L as Guinglain, the name given to him by Arthur (Lybeaus Desconus) is the name that accrues recognition and authority in the chivalric world. This is the name that is cited on the Winchester Round Table.

2280   N: *Qui scripcit carmen sit benedictis. Amen*. A formulaic ending which often concludes secular as well as religious manuscript entries. The correct spelling is *scripsit*; however, the variant *scripcit* also frequently appears in manuscript colophons.

For instance, the exact phrasing and spelling closes *The Prick of Conscience* in Manchester, John Rylands Library, Eng. 51 [olim Quaritch Sale Cat. 344, Item 28], fol. 116v (see *The IMEV: An Open-Access, Web-Based Edition of The Index of Middle English Verse*, ed. Linne R. Mooney et al., Number 3428: http://www.cddc. vt.edu/host/imev/record.php?recID=3428.). This is the first of a hierarchy of display scripts in the Lybeaus portion of N, here a bastard display script composed of a mix of more formal bookhand scripts, including an approximation of *textualis semiquadrata* with its occasional feet in the minims, occasional separate letters, angular letters, and a more formal cursive blend of mainly Secretary forms (the letter *a*) together with some Anglicana forms (the long *s*).

2281   N: *Hic Explicit Libeus Disconyus*. This colophon is written in the scribe's most elevated and formal bastard display script.

2282–85   N: *He that lovyth welle to fare / . . . . / His here wol grow throw his hood*. This homely verse, which apart from the more formal capital *h* and top line with its stylistic decorative features, is written in the same script as the text (a mix of Secretary and Anglicana features) and inserts a conventional moral on the page, although it is not clear whether or not it is meant as a commentary on *LD*. These moralizing verses appear in Bodley MS 315 (SC 2712) which was presented to the Dean and Chapter of Exeter Cathedral in the mid-1470s by Magister John Stevens, a canon at Exeter. According to the manuscript, the Naples verses are among several which appeared on the wall of the dining hall of the Augustinian Canons' Priory of St. Stephen of Launceston in Cornwall. See Rossell Hope Robbins, "Wall Verses at Launceston Priory." The sense is that indiscriminate spending leads to poverty, a condition marked by the wear and thinness of the material of the hood that allows the wearer's hair to poke through the material. The scribe signs his name here as More, whom Manly and Rickert identify as a Harry More, although they offer three other potential scribal candidates who were writing/ copying at the same time: an Oxford stationer John More, a London stationer Richard More, and a Bristol scrivener William More (*Text of the Canterbury Tales*, 1:376). There is, however, no scholarly agreement on these suggestions. Verses from Lydgate's "Beware of Doubleness" as well as a disguised signature of the scribe as More conclude the final item in N, *Grisilde* or *The Clerk's Tale* on p. 146 of the manuscript.

2286   N: *Hic pennam fixi penitent me si male scripsi*. This is a smaller script than that used for line 2281 and less formal, although here, too, there are suggestions of *textualis*. The same Latin phrase is repeated at the end of the Naples manuscript, concluding the tale of *Griselde* (Chaucer's Clerk's Tale). See Weldon, "Naples Manuscript." See the note for lines 2282–85 above.

ABBREVIATIONS: A: Ashmole 61 (Oxford, Bodleian Library, MS 6922) (see Shuffelton); **C:** London, British Library, MS Cotton Caligula A.ii (see Mills); **L:** London, Lambeth Palace, MS 306; ***LD***: *Lybeaus Desconus*; **LI**: London, Lincoln's Inn, MS 150 (formerly known as Lincoln's Inn, MS Hales 150) (see Cooper); **N**: Naples, Biblioteca Nazionale, MS XIII.B.29; **P**: London, British Library, MS Additional 27879 (also known as the Percy Folio); ***LBD***: *Li Biaus Descouneüs*.

Incipit	L: *A tretys of one Gyngelayne othir wyse Namyd by Kyng Arthure Lybeus Dysconeus that was bastard son to Sir Gaweyne.*
1	*oure.* Mills notes superscript *r* added later (*LD*, p. 75), though it is difficult to determine when that insertion was made.
11	*Roun Table.* L: *rountable.* As is the case with most proper nouns in ME manuscripts, Roun(d) Table appears as one word uncapitalized. Conventions of capitalization vary widely, though rubrics (historiated or not) are most often the exception. Mills detects an erasure under the *r* (*LD*, p. 75).
12	*Herde I never of redde.* L: *Herde J neuer of nor redde. Nor* added above *redde.*
16	*kepte.* L: *kept.* We have added a final *e* to *kepte.*
19	*savage.* L: *savage* crossed out and followed by *sawge.* Mills emends to *savage* (*LD*, p. 75) in accordance with the *Middle English Dictionary* citation.
20	*And gladly wold do outerage.* L: *do* is crossed out and *not* is added above. The sense is that if Lybeaus is *full savage* (*sawge*) as the previous line suggests, then he would more likely *do* outrageous violence than refrain from doing it. We have restored the appropriate verb.
26	*clepte.* L: *clept.* The final *e* has been restored in accordance with Mills (*LD*, p. 75).
30	*Whate hight of his dame.* L: *Whate hight off his dame.* Mills notes correctly that there is another word above *off* which appears to be added after an attempt to cross out that word. The replacement superscript is *onys.* He retains *off* to maintain the orthography of the manuscript (*LD*, p. 77). We have eliminated the second *f* for the sake of clarity.
38	*can shrede.* L: *gan shrede.* Mills emends *gan* to *can* based on his observation that *c* appears to be written over *g* (*LD*, p. 77).
70	*Whan that he wold be made a knyght.* L: *Whan that wold be made a knyght.* There is an erasure and a lacuna in this line in which Mills has inserted an appropriate pronoun. N: *When he wol ben a knyght* (line 70).
71	*hyght.* L: *heght.* Mills detects an *e* written over the *y* in *hyght* (*LD*, p. 79). We have retained the *y*.

74   *same*. L: *fame*. Mills sees a cross-stroke in the *s* of *same* (*LD*, p. 79); the sense
      is better retained by this emendation.

86   *Con*. L: *Gon*. Mills detects a *c* written over the *g* (*LD*, p. 79), an emendation
      that makes more sense of the line.

92   *strok of myght*. L: *stroke of myght*. The final *e* on *stroke* is blurred. Cooper
      emends to *strokes* (p. 15).

114   *Att his tabyll sett*. L: there is a word crossed out before *sett*. Mills identifies it
      as *sete* (*LD*, p. 81).

115   *Ther*. L: *The*. Mills adds *r* (*LD*, p. 81).

118   *The may hight Ellene*. Mills reads *Ellyne* explaining that the *y* has been erased
      and *e* written over the erasure (*LD*, p. 81).

122   *on*. L: *one*. There is clearly a final *e* on *one*. We have emended to retain the
      sense of the line.

129   *Milke*. In L, the first letter is blurred.

130   *The dwerf was clothed in ynde*. L: *The dew dwerff was clothed in ynde*. Mills sees a
      mark of deletion through the word "dew," though it appears not to be
      fully expunged (*LD*, p. 83). This may be evidence of scribal error and
      revision.

131   *Byfore*. L: *fore* is added above the line. It appears to be filling in the gap
      before the partially deleted word *fore* that follows, making the beginning
      of the line read: *Byfore fore*.

135   *His surcote*. L: *Hi surcote*. Mills has added the *s* to the pronoun as have we
      (*LD*, p. 83). The final *e* in *surcote* appears smudged.

143   *Wyde were*. L: *Whyde wher*. Mills detects an erasure here, *were* written over
      wher (*LD*, p. 83). He has restored the original word as have we.

152   *erende*. Mills notes an erasure in the middle of this word (*LD*, p. 83).

167   *hert*. L: *her*. We have completed the word *hert* to make sense of the line.

174   *bere recorde*. L: *bererecorde*. We have noted the oblique stroke between *bere*
      and *recorde* to separate the two words.

177   *sper and swerde*. L: *sperand swerde*. We have separated the word *sper/and*
      according to the stroke that appears in the manuscript.

188   *Persyfal*. L: *Persyfale*. We have deleted the final *e*.

189   *ben abled*. L: *beneabled*. We have emended according to the oblique line in the
      middle of this word.

196   *Or that he that lady see*. L: *that lady see*. Two words before *lady see* have been
      crossed out. Mills reads *lay see* (*LD*, p. 87).

206   *I lernede*. L: *J leerde*. There is a crossed-out word before *leerde*, which appears
      to be inserted in another hand. In agreement with Mills we have
      emended to *lerned* (*LD*, p. 87).

207   *Ther many man hathe be slawe*. There is a crossed-out word, *may*, before *many*.

215   *forsake*. L: *for forsake*. The preposition appears to be crossed out.

216   *As hit is londes lawe*. N: *For suche is Arthouris lawe* (line 213). This stanza in L
      contains three additional lines not present in N (fifteen rather than
      twelve).

218   *gettist*. L: *getist*.

226   *dismayde*. L: *dismaysed*. Mills's emendation of *dismaysed* makes more sense of
      the line (*LD*, p. 89).

236	*hightis.* L: *hightth.* Mills emends to *hightis* as have we (*LD*, p. 89).
239	*fyghtis.* L: *fyghtth.* Emended to maintain consistency with line 236.
253	*aboute.* Mills detects a *w* written over the *u* (*LD*, p. 89).
254	*A shelde with one cheferon.* N: *A schilde with on griffoun* (line 264).
260	*And a fell fauchone.* L: *And fell a ffawchone.*
276	*stoute and gaye.* Mills detects a *w* written over *u* (*LD*, p. 91).
282	*caytyfe.* L: *catyve.* Mills detects an erased *ff* under the *v*. We have emended accordingly.
286	*with eche.* The considerable gap between these words suggests an erasure. Mills notes an extra *h* and *e* in the space and something in the left margin that appears to be erased words "the which" (*LD*, p. 91).
288	*Delaraunche.* L: *delarawnche.* There appears to be another letter under the *w*. What is most notable about this line, however, is that the name of this character has changed from "Salebrant" as it appears in *LBD*.
315	*ridis.* L: *ridith.* Emended to *ridis* to maintain consistency with other words ending with *th*, e.g., *knightis.* The *-is* suffix indicates the plural form.
331	*non other.* L: *no nother.* Mills emends correctly to *non other* (*LD*, p. 95).
332	*In haste.* L: *J haste.* Adding a preposition makes sense of the phrase.
342	*William.* L: *Will* appears to have an abbreviation mark indicating the full name.
352	*afor.* L: *afore.* Mills notes that the final *e* was added later (*LD*, p. 95).
386	*plasse.* L: *plase.* The second *s* is barely visible.
388	*love.* L: *lesse.* Mills emends to *love* (*LD*, p. 99), an emendation with which we agree based on readings from other versions.
393	*knele thu downe.* L: *knele downe.* Mills notes a caret insert after *knele* (*LD*, p. 99).
394	*fauchon.* L: *ffauchone.* Mills emends to *ffauchon* presumably to maintain the rhyme with *renon* (*LD*, p. 99).
401	*kynde.* L: *kyende.* Partially visible *y* with *e* inserted over *kynde* emended for clarity's sake.
404	*forward.* Caret indicates place where first *r* is inserted over the word.
421	*nought.* L: *nougthte.* We have emended to *nought* in order to maintain the meter of the line.
426	*rydis.* L: *rideth.* Emended for greater consistency among plural verbs.
429	*But o thinge.* L: *But othinge.* We have emended to indicate the word *one.*
457	*togeder.* L: *to geder.* Emended to make sense of the line.
461	*foryave.* L: *for yave.*
469	*knyghtis.* L: *knighth.*
482	*rede.* L: *ryde.* *y* written over *e*.
487	*so neghe.* L: *so nygh.* *y* written over *e* and final *e* is erased.
502	*beheld.* L: *be helde.*
514	*The yongest brother full yerne.* L: *the yongest brother* appear as guide words at the bottom of the folio page.
518	*yerne.* L: *yern.* Final *e* appears to be erased. We have restored it.
519	*Ber.* L: *Bere.* Mills identifies a final *e* added by a later hand (*LD*, p. 107).
523	*styffe.* *fe* ending added later as indicated by a different hand.
	sett. Second *t* appears to be partially erased.

524	*basnett*. Second *t* appears to be partially erased as in *sett* above.
527	*hede*. L: *hed*. Final *e* partially erased.
531	*Alse*. L: *Als*. Final *e* partially erased. We have restored it to preserve the sense of the line.
532	*thoo*. L: *tho*. Second *o* thoroughly erased.
536	*gryme*. L: *grym*. Final *e* partially erased.
540	*thoo*. L: *tho*. Final *o* partially erased.
543	*atwoo*. L: *atwo*. Final *o* partially erased.
545	*no myght*. L: *nemyght*. Oblique line separating *ne myght*. Mills reads *no* for *ne* as do we (*LD*, p. 109).
557	*of*. Under erasure.
562	L: rubricated capital A, two lines deep, begins line.
571	*therd day*. L: *therday*. Emended to make sense of the line.
579	*towne*. L: *towe*. Emended to make sense of the line.
582	*browne*. L: *browe*.
588	*Here*. L: *Her*. Final *e* is under erasure.
595	*hire*. L: *hre*.
602	*fyre*. L: *fere*.
605	*pyche*. L: *pytche*.
624	*enprice*. L: *enprise*.
632	*Thorugh lounge and hert*. L: *eke thorugh* inserted above *hert*.
645	*ner*. L: *ne*. We have emended to maintain the sense of the line.
650	*therefore*. L: *there fore*.
718	*The Erle*. L: large unhistoriated capital *T* in red.
739	*him*. L: *ho*.
813	*Quod*. L: *Qud*.
819	*And amyddis the market*. L: Large unhistoriated capital *A* in red with guide letter in lower case.
852	*Thow*. L: *Tow*.
862	*samyte*. L: *sanyte*.
863	*hir atyre*. L: there appears to be a word crossed out between these two.
901	*back*. L: *backis*.
935	*hauk*. L: *haukys*. The sense of the line calls for one hawk rather than many.
936	*Quod*. L: *Qud*.
943	*hauk*. L: *haukis*.
1001	*rowne*. L: *rowme*.
1007	*hauk*. L: *haukis*.
1021	*forty* L: *xlti*. *Xlti* is crossed out in the body of the narrative and reinserted in the left margin.
1029	*As they redyn by a lowe*. Large unhistoriated capital *A*. Catchwords *hornes herd* at bottom of folio page.
1089	*Quod*. L: *Qud*.
1101	*Quod*. L: *Qud*.
1106	*dwerf hem*. L: *dewerff hen*.
1110	*rightis*. L: *righth*.
1269	In L, large unhistoriated capital *N* in red.
1275	In L, large unhistoriated capital *H* in red.

1376	*felde*. L: *flelde*.
1495	*Thus*. L: *This*.
1544	*I tell thee whate hit is.* L: Catchwords *no knyghth* follow at bottom of folio page.
1572	*prophyte*. L: *profyte*. Mills reads *propfyte* (*LD*, p. 169).
1589	*myghtis*. L: *myghth*.
1592	*fightis*. L: *fyghth*.
1609	*greyhounde*. L: *geyhounde*.
1652	*myghtis*. L: *myghth*.
1665	*they*. L: *the*.
1702	*Quod*. L: *Qud*.
1787	*welde*. L: *wele*.
1799	*souped*. L: *stoupeth*.
1876	*mynstrales*. L: *mynstales*.
1947	*Her*. L: *He*.
1976	*Downe*. L: *Dowe*.
2017	*my powsté*. L: there appears to be a word crossed out between these two.
2071	*thynchis*. L: *pynchis*.
2074	L: Catchwords at bottom of folio page, *hyr peynis*.
2106	*I*. L: this word has been inserted with a caret.
2113	*stryfe*. L: this word has been inserted with a caret.
2114	*be*. L: this word has been inserted with a caret
2118	*he*. L: this word has been inserted with a caret.
2130	*her lady*. L: there appears to be a word crossed out between these two.

TEXTUAL NOTES TO NAPLES, MS XIII.B.29

ABBREVIATIONS: A: Ashmole 61 (Oxford, Bodleian Library, MS 6922) (see Shuffelton); **C**: London, British Library, MS Cotton Caligula A.ii (see Mills); **L**: London, Lambeth Palace, MS 306; **LI**: London, Lincoln's Inn, MS 150 (formerly known as Lincoln's Inn, MS Hale 150) (see Cooper); **N**: Naples, Biblioteca Nazionale, MS XIII.B.29; **P**: London, British Library, MS Additional 27879 (also known as the Percy Folio).

1	N: guide letter *J* and space three lines deep for later insertion of decorated capital.
111	*Thei.* N: *the.*
122	*and.* N: *an.*
133	*ynd.* N: *hynd.*
140	*henge.* N: *kyenge?* This word is ill-formed, and the scribe appears to have attempted a correction by superimposing a *y*, with the result that the first letter of the word is illegible. It may be a *k* or a *b*.
149	*sawtre.* N: *swithe.* L, C, and A have a version of *sawtre* here.
152	*telle.* N: *telle me* (makes no sense in context).
154	*knelid.* N: *kene.*
188	*Sir.* N: *si.*
190	*errour.* N: *errout.*
202	*Lybeus.* N: *.l.,* which is N's typical abbreviation for the name of the hero.
225	Scribal ink blot over *g* of *degré*.
239	*Commaundid.* Linear scribal correction *commaandid* corrected to *commaundid*.
254	Compare the fourth person: Agrafrayn (C, line 221), Agfayne (L, line 244).
257	*A.* N: *at.*
282	*As.* N: *and.*
287	*palfray.* N: *palfaray.*
325	*here furth rides.* N: *he furth right.*
327	*his.* N: *hir.*
337	*two.* N: *to.*
345	*her.* Interlinear scribal correction with the addition of *r* after *he*. The scribe has also corrected the *a* in *al*.
384	*slygh.* N: *slyght.*
392	*his.* N: *is.*
399	*a.* N: missing.
409	*sei.* N: *seid.*
414	*Unkouth.* N: *unkough.*
415	*on.* N: *un.*
429	*Thei.* N: *the.*

439	Scribal correction of *e* in *bifore*.
491	Interlinear scribal correction over *m* in *ame*, which is then crossed out.
494	Following this line, L reads: *And to them stoutly con rede* (line 482), giving the stanza an unusual thirteen lines. N omits this line and corrects the stanza.
498	*his*. N: *is*.
499	*Libious*. N: *.l.*
519	L has three lines here that are missing in N, A, P. The stanza is missing in C and LI. The following stanza also has some missing lines and some new ones added. These words of the youngest brother, for example, are only in N, A.
533	*Sir*. N: *sir*. The letter combination *ir* is ill-formed. The stem of the *r* touches the stem of the *i*, and the headstroke of the *r* is exaggerated.
538	*Than*. N: *That*.
554–55	*And in that ilke spaas, / The right arme fille him fro*. So A. L reads "And in that selfe space / His lyfte arme brast atwoo" (lines 542–43).
574	*so*. N: *se*.
592	Scribal interlinear correction — *geuy* crossed out and *greuys* written after.
593	*Thei*. N: *the*.
594	*broun*. N: *bron*.
649	*bisoughte*. N: *bisoughe*.
663	*geaunt his*. N: *geauntis*.
665	*With*. N: *but*. Scribal error perhaps because of following *butte*.
691	Boxed catchwords at bottom of p. 94b, *tille that othir*.
692	Underlined catchwords at top of p. 95a, *it is founde*. These catchwords refer back to p. 94b, the last words of which are "it is found" (line 691).
694	*Tho*. N: *the*.
698	*thonkid*. N: *thongid*.
705	*biforne*. N: *biforme*.
763	*feirer*. N: *feire*.
778	What appears to be a partially boxed catchword on p. 95b, *turne over*, is not actually a catchword. It seems to be the scribe's note to himself.
787	*Geffron le Frediens*. N: *Geffron Jle Frediens*. See line 808 below.
793	*his*. N: *is*.
797	*dwellid*. N: *leftin*; L: *dwellyd* (line 778).
813	*prins*. The scribe uses Latin abbreviations but often modifies or adapts them to the English spellings of his dialect. Here, for instance, the abbreviated *p* form (see C, lines 256 ff.), which usually signals a Latin abbreviation for *per* or *pre* (or *pro*) but which here represents *pri*. *Prins* (not *prens*) is the usual N spelling: see line 849 below, where *prins* is written out fully. See also the notes for lines 849 and 1462.
817	*schrille*. N: *schille*.
842	*graunt*. N: *gaunt*.
849	*prout*. Another example where the scribe uses the Latin *pre* abbreviation for simply *pr*. See note 813 above and line 318, where the word *proute* is written out in full.
903	*border*. N: *borders*. The plural noun makes no sense here.

ryngid with floris. N: *ryng flor*, where the scribe has inserted an *r* above the *o*. In C and L, the word "floures" (C, line 860; L, line 889) refers to color: e.g., "And of that same colours / And of that other floures" (L, lines 888–89). In the A, N, LI, P tradition, however, flowers are decorative items on the shield; e.g., "Of gold was the border, / And of the same colorus, / Dyght with other floures" (A, lines 914–16). N's line seems to be a scribal error connected with the A, N, P sense. A plausible rendering of the line, then, is "ryngid with floris."

906	*cromponis*. This word "cromponis" and line 903 above are unique to N.
919	*ruffyne*. Compare LI: *rosyn*.
926	*on*. N: *in*.
927	*schyning*. N: *schynding*.
933	*straight*. N: *stranght*.
949	*Geffron le Fredus*. N: *Geffron Ile Fredus*. See Explanatory Note 768. All versions of *LD* have difficulty with this name. Here the French article *le* is misspelled as *Ile*.
·1051	*de la Ile*. N: *de a Ile*.
1078	*greyhoundis*. N: *grewhondis*.
1102	*wile*. N: *while*. The other manuscripts have *gile*.
1136	*ther*. N: *the*.
1178	*cler*. N: *cleir*. See *clere*, line 943.
1215	*actowne*: N: *attowne*.
1220	*an ax*. N: missing word, as attested in L, C, A, P (stanza missing in H).
1248	*Sir Libeous* written over illegible erasure.
1280 ff.	Guide letter *r* and space three lines deep for later insertion of a decorated capital.
1287	*buskis*. N: *buskid*.
1307	*Maugus*. The scribe writes a Latin abbreviation stroke over the *a*, and it is likely that he intends the abbreviation to represent *au* rather than *an*, *Mangus*. Elsewhere the spelling Maugus is used.
1318	*knyghtis*. N: *knighti*.
1373	*turne*. N: *turine*.
1407	*nekke*. N: *hekke*.
1420	*there* seems to be a scribal error. The rhyme scheme is broken: A has "tho" (line 1434); L, "throo" (line 1397).
1440	*swore*. N: *swere*.
1462	*othir*. The scribe has written a thorn with a Latin abbreviation symbol for *er*, so that the word technically should be *other*. However, the scribe again adapts the Latin symbol for his normal spelling of *othir*, the usual form which appears throughout the manuscript. See the note for line 813 above.
1464	*After*. N: *Afer*.
1471	*sans faile*. N: *sam faile*.
1483a	Missing line. L, line 1461: *A lady bright as floure*. The text in N is supplied from C.

1509	*Than othir wicchis fyve.* L has "other suche fyve" (line 1487), as does A (line 1522). This is one of the interesting variations where N (and LI) agrees with C, line 1425, as Mills points out (*LD*, p. 235n1425).
1520	*He.* N: *the.*
1548	*Men.* N: *me.* L, line 1526: *men clepen hit.*
1554	The word *towne* is written over an illegible erasure.
1554	A, N omit the lines L:1530–41 and the stanza L:1557–68 where the inhabitants of the castle gather refuse in order to throw it on the heads of challengers to humiliate Arthurian knights, thereby embarrassing Arthur further. A and N thus delete this insult to Arthurian knights.
1594	*porter.* N: *portelle.*
1603	*prestabelle* is unique to N: other manuscripts have some form of L's *prophitable* (line 1593).
1619	Scribal interlinear correction with *r* inserted above the *g* of *greyhound.*
1677	*renoune.* L has *raundon* (line 1667), C *resoun* (line 1605), and A *rawndon* (line 1684).
1679	*To.* N: *And. And* does not make sense since neither really does deliver a mortal wound. They are attempting to do so, however, so "To" is a better choice of expression here.
1684	*he him.* N: *have and.* We have corrected this following L, line 1674, *So harde he hym hitte.*
1690	*and.* N: *an.*
1761	*Libeous.* N: *Libeouc.* Compare with the *c* in "chast" (line 1735) and in "clerkis" (line 2130). The scribe forms a miniscule *c* in two ways, the more common angular variety, and the one here where the angularity disappears. Unlike a *t* formation, the headstroke differs from the *t* headstroke and does not cross the stem, as it does in *Lambart* in the same line. This scribe often alters *s* and *c* for spellings; see the *certeyne / serteyne* shifts and the unique *Cinadowne* for Sinadowne (line 1548). *Libeouc* makes more sense as the manuscript reading in this context.
1779	*one.* N: *one is.*
1811	Scribal correction of *g* in *bring.*
1820	An *e* has been inserted above *makith.*
1834	Scribal correction of *h* to *f* in *of.*
1843	*Libeousis.* N: *l is.*
1923	*onis.* N: *enis.*
1967	*sans faile.* N: *samfaile.*
1984	Scribal correction of the *r* of *provid* over illegible erasure.
2017	*and.* N: *an.*
2024	*lame.* N: *lane.*
2063	*Sir Libeous.* N: *si.L.*
2134 ff.	Missing lines. L: *Thorowe ther chauntement / To a worme thei had me went / In wo to leven and lende, / Tyll I had kyssed Gaweyne* (lines 2103–06).
2165	Scribal correction. The scribe has written *t* above the *r* of *pertly.*
2184	*pris.* Once more the scribe adapts the Latin abbreviation for his English spelling so that the word reads *pris,* not *pres.* See the note for line 813

    above. The spelling of this word throughout the manuscript is *pris*: see
    lines 2237 and 1304.

2197   *a precious.* N: *a precious a.*

2239   *delaye.* N: *delayne.*

2283   *Ever.* N: *eur.*

LIST OF NAMES, PLACE-NAMES, AND VARIANT SPELLINGS

Agrafrayn, Agafayne
Alysander, Alysaunder, Alexaundre
Antore, Anctour, Anter, Antory, Arthore, Aunctours, Auntouris
Artour, Arthour, Arthur

Bewfiz, Beaufice, Bewfys, Beufise, Beuys

Cadas, Clewdas, Gludas, Caudas, Cludas, Claudas, Lucus
Cardiff, Cordile, Cardelof, Karlof, Cardeuyle, Kardeuyle, Kardill, Karlille, Cardigan
Carleon, Carboun, Carlioun, Karlowne, Caerleon, Skarlyon
Chapell of Awntrous, Chapel of Auentours, Aduentrous Chappell, Chapell of Antrus

Dame D'Amore, Dame Amoure, Diamour, Damore, Damour, Madam de Armoroure,
    Denamowre
Delaraunche, Delarawnche, Celabronche, Celebronche, la Braunche, la Brawnche,
    Dolebraunche
Denys, Denyse, Denyce

Edward, Leonarde
Elene, Ellene, Ellyne, Elyne, Hellen, Elyn
Eweyn, Iwayne

Gaweyne, Gawain, Gawyn, Gawayn
Glastynbury, Glastonbury
Gower, Gawer, Baner, Gauerer
Gyfflet, Gyrflete, Jerflete, Jeffelot, Gesloke, Gyfflet, Gyffet, Turfete
Gyffroun le Flowdous, Jeffrond le Frendys, Jeffron le Freudous, Gyffroun le Fludous,
    Gyffron la Fraudeus, Gefferon Lefrenceus, Geffron la Fredicus
Gyngeleyn, Gyngelayn, Guinglain, Gyngelayne, Ginnglaine

Iran, Irayn, Yrayn, Iran, Irowne, Yrayne

Lambard, Lambert, Lancharde, Lanwarde, Lambarte, Lamberd, Lambardys
Launcelet, Lawncelett, Lawncelot, Launselake
Lybeaus Desconus, Libious Discoinous, Libeous Disconious, Libeus Desconuz,
    Lybeus Disconeus, Libius, Libeus, Libious, Lebeous, Libeous

Maboun, Mabon, Mabownys
Maugys, Maugis, Maugus

Otes de Lyle, Otis de Lile, Otyl de la Byle

Persyfal, Persyfale, Persavale, Perceval, Percivall, Persyvall, Persyvall

Synadoun, Synadown, Synadowne, Cinadowne

Termagaunt, Turrmmagaunt
Theodeley, Deodelyne, Wyndelyn, Teddelyne

Vyolette, Violette, Violet

Wales, Walys, Walis
Wirral, Wyralle, Wirale
Wylleam, William, Will

BIBLIOGRAPHY

MANUSCRIPTS INDICATING FOLIO PLACEMENTS OF *LYBEAUS DESCONUS*

London, British Library, MS Cotton Caligula A.ii, fols. 42vb–57rb (C)
Oxford, Bodleian Library, MS Ashmole 61 (Bodleian 6922), fols. 38v–59v (A)
London, British Library, MS Additional 27879 (Percy Folio, 2:404; fols. 156v–171r) (P)
London, Lambeth Palace, MS 306, fols. 73r–107r (L)
London, Lincoln's Inn, MS 150, fols. 1 and 4r–12v (LI)
Naples, Biblioteca Nazionale, MS XIII.B.29, pp. 87–113 (N)

BIBLIOGRAPHY

Ackerman, R. W. *An Index of the Arthurian Names in Middle English*. Stanford: Stanford University Press, 1952.

The Alliterative Morte Arthure: A Critical Edition. Ed. Valerie Krishna. New York: Burt Franklin, 1976. See also Benson, ed.

Almond, Richard. *Medieval Hunting*. Stroud: Sutton, 2003.

Amidei, Beatrice Barbiellini. "Il tema del fiero bacio nel *Bel Inconnu* e la sua permanenza nella tradizione cantarina." In *Carte Romanze*. Series 1. Quaderni di Acme 23. Bologna: Cisalpino, 1995. Pp. 9–38.

Anderson, Earl R. *Folk-Taxonomies in Early English*. Madison, NJ: Fairleigh Dickinson University Press, 2003.

Archibald, Elizabeth. "The Breton Lay in Middle English: Genre, Transmission and the Franklin's Tale." In *Medieval Insular Romance: Translation and Innovation*. Ed. Judith Weiss, Jennifer Fellows, and Morgan Dickson. Cambridge: D. S. Brewer, 2000. Pp. 55–70.

Arthur at Tamelide. In *Prose Merlin*. Ed. John Conlee. Kalamazoo, MI: Medieval Institute Publications, 1998. Pp. 137–55.

Ashley, Kathleen M. "Medieval Courtesy Books and Dramatic Mirrors of Female Conduct." In *The Ideology of Conduct: Essays on Literature and the History of Sexuality*. Ed. Nancy Armstrong and Leonard Tennenhouse. New York: Methuen and Co., 1987. Pp. 25–38.

Ashley, Kathleen, and Robert L. A. Clark, eds. *Medieval Conduct*. Minneapolis: University of Minnesota Press, 2001.

Augustine. *De bono coniugali, De sancta virginitate*. Ed. and trans. P. G. Walsh. Oxford: Clarendon Press, 2001.

The Babees Book: Aristotle's A B C, Urbanitatis, Stans Puer Ad Mensam, The Lytille Childrenes Lytil Boke, Etc. Ed. Frederick J. Furnivall. EETS o.s. 32. London: Trübner, 1868. Reprint, New York: Greenwood Press, 1969.

Badham, Sally, and Martin Biddle. "Inscriptions in the Painting." In *King Arthur's Round Table: An Archaeological Investigation*. Ed. Martin Biddle et al. Woodbridge: Boydell Press, 2000. Pp. 253–83.

Benson, Larry D, ed. *King Arthur's Death: The Middle English Stanziac Morte Arthur and Alliterative Morte Arthure*. Rev. ed. Edward E. Foster. Kalamazoo, MI: Medieval Institute Publications, 1994.

Bevis of Hampton. In *Four Romances of England: King Horn, Havelok the Dane, Bevis of Hampton, Athelston*. Ed. Ronald B. Herzman, Graham Drake, and Eve Salisbury. Kalamazoo, MI: Medieval Institute Publications, 1997. Pp. 187–340.

Blamires, David. "The Sources and Literary Structure of *Wigamur*." In *Studies in Medieval Literature and Languages: In Memory of Frederick Whitehead*. Ed. W. Rothwell, W. R. J. Barron, David Blamires, and Lewis Thorpe. Manchester: Manchester University Press, 1973. Pp. 27–46.

Blanchfield, Lynne S. "The Romances in MS Ashmole 61: An Idiosyncratic Scribe." In *Romance in Medieval England*. Ed. Maldwyn Mills, Jennifer Fellows, and Carol M. Meale. Cambridge: D. S. Brewer, 1991. Pp. 65–87.

Bliss, Jane. *Naming and Namelessness in Medieval Romance*. Cambridge: D. S. Brewer, 2008.

The Book of John Mandeville. Ed. Tamarah Kohanski and C. David Benson. Kalamazoo, MI: Medieval Institute Publications, 2007.

Bradbury, Jim. *The Routledge Companion to Medieval Warfare*. London: Routledge, 2004.

Brand, Paul. "Family and Inheritance, Women and Children." In *An Illustrated History of Late Medieval England*. Ed. Chris Given-Wilson. Manchester: Manchester University Press, 1996. Pp. 58–81.

Braswell, Mary Flowers, ed. *Sir Perceval of Galles and Ywain and Gawain*. Kalamazoo, MI: Medieval Institute Publications, 1995.

Brereton, Georgine E. "A Thirteenth-Century List of French Lays and Other Narrative Poems." *Modern Language Review* 45 (1950): 40–45.

Broadus, Edmund Kemper. "The Red Cross Knight and *Lybeaus Desconus*." *Modern Language Notes* 18.7 (1903): 202–04.

Brown, Howard Mayer, and Keith Polk. "Instrumental Music, *c*.1300–*c*.1520." In *Music as Concept and Practice in the Late Middle Ages*. Ed. Reinhard Strohm and Bonnie J. Blackburn. Oxford: Oxford University Press, 2001. Pp. 97–161.

Bruce, Christopher W. *The Arthurian Name Dictionary*. New York: Garland, 1999.

Burrow, J. A. "Explanatory Notes: 'The Tale of Sir Thopas.'" In *The Riverside Chaucer*. Gen. ed. Larry D. Benson. Third ed. Boston: Houghton Mifflin, 1987. Pp. 917–23.

Calin, William. *The French Tradition and the Literature of Medieval England*. Toronto: University of Toronto Press, 1994.

Cantari di Carduino. In *Cantari Fiabeschi Arturiani*. Ed. Daniela Delcorno Branca. Milan: Luni, 1999. Pp. 39–64.

I Cantari di Carduino giuntovi quello di Tristano e Lancielotto quando combattettero al petrone di Merlino. Ed. P. Rajna. Bologna: Romagnoli, 1873.

Caxton, William. "Caxton's Prologue." In *Caxton's Malory: A New Edition of Sir Thomas Malory's Le Morte Darthur, Based on the Pierpont Morgan Copy of William Caxton's Edition of 1485*. Ed. James W. Spisak. 2 vols. Berkeley: University of California Press, 1983. 1:1–4.

Chaucer, Geoffrey. *The Riverside Chaucer*. Gen. ed. Larry D. Benson. Third ed. Boston: Houghton Mifflin, 1987.

Child, Francis James, ed. *The English and Scottish Popular Ballads*. 10 vols. 1884. Reprint, New York: Dover Publications, 1965.

Chrétien de Troyes. *The Complete Romances of Chrétien de Troyes*. Trans. David Staines. Bloomington: Indiana University Press, 1990.

Chudley, Margaret C., and P. J. C. Field. "A Source for Spenser's House of Busirane Episode." *Notes and Queries* 27 (1980): 304–06.

Cohen, Jeffrey Jerome. *Of Giants: Sex, Monsters, and the Middle Ages*. Minneapolis: University of Minnesota Press, 1999.

———. *Medieval Identity Machines*. Minneapolis: University of Minnesota Press, 2003.

Cooper, Helen. *The English Romance in Time: Transforming Motifs from Geoffrey of Monmouth to the Death of Shakespeare*. Oxford: Oxford University Press, 2004.

Cooper, Nancy Margaret Mays. "*Libeaus Desconus*: A Multi-Text Edition." Ph.D. dissertation, Stanford University, 1961. Dissertation Abstracts 21 (1961), 3449.

Corèdon, Christopher, with Ann Williams. *A Dictionary of Medieval Terms and Phrases*. Cambridge: D. S. Brewer, 2004.

Crane, Susan. *Insular Romance: Politics, Faith, and Culture in Anglo-Norman and Middle English Literature*. Berkeley: University of California Press, 1986.

Crosse, Henry. *Vertues Common-Wealth or The High-Way to Honour*. 1603. Ed. Alexander B. Grosart. London: Printed for Subscribers, 1878.

Daileader, Celia R. "When a Sparrow Falls: Women Readers, Male Critics, and John Skelton's *Phyllyp Sparowe*." *Philological Quarterly* 75 (1996): 391–409.

Dalrymple, Roger. *Language and Piety in Middle English Romance*. Cambridge: D. S. Brewer, 2000.

Dickson, Arthur. "The Earl of Westmoreland and Bueve de Hantone." *PMLA* 43.2 (1928): 570.

Dickson, Morgan. "Female Doubling and Male Identity in Medieval Romance." In *The Matter of Identity in Medieval Romance*. Ed. Phillipa Hardman. Cambridge: D. S. Brewer, 2002. Pp. 59–72.

Djordjević, Ivana, and Jennifer Fellows. "Introduction." In *Sir Bevis of Hampton in Literary Tradition*. Ed. Jennifer Fellows and Ivana Djordjevič. Woodbridge: D. S. Brewer, 2008. Pp. 1–8.

The Erle of Tolous. In Laskaya and Salisbury, *Middle English Breton Lays*. Pp. 309–65.

Evans, Joan. *Dress in Mediaeval France*. Oxford: Clarendon Press, 1952.

Evans, Murray J. *Rereading Middle English Romance: Manuscript Layout, Decoration, and the Rhetoric of Composite Structure*. Montreal: McGill-Queen's University Press, 1995.

Everett, Dorothy. "The Relationship of Chestre's *Launfal* and *Lybeaus Desconus*." *Medium Ævum* 7 (1938): 29–49.

Farmer, David Hugh. *The Oxford Dictionary of Saints*. Oxford: Oxford University Press, 2004.

Ferlampin-Acher, Christine. "La Fée et la Guivre — *Le Bel Inconnu* de Renaut de Beaujeu: Approche Littéraire." In *La Fée et la Guivre — Le Bel Inconnu de Renaut de Beaujeu: Approche Littéraire et Concordancier (v. v. 1237–3252)*. Ed. Christine Ferlampin-Acher et concordancier établi par Monique Léonard. Champion-Varia 8. Paris: Champion, 1996. Pp. ix–lxxi.

Fewster, Carol. *Traditionality and Genre in Middle English Romance*. Cambridge: D. S. Brewer, 1987.

Field, Rosalind. "Popular Romance: The Material and the Problems." In *A Companion to Medieval Popular Romance*. Ed. Raluca L. Radulescu and Cory James Rushton. Cambridge: D. S. Brewer, 1999. Pp. 9–30.

Flanagan, Sarah Patricia. "The Male Cinderella in English Metrical Romance." MA thesis, Brown University, 1931.

Fleming, John V. "The Round Table in Literature and Legend." In *King Arthur's Round Table: An Archaeological Investigation*. Ed. Martin Biddle et al. Woodbridge: Boydell Press, 2000. Pp. 5–30.

Friar, Stephen, ed. *A Dictionary of Heraldry*. New York: Harmony, 1987.

Furrow, Melissa. *Expectations of Romance: The Reception of a Genre in Medieval England*. Cambridge: D. S. Brewer, 2009.

Gairdner, James. *Three Fifteenth-Century Chronicles, with Historical Memoranda by John Stowe, and Contemporary Notes of Occurrences Written by Him in the Reign of Queen Elizabeth*. Westminster: J. B. Nichols and Sons, 1880. Reprint, New York: Johnson Reprint, 1965.

Geoffrey of Monmouth. *The History of the Kings of Britain: An Edition and Translation of De gestis Britonum (Historia regum Britanniae)*. Ed. Michael D. Reeve. Trans. Neil Wright. Woodbridge: Boydell Press, 2007.

Geoffrey of Vinsauf. *Poetria Nova*. Trans. Margaret F. Nims. Toronto: Pontifical Institute of Mediaeval Studies, 1967.

Goldsmid, Edmund. "Libius Disconius." In *Ancient English Metrical Romances*. Edinburgh: E. & G. Goldsmid, 1884. 2:404–99.

Guddat-Figge, Gisela. *Catalogue of Manuscripts Containing Middle English Romances*. Munich: Wilhelm Fink, 1976.

Guy of Warwick, Couplets. The Auchinleck Manuscript Project. Ed. David Burnley and Alison Wiggins. July 2003. National Library of Scotland: http://www.nls.uk/auchinleck/mss/guy_cp.html.

Hahn, Thomas, ed. *Sir Gawain: Eleven Romances and Tales*. Kalamazoo, MI: Medieval Institute Publications, 1995.

Hanning, Robert W. "Uses of Names in Medieval Literature." *Names* 16 (1968): 325–38.

Hales, John W., and Frederick J. Furnivall, eds. "Libius Disconius." In *Bishop Percy's Folio Manuscript: Ballads and Romances*. 3 vols. London: N. Trübner and Co., 1867–68. 2:404–99.

Harward, Vernon J., Jr. *The Dwarfs of Arthurian Romance and Celtic Tradition*. Leiden: E. J. Brill, 1958.

Hazell, Dinah. "The Blinding of Gwennere: Thomas Chestre as Social Critic." *Arthurian Literature* 20 (2003): 123–43.

Hebert, Jill M. *Morgan Le Fay, Shapeshifter*. New York: Palgrave Macmillian, 2013.

Heng, Geraldine. *Empire of Magic: Medieval Romance and the Politics of Cultural Fantasy*. New York: Columbia University Press, 2003.

Hewitt, John. *Ancient Armour and Weapons in Europe: From the Iron Period of the Northern Nations to the End of the Seventeenth Century: With Illustrations from Contemporary Monuments*. Vol. 2, *The Fourteenth Century*. 3 vols. Oxford: J. Henry and J. Parker, 1855.

Hibbard, Laura A. *Mediæval Romance in England: A Study of the Sources and Analogues of the Non-Cyclic Metrical Romances*. New York: Oxford University Press, 1924.

Hoffman, Donald L. "Malory's 'Cinderella Knights' and the Notion of Adventure." *Philological Quarterly* 67 (1988): 145–56.

Honemann, Volker. "The Wigalois Narratives." In *The Arthur of the Germans: The Arthurian Legend in Medieval German and Dutch Literature*. Ed. W. H. Jackson and S. A. Ranawake. Cardiff: University of Wales, 2000. Pp. 142–54.

How Culhwch Won Olwen. In *The Mabinogion*. Trans. Gwyn Jones. New York: Knopf, 1949. Pp. 85–121.

Hunt, Tony. "Editing Arthuriana." In *The History of Arthurian Scholarship*. Vol. 2. Ed. Norris J. Lacy. Arthurian Studies. Cambridge: D. S. Brewer, 2006. Pp. 37–48.

———. "Texte and Prétexte: Jaufré and Yvain." In *The Legacy of Chrétien of Troyes*. Ed. Norris J. Lacy et al. 2 vols. Amsterdam: Rodopi, 1988. 2:125–41.

James, Montague Rhodes, and Claude Jenkins. *A Descriptive Catalogue of the Manuscripts in the Library of Lambeth Palace*. Cambridge: Cambridge University Press, 1930–32.

Jewers, Caroline. "Slippery Custom(er)s: On Knight and Snake in the *Bel Inconnu*." *Neophilologus* 94 (2010):17–31.

Johnston, Mark D., ed. *Medieval Conduct Literature: An Anthology of Vernacular Guides to Behaviour for Youths, with English Translations*. Toronto: University of Toronto Press, 2009.

Jones, Mark. "The Life of St. Eustace: A Saint's Legend from Lambeth Palace MS 306." *ANQ* 20.1 (2007): 13–23.

Kaeuper, Richard W. *Bankers to the Crown: The Riccardi of Lucca and Edward I*. Princeton, NJ: Princeton University Press, 1973.

Kaluza, Max, ed. *Libeaus Desconus: Die Mittelenglishche Romanze vom Schönen Unbekannten*. Leipzig: O. R. Reisland, 1890.

———. "Thomas Chestre, Verfasser des Launfal, Libeaus Desconus und Octovian." *Englische Studien* 18 (1893): 165–90.

Karras, Ruth Mazo. *From Boys to Men: Formations of Masculinity in Late Medieval Europe*. Philadelphia: University of Pennsylvania Press, 2003.

Ker, N. R., and A. J. Piper. *Medieval Manuscripts in British Libraries*. Vol. 4, *Paisley to York*. Oxford: Oxford University Press, 1992.

Kibler, William W. "Three Old French Magicians: Maugis, Basin, and Auberon." In *Romance Epic: Essays on a Medieval Literary Genre*. Ed. Hans-Erich Keller. Kalamazoo, MI: Medieval Institute Publications, 1987. Pp. 173–87.

Knight, Stephen. "The Social Function of the Middle English Romances." In *Medieval Literature: Criticism, Ideology and History*. Ed. David Aers. New York: St. Martin's Press, 1986. Pp. 99–112.

The Knight of the Parrot (Le Chevalier du Papegau). Trans. Thomas E. Vesce. New York: Garland, 1986.

Kooper, Erik, ed. *Sentimental and Humorous Romances: Floris and Blancheflour, Sir Degrevant, The Squire of Low Degree, The Tournament of Tottenham, and the Feast of Tottenham*. Kalamazoo, MI: Medieval Institute Publications, 2006.

Lacy, Norris J., ed. *The New Arthurian Encyclopedia*. New York: Garland, 1996.

Larrington, Carolyne. *King Arthur's Enchantresses: Morgan and Her Sisters in Arthurian Tradition.* London: I. B. Tauris, 2006.

Laskaya, Anne, and Eve Salisbury, eds. *The Middle English Breton Lays.* Kalamazoo, MI: Medieval Institute Publications, 1995.

Lay le Freine. In Laskaya and Salisbury, *Middle English Breton Lays.* Pp. 61–87.

L'Hystoire de Giglan Filz de Messire Gauvain Qui Fut Roy de Galles. Et de Geoffroy de Maience Son Compaignon: Tous Deux Chevaliers de la Table Ronde. Lesquelz Feirent Plusieurs et Merveilleuses Enterprises. Et Eurent de Grandes Fortunes et Adventures, Autant Que Chevaliers de Leur Temps: Desquelles par Leur Noble Prouesse et Cueur Chevaleureux Vindrent a Bout et Honourable Fin, comme on Pourra Veoir en Ce Present Livre. Lequel a este Nouvellement Translate de langaiges Espaignol en Nostre Langaige Francoys. Trans. Claude Platin. Lyon: Claude Nourry. London, British Library, C.47.f.5, 1530.

Loomis, Roger Sherman. "From Segontium to Sinadon: The Legends of a *Cité Gaste.*" *Speculum* 22 (1947): 520–33.

———. "The Fier Baiser in Mandeville's Travels, Arthurian Romance, and Irish Saga." *Studi Medievali* 17 (1951): 104–13.

———. *The Development of Arthurian Romance.* New York: Harper and Row, 1964. Reprint, Mineola, NY: Dover Publications, 2000.

Lull, Ramón. *The Book of the Ordre of Chyuvalry,* trans. and printed by William Caxton from a French Version of Ramón Lull's "Le Libre del Orde de Cauayleria," Together with Adam Loutfuts Scottish Transcript (Harleian MS 6149, ed. Alfred T. P. Beyles). EETS o.s. 168. London: Oxford University Press, 1926.

Lumby, J. Rawson. *Ratis Raving, and Other Moral and Religious Pieces, in Prose and Verse.* EETS o.s. 43. London: Trübner and Co., 1870.

Lupack, Alan, ed. *Lancelot of the Laik and Sir Tristrem.* Kalamazoo, MI: Medieval Institute Publications, 1994.

———. *The Oxford Guide to Arthurian Literature and Legend.* Oxford: Oxford University Press, 2005.

Maddox, Donald. *The Arthurian Romances of Chrétien de Troyes: Once and Future Fictions.* Cambridge: Cambridge University Press, 1991.

Magoun, Francis P., Jr. "The Source of Chaucer's Rime of Sir Thopas." *PMLA* 42 (1927): 833–44.

Malory, Thomas. *The Works of Sir Thomas Malory.* Ed. Eugène Vinaver. Second ed. 3 vols. Oxford: Clarendon Press, 1973.

Manly, John M., and Edith Rickert, eds. *The Text of the Canterbury Tales: Studied on the Basis of All Known Manuscripts.* 8 vols. Chicago: University of Chicago Press, 1940.

Mann, Jill. "The Power of the Alphabet: A Reassessment of the Relation between the A and B Versions of *Piers Plowman.*" *Yearbook of Langland Studies* 8 (1994): 21–50.

Marie de France. *Laüstic.* In *The Lais of Marie de France.* Trans. Glyn S. Burgess and Keith Busby. New York: Penguin, 2003.

Maugis D'Aigremont: Chanson de Geste. Ed. Philippe Vernay. Bern: A. Francke, 1980.

McCracken, Peggy. *The Romance of Adultery: Queenship and Sexual Transgression in Old French Literature.* Philadelphia: University of Pennsylvania Press, 1998.

McHugh, Sheila Joyce. "*The Lay of the Big Fool*: Its Irish and Arthurian Sources." *Modern Philology* 42 (1945): 197–211.

McSparran, Frances, ed. "British Library Manuscript Cotton Caligula A.II." In *Octovian Imperator: Edited from MS BL Cotton Caligula A.II.* Heidelberg: Carl Winter, 1979. Pp. 55–58.

Mills, Maldwyn. "The Composition and Style of the 'Southern' *Octavian, Sir Launfal* and *Libeaus Desconus.*" *Medium Ævum* 31 (1962): 88–109.

———. "A Mediaeval Reviser at Work." *Medium Ævum* 32 (1963): 11–23.

———. "The Huntsman and the Dwarf in *Eric* and *Libeaus Desconus.*" *Romania: Revue Consacree a l'Etude des Langues et des Literatures Romanes* 87 (1966): 33–58.

———, ed. *Lybeaus Desconus.* EETS o.s. 261. Oxford: Oxford University Press, 1969.

Mitchell-Smith, Ilan. "Defining Violence in Middle English Romances: 'Sir Gowther' and 'Libeaus Desconus.'" *Fifteenth Century Studies* 34 (2009): 148–61.

Le Morte Darthur. See Malory.

Neal, Derek G. *The Masculine Self in Late Medieval England*. Chicago: University of Chicago Press, 2008.

Nicholls, Jonathan. *The Matter of Courtesy: Medieval Courtesy Books and the Gawain-Poet*. Woodbridge: D. S. Brewer, 1985.

Nicolle, David. *Arms and Armour of the Crusading Era 1050–1350*. London: Greenhill, 1999.

"Nix Nought Nothing." In *English Fairy Tales; and, More English Fairy Tales*. Ed. Joseph Jacobs and Donald Haase. Illustrated by John D. Batten. Santa Barbara, CA: ABC-CLIO, 2002. Pp. 37–40.

Oakeshott, R. Ewart. *The Sword in the Age of Chivalry*. New York: Frederick A. Praeger, 1964.

———. *The Archaeology of Weapons: Arms and Armour from Prehistory to the Age of Chivalry*. Woodbridge: Boydell Press, 1996.

———. *European Weapons and Armour: From the Renaissance to the Industrial Revolution*. Woodbridge: Boydell, 2000.

Octavian: Zwei Mittelenglische Bearbeitungen Der Sage. Ed. Gregor Sarrazin. Heilbronn: Gebr. Henninger, 1885.

Orme, Nicholas. *Medieval Children*. New Haven: Yale University Press, 2001.

Oswald, Dana M. *Monsters, Gender, and Sexuality in Medieval English Literature*. Woodbridge: D. S. Brewer, 2010.

Otuel and Roland. In *Firumbras and Otuel and Roland: Edited from MS. Brit. Mus. Addit. 37492*. Ed. Mary Isabelle O'Sullivan. EETS o.s. 198. London: Oxford University Press, 1935. Pp. 59–146.

Painter, Sidney. *William Marshal: Knight-Errant, Baron, and Regent of England*. Toronto: University of Toronto Press, 1992.

Passmore, S. Elizabeth, and Susan Carter, eds. *The English "Loathly Lady" Tales: Boundaries, Traditions, Motifs*. Kalamazoo, MI: Medieval Institute Publications, 2007.

Pearsall, Derek, and I. C. Cunningham. "Introduction." In *The Auchinleck Manuscript: National Library of Scotland Advocates' MS. 19.2.1*. London: Scolar Press, 1977. Pp. vii–xxiv.

Peck, Russell A. "Folklore and Powerful Women in Gower's 'Tale of Florent.'" In *The English "Loathly Lady" Tales: Boundaries, Traditions, Motifs*, ed. S. Elizabeth Passmore and Susan Carter. Kalamazoo, MI: Medieval Institute Publications, 2007. Pp. 100–45.

Percy, Thomas. *Reliques of Ancient English Poetry*. 3 vols. Edinburgh: James Nicol, 1858.

Pickering, O. S., and V. M. O'Mara. *The Index of Middle English Prose, Handlist XIII: Manuscripts in Lambeth Palace Library, Including Those Formerly in Sion College Library*. Cambridge: D. S. Brewer, 1999.

Ponzela Gaia: Galvano e la Donna Serpente. Ed. Beatrice Barbiellini Amidei. Milan: Luni, 2000.

Predelli, Maria Bendinelli. *Alle Origini del Bel Gherardino*. Florence: Leo S. Olschki, 1990.

Promptorium Parvulorum Sive Clericorum, Lexicon Anglo-Latinum Princeps. 3 vols. Ed. A. L. Mayhew. EETS e.s. 102 London: Trubner & Co, 1908.

Purdie, Rhiannon. *Anglicising Romance: Tail-Rhyme and Genre in Medieval English Literature*. Cambridge: D. S. Brewer, 2008.

Radulescu, Raluca L. "Genre and Classification." In *A Companion to Medieval Popular Romance*. Ed. Raluca L. Radulescu and Cory James Rushton. Cambridge: D. S. Brewer, 1999. Pp. 31–48.

Renaut de Bâgé. *Le Bel Inconnu (Li Biaus Descouneüs: The Fair Unknown)*. Ed. Karen Fresco. Trans. Colleen P. Donagher. New York: Garland, 1992.

Reno, Frank D. *Arthurian Figures of History and Legend: A Biographical Dictionary*. Jefferson, NC: McFarland, 2011.

Richmond, Velma Bourgeois. *The Popularity of Middle English Romance*. Bowling Green, OH: Bowling Green University Popular Press, 1975.

The Rise of Gawain, Nephew of Arthur (De ortu Waluuanii nepotism Arturi). Ed. and trans. Mildred Leake Day. New York: Garland, 1984.

Roach, William, ed. *The Continuations of the Old French Perceval of Chretien de Troyes*. 5 vols. Philadelphia: University of Pennsylvania Press, 1949.

Robbins, Rossell Hope. "Wall Verses at Launceston Priory." *Archiv für das Studium der neuere Sprachen und Literaturen* 200 (1963): 338–43.

Romance of Guy of Warwick. Ed. from the Auchinleck MS. In the Advocates' Library, Edinburgh and from MS. 107 in Caius College, Cambridge. Ed. Julius Zupitza. EETS e.s. 42, 49, 59. One Volume Reprint, London: Oxford University Press, 1966.

Rushton, Cory. "Absent Fathers, Unexpected Sons: Paternity in Malory's *Morte Darthur*." *Studies in Philology* 101 (2004): 136–52.

Salisbury, Eve. "(Re)dressing Cinderella." In *Retelling Tales: Essays in Honor of Russell Peck*. Ed. Thomas Hahn and Alan Lupack. Cambridge: D. S. Brewer, 1997. Pp. 275–92.

———. "*Lybeaus Desconus*: Transformation, Adaptation, and the Monstrous-Feminine." *Arthuriana* 24.1 (2014): forthcoming.

Salter, David. *Holy and Noble Beasts: Encounters with Animals in Medieval Literature*. Cambridge: D. S. Brewer, 2001.

Sanders, Arnold. "Sir Gareth and the 'Unfair Unknown': Malory's Use of the Gawain Romances." *Arthuriana* 16 (2006): 34–46.

Saunders, Corinne. *Rape and Ravishment in the Literature of Medieval England*. Cambridge: D. S. Brewer, 2001.

———, ed. *Cultural Encounters in the Romance of Medieval England*. Cambridge: D. S. Brewer, 2005.

———. "Erotic Magic: The Enchantress in Middle English Romance." In *The Erotic in the Literature of Medieval Britain*. Ed. Amanda Hopkins and Cory James Rushton. Cambridge: Boydell and Brewer, 2007. Pp. 38–52.

———. *Magic and the Supernatural in Medieval English Romance*. Cambridge: D. S. Brewer, 2010.

———. "Subtle Crafts: Magic and Exploitation in Medieval English Romance." In *The Exploitations of Medieval Romance*. Ed. Laura Ashe, Ivana Djordjević, and Judith Weiss. Cambridge: D. S. Brewer, 2010. Pp. 108–24.

Scala, Elizabeth. "Pretty Women: The Romance of the Fair Unknown, Feminism, and Contemporary Romantic Comedy." *Film & History* 29 (1999): 34–45.

Scherb, Victor I. "John Skelton's 'Agenst Garnesche': Poetic Territorialism at the Court of Henry VIII." *Quidditas* 19 (1998): 123–42.

Schibanoff, Susan. "Taking Jane's Cue: *Phyllyp Sparowe* as Primer for Women Readers." *PMLA* 101 (1986): 832–47.

Schofield, William Henry. *Studies on the Libeaus Desconus*. Boston: Ginn & Co., 1895.

Shuffleton, George, ed. "Lybeaus Desconus." In *Codex Ashmole 61: A Compilation of Popular Middle English Verse*. Kalamazoo, MI: Medieval Institute Publications, 2008. Pp. 111–64, 471–84.

Simons, Penny. "The 'Bel Sanblant': Reading *Le Bel Inconnu*." *French Studies* 50.3 (1996): 257–74.

Sir Degaré. In Laskaya and Salisbury, *Middle English Breton Lays*. Pp. 89–144.

Sir Degaré. The Auchinleck Manuscript. Ed. David Burnley and Alison Wiggins. July 2003. National Library of Scotland <http://www.nls.uk/auchinleck/mss/degare.html>.

Sir Gawain and the Carle of Carlisle. In Hahn, *Sir Gawain*, Pp. 81–112.

Sir Gawain and the Green Knight. Ed. J. R. R. Tolkien and E. V. Gordon. Second edition. Ed. Norman Davies. Oxford: Clarendon Press, 1972.

Sir Gawain and the Green Knight. In *The Poems of the Pearl Manuscript: Pearl, Cleanness, Patience, Sir Gawain and the Green Knight*. Ed. Malcolm Andrew and Ronald Waldron. Exeter: University of Exeter Press, 2007. Pp. 207–300.

Sir Gowther. In Laskaya and Salisbury, *Middle English Breton Lays*. Pp. 263–307.

Sir Launfal. In Laskaya and Salisbury, *Middle English Breton Lays*. Pp. 201–62.

Sir Orfeo. In Laskaya and Salisbury, *Middle English Breton Lays*. Pp. 15–59.

Sir Perceval of Galles. In Braswell, *Sir Perceval of Galles*. Pp. 7–68.

Skelton, John. *The Complete English Poems*. Ed. John Scattergood. Harmondsworth: Penguin Books, 1983.

———. *The Poetical Works of John Skelton.* Ed. Alexander Dyce. 3 vols. Boston: Little, Brown & Co., 1856. Reprint, Whitefish, MT: Kessinger Publishing, 2006.

The Squire of Low Degree. In Kooper, *Sentimental and Humorous Romances.* Pp. 127–71.

Stanzaic Guy of Warwick. Ed. Alison Wiggins. Kalamazoo, MI: Medieval Institute Publications, 2004.

Taylor, A. "The Motif of the Vacant Stake in Folklore and Romance." *Romanic Review* 9 (1918): 21–28.

Thomas, Neil. *A German View of Camelot: Wirnt von Gravenberg's "Wigalois" and Arthurian Tradition.* Bern: Peter Lang, 1987.

———. "The Sources of *Wigamur* and the German Reception of the Fair Unknown Tradition." *Reading Medieval Studies* 19 (1993): 97–111.

Todd, Henry J. *A Catalogue of the Archiepiscopal Manuscripts in the Library of Lambeth Palace.* London: Law and Gilbert, 1812.

Trounce, A. McI. "The English Tail-Rhyme Romances - I." *Medium Ævum* 1 (1932): 87–108.

Tyler, Margaret. *The Mirrour of Princely Deedes and Knighthood, a Translation of Book 1 of Part 1 of Espejo de Principes y Cavalleros by Diego Ortúñez de Calahorra.* Trans. Margaret Tyler. London: Thomas East, 1578.

Tyssens, Madeleine. "Les Sources de Renaut de Beaujeu." In *Mélanges de Langue et de Littérature du Moyen Age et de la Renaissance Offerts a Jean Frappier.* Publications Romanes et Françaises 112. 2 vols. Geneva: Droz, 1970. 2:1043–55.

Verner, Lisa. *The Epistemology of the Monstrous in the Middle Ages.* New York: Routledge, 2005.

Vesce, Thomas. "The Greening of *Carduino.*" *Mid-Hudson Language Studies* 3 (1980): 13–24.

Vives, Juan Luis. *The Instruction of a Christen Woman.* Trans. Richard Hyrde [c. 1529]. Ed. Virginia Walcott Beauchamp, Elizabeth H. Hageman, and Margaret Mikesell. Urbana: University of Illinois Press, 2002.

von Grafenberg, Wirnt. *Wigalois: The Knight of Fortune's Wheel.* Trans. J. W. Thomas. Lincoln: University of Nebraska Press, 1977.

Walters, Lori. "'A Love That Knows No Falsehood': Moral Instruction and Narrative Closure in the *Bel Inconnu* and *Beaudous.*" *South Atlantic Review* 58.2 (1993): 21–39.

Walter, Philippe. *Le Bel Inconnu de Renaut de Beaujeu: Rite, mythe et roman.* Paris: Presses Universitaires de France, 1996.

Ward, Renée. "Challenging the Boundaries of Medieval Romance: Thomas Chestre's *Lybeaus Desconus.*" *Florilegium* 21 (2004): 119–34.

Wace. *Wace's Roman de Brut: A History of the British.* Ed. and trans. Judith Weiss. Rev. ed. Exeter: University of Exeter Press, 2002.

The Wedding of Sir Gawain and Dame Ragnelle. In Hahn, *Sir Gawain.* Pp. 41–80.

Weldon, James. "Jousting for Identity: Tournaments in Thomas Chestre's *Sir Launfal.*" *Parergon* 17.2 (2000): 107–23.

———. "'Naked as she was bore': Naked Disenchantment in *Lybeaus Desconus.*" *Parergon* 24.1 (2007): 67–99.

———. "The Naples Manuscript and the Case for a Female Readership." *Neophilologus* 93 (2009): 703–22.

Weston, Jessie L., trans. *Sir Cleges, Sir Libeaus Desconus: Two Old English Metrical Romances.* London: David Nutt, 1902.

———. "Sir Libeaus Desconus." The Camelot Project at the University of Rochester. Ed. Alan Lupack and Barbara Tepa Lupack. March 7, 2011 <http://www.lib.rochester.edu/camelot/libeaus.htm>.

Westwood, Jennifer, and Jacqueline Simpson. *The Lore of the Land: A Guide to England's Legends, from Spring-Heeled Jack to the Witches of Warboys.* London: Penguin, 2005.

Whiting, Bartlett Jere, and Helen Wescott Whiting. *Proverbs, Sentences, and Proverbial Phrases.* Cambridge, MA: Belknap Press of Harvard University Press, 1968.

Wigamur. Ed. Nathanael Busch. Berlin: Walter de Gruyter, 2009.

Wilson, Robert H. "The 'Fair Unknown' in Malory." *PMLA* 58 (1943): 1–21.

Ywain and Gawain. In Braswell, *Sir Perceval of Galles.* Pp. 84–187.

Zaerr, Linda Marie. "Music and Magic in *Le Bel Inconnu* and *Lybeaus Desconus*." *Medieval Forum* 4 (2004) <http://www.sfsu.edu/~medieval/Volume4/Zaerr.html>.

~ GLOSSARY

We have made ample use of the *Middle English Dictionary* in compiling this glossary. If there is variation in spelling, the Lambeth spelling occurs first, followed by the Naples spelling.

aketowne, actowne, acton *a quilted or padded jacket worn under armor*

algate *straightaway, at once*

aplyght, aplight *an expression used to add emphasis*

ar *see* **or**

arblast *weapon consisting of a bow set on a shaft, i.e., a crossbow*

arsoun *uptilted front or back of a saddle*

asise *custom or practice; a standard of measure*

barme *breast, bosom; arms*

bassnet, basnet *a light helmet worn under the fighting helmet*

bawndon, bandowne *control, power, governance*

besette *surround, besiege; simply protect*

beyete, bigete *advantage, gain*

bidene *all together; all told*

bileve *leave it where it is, turn away from*

bilevyd *departed; died*

blawndenere, blandere *rich fur, possibly ermine*

blynne *stop, cease*

bone *petition, request*

borde *dining table, table of honor*

bowne, bownde, boune *ready, prepared*

braid, breid *a moment*

bras *impale; break to pieces*

brond(e) *torch; torch stick*

bround *burnt; blackened*

browne, broun *polished brightly*

bryght, bright *fresh, beautiful, splendid*

burgeys, burgeis *free citizen of a town*

can *see* **con**

cantel *chunk, piece, slice*

cheiris, cheyers *chairs*

chepyng *marketplace*

chorle *any person not belonging to the nobility or clergy*

con, can *understands how to use; knows*

coped, kopid *wearing a cloak*

cor, corps, course, kose *a dead body, corpse; the body (as distinct from soul); head or limbs*

corcis *corset or corselet; breastplate*

cornelle *corner or angle of a building; front*

covery, coverid *recover, recovered*

cromponis *setting for jewelry*

cropoune *hindquarters of an animal*

destere, desture *a riding horse (as opposed to a warhorse)*

dight *arranged; adorned*

dissoures *storytellers, minstrels*

doughti, doughty *valiant, fierce in combat, bold*

drawght, draught *blow of a sword*

durye, dury *endure*

egir *fierce, enraged; eager*
empris *enterprise, chivalric adventure*
entent *wish, desire, will*
envye *hatred, ill will*
errour(e) *anger, wrath*

falle *many*
fange, fynge *seize*
fare *travel*
fassyon, facion *physical appearance, figure, shape, face, presence; fashion*
fauchone, fouchone *sword*
fax *hair of the head*
fellowne, feloun *treachery*
felwet *velvet*
fenne *swamp, mud, dirt, trash*
ferde *suitable, appropriate to*
ferli *terrifying, terrible*
fond *put forth one's best effort*
foreward *agreement*
frede *experienced, felt*
freke *a brave man, warrior, man-at-arms*
fynge *see* **fange**

gestours *reciters, storytellers*
gorger, gorgare *the piece of armor that protects the neck*
grede *proclaim or announce*
grise *terrible, frightening*
grom, grome *a boy, youth, young man*
gryce, grys *gray; robe made of fur (possibly Russian gray squirrel)*
gynne, gyne *ingenious device*

hende, hynde *courtly, gracious, noble*
hete *anger*
hight, yhight *was called; had promised*

ilke *each; the same; that*

jepowne *a light tunic*

kopid *see* **coped**
korvelle *corbel, an ornamental projection jutting out from a wall, supporting the weight of a tower or window*

kythe, kithe *make known, reveal*

lavender *laundry*
lawnder, lavender *washerwoman, laundress*
laye, lei *obedience to law, allegiance to oath, faith*
laynore *a thong or strap, possibly of a helmet*
lefe *eager, willing*
leman, lemmoun *lover, paramour*
lende *dwell, rest*
leese, les *lies, used in the formula "withoute lees" (without lies, truly)*
lesynge *lying*
lewte *honor*
lithe *be attentive*
loose, loce, lose, los *reputation*
lorne *lost*
louge, lought(e) *laughed*
loute, lowte *bow, prostrate oneself*
lowe *hill, mountain*
lynnell, lengels *straps of a charger's harness*

mawmentis *representations of a pagan deity, idols*
mayne, maigne *retinue, attendants*
moolde, molde *head, crown of the head*

nete *beast; ox, heifer, cow*
noye *annoyance, wrath*

or, ar, er *before*
outrage *inappropriate or excessive action, possibly violence; unchivalric deed(s)*
overthwart *across, lying crossways*

palfaray, palfray *a riding horse (as opposed to a warhorse)*
pare *cut, trim*
pay(e) *pleasure, satisfaction, liking*
pertte, pert *attractive*
pesawe, pesyn *ornamental collar attached to helmet*
plax *braided hair of head, beard*

preson, presond *present, gift*
prestabelle (v.) *eager to serve, capable in service*
prestabelle (adj.) *remarkable*
pris, price *fame, renown, worthiness, nobility, reputation; worthy*
prove, preve *test, put to trial*
prowe *well-being, honor*

quede *evil; wickedness*
quyte, quite *repay, requite*
qwelled, yquelde *killed, destroyed*

rasshe *tear up (see to-rasshe)*
raught *reached*
redde, rede *tell, recount, narrate*
resound *speech, discourse, debate*
rice *branch, stem*
ruffyne *reddish in color*
ryffe, ryve *abundantly, frequently*

sawe *declaration, proverb*
shawe, schawe *forest, thicket, foliage*
shent, yschent *harmed, defiled*
socoure *help, assistance*
soth(e) *truth*
splete *metal plate for reinforcing armor*
stark(e) *strongly made, solid*
stent(e) *an assessed value*
stert *jumped up and faced; turned abruptly*
stif(e) *mighty, stalwart, fierce*
store *powerful, unyielding, solid, strongly built*
stound *period of time, time*
stout(e) *strong or valiant; noble or arrogant; proud, splendidly built*
stythe, stithe *hardy, strong*

tho *then, at that time*
thore *there, at that time*
thorowe, throwe *short period of time; quickly*
thrytte *tested, proven, faithful*
to-rasshe *tear up*
trappes, trappis *ornamental, usually decorated, coverings of a horse*
trewthe *oath, promise*
trompours *trumpeters*
tyte, tide *quickly, hastily*

uncowthe *unknown, unidentified*
unsaught *hostile, angry; engaged in combat*

ventayle, ventaile *lower part of a helmet*
vis, vise *face*

warra, ware *shrewd, alert, wise*
wende, wynde *travel, depart*
were, weire *protect, provide defense*
wight *courageous, valiant; powerful*
witen, wote *know(s), understand(s)*
witty, witti *intelligent, discerning*
wode *deranged, insane*
wone *building, residence*
wowe *affliction, distress*

yare *ready, prepared*
yave *gave*
yfett, yfette *provided, procured, fetched*
ykidde *born*
ylore *received instruction, taught*
yode *went*
yorne *enthusiastic, keen, eager*

✒ MIDDLE ENGLISH TEXTS SERIES

The Floure and the Leafe, The Assembly of Ladies, The Isle of Ladies, edited by Derek Pearsall (1990)

Three Middle English Charlemagne Romances, edited by Alan Lupack (1990)

Six Ecclesiastical Satires, edited by James M. Dean (1991)

Heroic Women from the Old Testament in Middle English Verse, edited by Russell A. Peck (1991)

The Canterbury Tales: Fifteenth-Century Continuations and Additions, edited by John M. Bowers (1992)

Gavin Douglas, *The Palis of Honoure*, edited by David Parkinson (1992)

Wynnere and Wastoure and The Parlement of the Thre Ages, edited by Warren Ginsberg (1992)

The Shewings of Julian of Norwich, edited by Georgia Ronan Crampton (1994)

King Arthur's Death: The Middle English Stanzaic Morte Arthur and Alliterative Morte Arthure, edited by Larry D. Benson, revised by Edward E. Foster (1994)

Lancelot of the Laik and Sir Tristrem, edited by Alan Lupack (1994)

Sir Gawain: Eleven Romances and Tales, edited by Thomas Hahn (1995)

The Middle English Breton Lays, edited by Anne Laskaya and Eve Salisbury (1995)

Sir Perceval of Galles and Ywain and Gawain, edited by Mary Flowers Braswell (1995)

Four Middle English Romances: Sir Isumbras, Octavian, Sir Eglamour of Artois, Sir Tryamour, edited by Harriet Hudson (1996; second edition 2006)

The Poems of Laurence Minot, 1333–1352, edited by Richard H. Osberg (1996)

Medieval English Political Writings, edited by James M. Dean (1996)

The Book of Margery Kempe, edited by Lynn Staley (1996)

Amis and Amiloun, Robert of Cisyle, and Sir Amadace, edited by Edward E. Foster (1997; second edition 2007)

The Cloud of Unknowing, edited by Patrick J. Gallacher (1997)

Robin Hood and Other Outlaw Tales, edited by Stephen Knight and Thomas Ohlgren (1997; second edition 2000)

The Poems of Robert Henryson, edited by Robert L. Kindrick with the assistance of Kristie A. Bixby (1997)

Moral Love Songs and Laments, edited by Susanna Greer Fein (1998)

John Lydgate, *Troy Book Selections*, edited by Robert R. Edwards (1998)

Thomas Usk, *The Testament of Love*, edited by R. Allen Shoaf (1998)

Prose Merlin, edited by John Conlee (1998)

Middle English Marian Lyrics, edited by Karen Saupe (1998)

John Metham, *Amoryus and Cleopes*, edited by Stephen F. Page (1999)

Four Romances of England: King Horn, Havelok the Dane, Bevis of Hampton, Athelston, edited by Ronald B. Herzman, Graham Drake, and Eve Salisbury (1999)

The Assembly of Gods: Le Assemble de Dyeus, or Banquet of Gods and Goddesses, with the Discourse of Reason and Sensuality, edited by Jane Chance (1999)

Thomas Hoccleve, *The Regiment of Princes*, edited by Charles R. Blyth (1999)

John Capgrave, *The Life of Saint Katherine*, edited by Karen A. Winstead (1999)

John Gower, *Confessio Amantis*, Vol. 1, edited by Russell A. Peck; with Latin translations by Andrew Galloway (2000; second edition 2006); Vol. 2 (2003; second edition 2013); Vol. 3 (2004)

Richard the Redeless and Mum and the Sothsegger, edited by James M. Dean (2000)

Ancrene Wisse, edited by Robert Hasenfratz (2000)

Walter Hilton, *The Scale of Perfection*, edited by Thomas H. Bestul (2000)

John Lydgate, *The Siege of Thebes*, edited by Robert R. Edwards (2001)

Pearl, edited by Sarah Stanbury (2001)

The Trials and Joys of Marriage, edited by Eve Salisbury (2002)

Middle English Legends of Women Saints, edited by Sherry L. Reames, with the assistance of Martha G. Blalock and Wendy R. Larson (2003)

The Wallace: Selections, edited by Anne McKim (2003)

Richard Maidstone, *Concordia (The Reconciliation of Richard II with London)*, edited by David R. Carlson, with a verse translation by A. G. Rigg (2003)

Three Purgatory Poems: The Gast of Gy, Sir Owain, The Vision of Tundale, edited by Edward E. Foster (2004)

William Dunbar, *The Complete Works*, edited by John Conlee (2004)

Chaucerian Dream Visions and Complaints, edited by Dana M. Symons (2004)

Stanzaic Guy of Warwick, edited by Alison Wiggins (2004)

Saints' Lives in Middle English Collections, edited by E. Gordon Whatley, with Anne B. Thompson and Robert K. Upchurch (2004)

Siege of Jerusalem, edited by Michael Livingston (2004)

The Kingis Quair and Other Prison Poems, edited by Linne R. Mooney and Mary-Jo Arn (2005)

The Chaucerian Apocrypha: A Selection, edited by Kathleen Forni (2005)

John Gower, *The Minor Latin Works*, edited and translated by R. F. Yeager, with *In Praise of Peace*, edited by Michael Livingston (2005)

Sentimental and Humorous Romances: Floris and Blauncheflour, Sir Degrevant, The Squire of Low Degree, The Tournament of Tottenham, and The Feast of Tottenham, edited by Erik Kooper (2006)

The Dicts and Sayings of the Philosophers, edited by John William Sutton (2006)

Everyman and Its Dutch Original, Elckerlijc, edited by Clifford Davidson, Martin W. Walsh, and Ton J. Broos (2007)

The N-Town Plays, edited by Douglas Sugano, with assistance by Victor I. Scherb (2007)

The Book of John Mandeville, edited by Tamarah Kohanski and C. David Benson (2007)

John Lydgate, *The Temple of Glas*, edited by J. Allan Mitchell (2007)

The Northern Homily Cycle, edited by Anne B. Thompson (2008)

Codex Ashmole 61: A Compilation of Popular Middle English Verse, edited by George Shuffelton (2008)

Chaucer and the Poems of "Ch," edited by James I. Wimsatt (revised edition 2009)

William Caxton, *The Game and Playe of the Chesse*, edited by Jenny Adams (2009)

John the Blind Audelay, *Poems and Carols*, edited by Susanna Fein (2009)

Two Moral Interludes: The Pride of Life and Wisdom, edited by David Klausner (2009)

John Lydgate, *Mummings and Entertainments*, edited by Claire Sponsler (2010)

Mankind, edited by Kathleen M. Ashley and Gerard NeCastro (2010)

The Castle of Perseverance, edited by David N. Klausner (2010)

Robert Henryson, *The Complete Works*, edited by David J. Parkinson (2010)

John Gower, *The French Balades*, edited and translated by R. F. Yeager (2011)

The Middle English Metrical Paraphrase of the Old Testament, edited by Michael Livingston (2011)

The York Corpus Christi Plays, edited by Clifford Davidson (2011)

Prik of Conscience, edited by James H. Morey (2012)

The Dialogue of Solomon and Marcolf: A Dual-Language Edition from Latin and Middle English Printed Editions, edited by Nancy Mason Bradbury and Scott Bradbury (2012)

Croxton Play of the Sacrament, edited by John T. Sebastian (2012)

Ten Bourdes, edited by Melissa M. Furrow (2013)

📖 COMMENTARY SERIES

Haimo of Auxerre, *Commentary on the Book of Jonah*, translated with an introduction and notes by Deborah Everhart (1993)

Medieval Exegesis in Translation: Commentaries on the Book of Ruth, translated with an introduction and notes by Lesley Smith (1996)

Nicholas of Lyra's Apocalypse Commentary, translated with an introduction and notes by Philip D. W. Krey (1997)

Rabbi Ezra Ben Solomon of Gerona, *Commentary on the Song of Songs and Other Kabbalistic Commentaries*, selected, translated, and annotated by Seth Brody (1999)

John Wyclif, *On the Truth of Holy Scripture*, translated with an introduction and notes by Ian Christopher Levy (2001)

Second Thessalonians: Two Early Medieval Apocalyptic Commentaries, introduced and translated by Steven R. Cartwright and Kevin L. Hughes (2001)

The "Glossa Ordinaria" on the Song of Songs, translated with an introduction and notes by Mary Dove (2004)

The Seven Seals of the Apocalypse: Medieval Texts in Translation, translated with an introduction and notes by Francis X. Gumerlock (2009)

The "Glossa Ordinaria" on Romans, translated with an introduction and notes by Michael Scott Woodward (2011)

🪶 DOCUMENTS OF PRACTICE SERIES

Love and Marriage in Late Medieval London, selected, translated, and introduced by Shannon McSheffrey (1995)

Sources for the History of Medicine in Late Medieval England, selected, introduced, and translated by Carole Rawcliffe (1995)

A Slice of Life: Selected Documents of Medieval English Peasant Experience, edited, translated, and with an introduction by Edwin Brezette DeWindt (1996)

Regular Life: Monastic, Canonical, and Mendicant "Rules," selected and introduced by Douglas J. McMillan and Kathryn Smith Fladenmuller (1997); second edition, selected and introduced by Daniel Marcel La Corte and Douglas J. McMillan (2004)

Women and Monasticism in Medieval Europe: Sisters and Patrons of the Cistercian Reform, selected, translated, and with an introduction by Constance H. Berman (2002)

Medieval Notaries and Their Acts: The 1327–1328 Register of Jean Holanie, introduced, edited, and translated by Kathryn L. Reyerson and Debra A. Salata (2004)

John Stone's Chronicle: Christ Church Priory, Canterbury, 1417–1472, selected, translated, and introduced by Meriel Connor (2010)

🪶 MEDIEVAL GERMAN TEXTS IN BILINGUAL EDITIONS SERIES

Sovereignty and Salvation in the Vernacular, 1050–1150, introduction, translations, and notes by James A. Schultz (2000)

Ava's New Testament Narratives: "When the Old Law Passed Away," introduction, translation, and notes by James A. Rushing, Jr. (2003)

History as Literature: German World Chronicles of the Thirteenth Century in Verse, introduction, translation, and notes by R. Graeme Dunphy (2003)

Thomasin von Zirclaria, *Der Welsche Gast (The Italian Guest)*, translated by Marion Gibbs and Winder McConnell (2009)

Ladies, Whores, and Holy Women: A Sourcebook in Courtly, Religious, and Urban Cultures of Late Medieval Germany, introductions, translations, and notes by Ann Marie Rasmussen and Sarah Westphal-Wihl (2010)

🪶 VARIA

The Study of Chivalry: Resources and Approaches, edited by Howell Chickering and Thomas H. Seiler (1988)

Studies in the Harley Manuscript: The Scribes, Contents, and Social Contexts of British Library MS Harley 2253, edited by Susanna Fein (2000)

The Liturgy of the Medieval Church, edited by Thomas J. Heffernan and E. Ann Matter (2001; second edition 2005)

Johannes de Grocheio, *Ars musice*, edited and translated by Constant J. Mews, John N. Crossley, Catherine Jeffreys, Leigh McKinnon, and Carol J. Williams (2011)

🪶 TO ORDER PLEASE CONTACT:

Medieval Institute Publications
Western Michigan University
Kalamazoo, MI 49008-5432
Phone (269) 387-8755
FAX (269) 387-8750
http://www.wmich.edu/medieval/mip/index.html

Typeset in 10/13 New Baskerville
and Golden Cockerel Ornaments display
Manufactured by Sheridan Books, Inc.

Medieval Institute Publications
College of Arts and Sciences
Western Michigan University
1903 W. Michigan Avenue
Kalamazoo, MI 49008-5432
http:/ /www.wmich.edu/medieval/mip

 WESTERN MICHIGAN UNIVERSITY